LEGALLY LEAN™

Sports Nutrition Strategies for Optimal Health & Performance

Lisa Dorfman, MS, RD, CSSD, LMHC, FAND

Cover Design: Trish Landsparger
Text Design: Sara Luciano
Illustrations: Gary Clark

Legally Lean
ISBN 978-0-9835831-9-6

Printed in the United States of America

MomentumMedia Sports Publishing
20 Eastlake Road
Ithaca, NY 14850
(607) 257-6970
info@MomentumMedia.com

TABLE OF CONTENTS

ACKNOWLEDGEMENTS

To my husband Bob for *fueling* me with love, support, and encouragement.

To my children, Rebecca, Danielle, and Joseph, for allowing me to share my nutritional passion through food at mealtimes, the conferences, and racing events we've taken together on this life journey.

To my dad Walter, for inspiring me and teaching me how to eat and compete successfully in sports.

To the athletes, colleagues (shout out to Leslie Bonci, RD, and Tavis Piattoly, RD), coaches, athletic trainers, massage therapists, acupuncturists, physical therapists, and personal trainers I have had the privilege to work with and learn from over the past three decades of practice.

To my training partners, fellow competitors, and friends for decades of comradery and fun.

To Damian Stephens, exercise physiologist and artist, who taught me to reach beyond and outside the "fitness" box.

To Mandy Twardowski, Culinary Dietitian, for her expertise and analysis of the recipes in this book.

To James Meder and Chris Herrera for their contribution to the first edition of this book.

To the Lord God for giving me the gift, joy, and love of coaching others to reach their personal best in health, sport, and life.

....

Ten percent of the proceeds from this book with be donated to the Taylor Hooton Foundation, dedicated to educating youth and their adult influencers about the dangers of anabolic steroids and other appearance & performance enhancement drugs (APEDs). http://taylorhooton.org

PREFACE

How to Use this Book

This program is for athletes, those striving to be athletes, and everyday fitness-minded men and women who desire a peak physique and optimal health and performance in sport and life. The best way to get started on the program is to read the book start to finish. Realistically, though, I know you are eager to get started on the plan.

As an athlete myself, I understand the desire to be stronger and to go faster and longer—tomorrow. You and I both know that's not possible. It takes more than a quick fix. Sometimes though, an athlete's frustration with poor performances, illness, and injuries can get the better of them, causing them to resort to surfing the Internet for the next magic solution. Even if you skip other parts of this book, I strongly suggest you read the Introduction. There you'll find information on the dangers of steroids, PEDs, and tainted supplements. Learn about the laws and safety issues involved so you will avoid having to pay the price for a bad decision.

Then, if you are eager to get started, begin with Sections I and II (the *Legally Lean* Principles and the *Legally Lean* Play Book) to learn about the system's guiding philosophy, ground rules, and food program. The information in these sections is intended for both non-athletes and competitive athletes.

Where you go next will depend upon your level of physical activity. If you are an athlete trying to make weight or anyone trying to lose weight fast, you will thrive on the Core Plan in Section III. However, if you are a competitive athlete, Section IV is for you. There you'll find higher calorie plans, formulas for calculating body composition, and food and meal guides for training and competition. Regardless of who you are, the Core Plan grocery list and A-Z performance foods are for you.

If you think you might be a candidate for taking supplements, there are two areas of the book specifically for you. In Section

V, you'll find a list of questions designed to help you evaluate whether taking a supplement is right for you as well as information on how to navigate the supplement label, laws, and certifications. If the answer is yes, you can check out the Supplement section in Appendix A to find out the nuts and bolts of the most popular vitamins, minerals, and compounds promoted for athletes, including the evidence, toxicity concerns, and certifications and emblems you need to look for on supplement labels prior to making the investment. In addition, a list of invaluable experts and organizations who research and test supplements can be found in Appendix B.

If you're interested in the science behind the program, check out Section III, where you'll find the A-Z Guide to natural sources of vitamins, minerals, and compounds that can possibly enhance your health and performance and accelerate your progress. If you want to learn even more about the scientific basis for this book and other topics pertaining to optimal health and performance, sift through the more than 200 selected scientific references, resources, and links listed in Appendix B. If you are a foodie, feel free to start cooking. Go to Section VI for delicious recipes prepared by renowned chefs, restaurateurs, and expert chef dietitians.

And if at any time throughout your journey, you are inspired to read about some of the Olympic-medal-winning, elite, professional, collegiate, or high school athletes who have transformed their physiques and performance by using this program, head to my website www.LegallyLean.com. While you're there, you can become a Legally Lean Ambassador, too!

You can also pick up new recipes and optimal health and sports performance tips by following me at Twitter@LegallyLean, www.Instagram.com/LegallyLean# or at www.Facebook.com/LegallyLean.

Ultimately, my goal is your goal: to help you reach your personal best—safely, nutritiously, healthfully, tastefully— and win your Olympic Gold in life.

Cheers to a healthy, leaner, and better you!

Your LEGALLY LEAN
JOURNEY to Optimal Health and Performance

The Warm Up
We all start from somewhere, a place & physique that we desire to change and transform. Embrace who you are, where you want to be & how you intend to get there.

The Work Out
The road to your personal best physique & health takes time, hard work and patience.

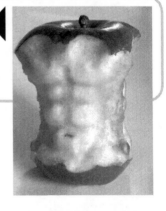

The Result
Congratulations, when you have reached your goals, it will show! Tell the world, share your success & inspire others to do the same.

Good luck with your Legally Lean Journey!

INTRODUCTION

Back in the day, athletes would do anything to improve their performance—safe or not, proven or not, tasty or otherwise. As far back as 776 B.C.E., Greek athletes used dried figs, mushrooms, and strychnine (an amphetamine) to improve performance.

Not much has changed.

Today's athletes still say they'll do whatever it takes—legal or otherwise—to look better, get stronger and faster, go farther, or simply to succeed in their sport. Pick up any newspaper, and you'll find that many of our superhero baseball and football players, track and field athletes, boxers and marathoners have tested positive for everything from amphetamines to steroids. *And they are not alone.*

The legal and illegal use of performance enhancing drugs has increased as a result of society's preoccupation with increasing muscle strength, size, and libido. Widespread availability via the Internet has also helped fuel the exponential growth of steroid use, according to the *Digital Citizen's Alliance*, a consumer-oriented coalition focused on educating the public and policy makers on the threats that consumers face on the Internet.

Steroid Statistics

Among Americans between 13 and 50 years of age, it's estimated that 2.9 to 4 million have used steroids, with about one million becoming dependent on their use.

According to the Taylor Hooton Foundation, a non-profit organization founded by the father of a high school athlete who committed suicide as a result of abusing anabolic steroids, more than eight percent of males aged 18 to 25 use steroids. Twenty-eight percent say they know someone who has taken some type of PEDs as the fast track to college scholarships and stardom.

According to the World Anti-Doping Association (WADA), about two percent of elite athletes use illegal substances.

Among NCAA male athletes who use steroids, more consistent unhealthy lifestyle behaviors were shown including heavier drinking, higher rates of cigarettes, marijuana, amphetamines, narcotics, and a variety of permissible and impermissible dietary supplements suggesting that the use of steroids may also lead to other risk-taking behaviors. Quick fixes like these are not only illegal, but are also dangerous to the athletes and to the sport culture.

Recent global studies also show steroid use increasing. A 2014 study looking at the lifetime prevalence rate for all ages was 3.3 percent. Among males, the rate was 6.4 percent, while for females, it was 1.6 percent. National survey results released by the Partnership for Drug Free Kids confirmed a doubling to 11 percent in the reported lifetime use of synthetic human growth hormone (hGH) without a prescription among teens grades 9 through 12, up dramatically from just 5 percent in 2012.

A 2013 study showed that steroid users begin later than users of most other drugs; 78 percent start after the age of 20. However, use is also growing among younger athletes. "Eating Amongst Teens," or Project EAT, looked at steroid use and behaviors associated with steroid use in middle- and high school athletes. Surveying 4,746 individuals, the study found that 5.4 percent of teenage males and 2.9 percent of females used steroids.

When prescribed by a medical doctor, hormones and steroids may have some valid uses in adolescents, such as for the treatment of delayed puberty and body wasting due to disease. But the use of these drugs is also known to have serious—sometimes permanent—physical and emotional consequences in adolescents, such as stunted bone growth, internal organ damage, and feminization in males and masculinization in females.

Steroid use in adolescents is also associated with other high-risk behaviors, such as the use of other illicit drugs; reduced involvement in school; poorer academic performance; engaging in unprotected sex, aggressive, and criminal behavior; and suicide, such as in the case of Taylor Hooten, the high school baseball player mentioned above.

With all the downsides, why do athletes use steroids? Improving performance at any cost is the most common reason cited followed by financial gain, increasing self-confidence and social recognition. One study noted that 10 to 24 percent of male athletes said they would "dope" if it would help them achieve better results without the risk of consequences, and an additional five to 10 percent indicate they might, regardless of health consequences. A 2010 study found 25 percent of male and female dancers surveyed would also "use" if it would ensure successful dance performance.

Other reasons given for using banned substances include improved recovery, and prevention of nutritional deficiencies. Still other athletes "use" based on the idea that others use, so it must be okay and fair (also known as the "false consensus effect"). And while athletes acknowledge that doping is cheating, unhealthy, and risky because of sanctions, its effectiveness is also widely recognized.

Dietary Supplements

Beyond steroids and illegal drugs, athletes are taking a myriad of other substances to try to improve performance. A billion dollar business, ergogenic aids are successfully marketed to athletes from middle schoolers to professionals.

Technically, an "ergogenic aid" can refer to any legal strategy for performance enhancement, including diet, training, mechanical devices or gear, and legitimate supplements such as vitamins, minerals to correct deficiencies, or sport drinks, shakes, bars, gels, and chews for energy and recovery. But the term also encompasses illegal pharmacological agents (such as metabolites, constituents, extracts, or a combination of these) designed to enhance performance or training adaptations and/or increase the speed of recovery from training and competition. In some cases, these performance enhancing aids can cause serious illness, irreversible physical damage, and even death.

The use of ergogenic aids in the form of dietary supplements is widespread in all sports. Many athletes, whether recreational, elite, or professional, use some form of dietary supplementation, whether it's a substance obtainable by prescription or by illegal means or one marked as a supplement, vitamin, or mineral, to improve athletic performance or to assist with weight loss.

In a 2008 study, 88 percent of collegiate athletes surveyed used one or more nutritional supplements. The reasons for taking supplements differ between the sexes. Female athletes say they take supplements for their health or to overcome deficient diets, while men take supplements to improve speed, agility, strength, and power or to build body mass and reduce weight or body fat.

A recent survey of track and field athletes competing in the world championships showed 89 percent of females and 83 percent of males reported using for the following reasons:

71% recovery from training
52% for health
46% improve performance
40% prevent or treat an illness
29% compensate for poor diet

Performance level may also dictate the prevalence and type of supplements used. In a study of close to 3,000 athletes, 37 percent of all athletes between 11 and 44 years old, of various performance levels, reported taking at least one dietary supplement, with a higher prevalence in individual (44 percent) compared to team sport athletes (35 percent), in more elite level athletes, and in men. The most popular supplement used in this study was amino acids.

The good news may be at the Olympic level, where supplement use is reported to be waning in popularity in some groups, according to a study published by the International Society of Sports Nutrition. In 2002, 81 percent of the athletes surveyed used dietary supplements compared with 73 percent in 2009. However, when age increased, so did use, even in 2009. The frequency of all dietary supplement use was 63 percent in those under 21 years old, 83 percent in 21-24 year olds, and 90 percent in those over 24 years old. Athletes in speed, power, and endurance events reported significantly more use of dietary supplements than team sport athletes in both years.

Competitive athletes aren't the only ones downing supplements—everyday people simply trying to get fit are taking them, too. The estimated use of supplements among gym participants is 36.8 percent, and use is nearly equal between men and women.

In one Brazilian study with over 1100 participants, five products consumed almost daily were those rich in proteins and amino acids (58 percent), isotonic drinks (32 percent), those rich in carbohydrates (23 percent), natural/herbs (20 percent), and multivitamin/mineral supplements (19 percent). In this study, individuals younger than 30 years old took the most protein supplements. In contrast, older participants reported taking supplements rich in multivitamin/minerals and natural/herbs.

What Are the Risks?

With so many people taking supplements, where are they getting advice about what to take? All too often, the advice comes from fellow athletes, trainers, advertisements, or the Internet, rather than well-informed and educated sports dietitians, physicians, certified coaches, and accredited exercise professionals.

This is a problem because the use of dietary supplements to improve performance can present grave risks. Take the report of 22-year-old Army Private Michael Lee Sparling, who died in 2011. Sparling died, not of a roadside bomb, but when he collapsed while running in formation, reportedly as a result of taking a popular supplement he bought on base. Unbeknownst to him, the supplement contained a powerful stimulant called dimethylamylamine (DMAA), which experts say has an effect on the body similar to that of amphetamine drugs.

Needless to say, the supplement is no longer available on military bases. It is, however, still available online and at retail outlets worldwide. Retailers claim that deaths cannot be directly traced back to the product, and therefore they should not be held responsible. They compare it to grocers who sell vegetables or meat with E.coli and are not held responsible for any associated illness or death. Another recent example comes from 2013. In this case, popular "fat burning" supplements were pulled from the market by the FDA when they were found to contain a methamphetamine-like substance called N, alpha-diethylphenylethylamine (N, a-DEPEA for short), despite having no listing on the label for this ingredient. Companies selling products with N, claim that the ingredient comes from a natural constituent of the dendrobium orchid extract. However, there is no evidence to suggest that this substance is actually a constituent of the plant, according to NSF International, the only accredited American Natural Standard lab for dietary supplements, which tests for more than 180 banned illegal athletic substances for sport.

And the stories don't stop there. In spring 2013, both younger and older athletes were admitted to hospital emergency wards with liver failure. *The common thread?* Tainted supplements.

Following actions by the FDA, a Texas-based company, USPLabs, agreed to recall and destroy a dietary supplement linked to dozens of cases of acute liver failure and hepatitis, including one death and illnesses so severe that several patients required liver transplants, according to the FDA website.

Why the delay in pulling the supplement from the market despite the reports? Unfortunately, the FDA didn't know about the reports for several months. Because existing laws protect the manufacturer and not the consumer, it is left up to companies to use the honor system and "fess up" to any cases of illness or death brought to their attention. In this situation, it took 97 cases linking the supplement to three liver transplants and even one death before the supplement was pulled.

For competitive athletes, there's an additional risk: Dietary supplements can be contaminated with banned substances that will result in a positive drug test. A wide range of stimulants, steroids, and other agents included in the WADA's prohibited list have recently been identified in supplements.

Of 25,000 supplement inquiries made to the Resource Exchange Center (REC) of the National Center for Drug Free Sport (see Appendix B), 30 percent of the most popular inquiries for amino acids/metabolites, vitamins and minerals, and herbal products were found to have banned substances.

Supplement contamination can happen here in the U.S. or because of the overseas preparation of raw ingredients included in the formulation of the finished product. Contamination puts athletes at risk for illness and positive drug tests.

Beyond the issue of contamination, there is another concern. In some supplements on the market, the amount of a vitamin, mineral, or herb may be exceptionally higher or lower than the therapeutic dose as reported by Consumer Lab (see APPENDIX B) (www.consumerlab.com). According to Chris Rosenbloom, PhD, RDN, CSSD, Sports Dietitian for the Georgia State Athletics Department and Editor-in-Chief of the *Sports Nutrition Care Manual for the Academy of Nutrition and Dietetics, "... the risk of toxicity from taking too much of a particular vitamin or mineral increases if athletes take supplements while also consuming fortified foods, sport shakes, bars, and beverages."*

In addition, different athletes may respond very differently to even a safe supplement. Some may experience negative effects such as gastrointestinal distress, neurological symptoms, or other physical consequences like headaches, nausea, or cramps. In 2008-2011, the FDA received 6,307 adverse event reports due to supplements. Of these, 71 percent were deemed serious, compared with only 63 percent of prescription drug reports found to be serious at that time. Poison control centers across the U.S. received 1,000 more adverse reports than the FDA. And many adverse events are not reported due to embarrassment, seeming insignificance, or because consumers do not know where to report them.

Who Monitors Supplements?

The truth is, there's little control over supplement safety, despite a 1994 law enacted under President Clinton that was designed to protect the public from tainted supplements. The Dietary Supplement Health and Education Act (DSHEA) has not achieved that result, for several reasons.

Part of the issue, as mentioned, is lack of money and manpower. For now, two government agencies, the FDA and the Federal Trade Commission (FTC), are responsible for regulating dietary supplements. The FDA oversees safety concerns, while the FTC regulates dietary supplement advertising, such as product information, labeling, claims, package inserts, and accompanying literature.

Prior to the enactment of DSHEA of 1994, it was the wild, wild, west—supplements were manufactured, marketed, and sold without *any* specific regulations. Sad to say, with thousands of products coming to market each day, not much has changed, even with new regulations in place.

After the passage of DSHEA, dietary supplements were defined as a subcategory of food, putting the burden on the FDA for proving that a dietary supplement is unsafe after it is on the market. This means that reports have to be submitted to the FDA to prove a supplement has caused an ill effect on the individual. However, this is a challenge for a few reasons.

You see, all supplements on the market prior to 1994 are cleared under a clause called "Generally Recognized as Safe," or GRAS, whether they are actually safe or not. Regulations are also limited to safety, not efficacy, which means a supplement could be safe, but not actually work or do what it says it is going to do. Any new dietary ingredient must be registered with the FDA and companies must submit proof of its safety before it is approved for sale.

Proving that a supplement has caused harm can be very difficult. It takes numbers; one, two, or three reports typically will not make a strong enough case to get a supplement pulled from the market. Also, as mentioned with the death of the U.S. Army private, it's nearly impossible to connect a death specifically to a supplement; and even if there were enough reports submitted, it's ultimately up to the manufacturer and/ or the consumer to report the incidents to the government. Sadly, without deaths or serious illnesses, the chances of getting a product pulled are slim, and it can take months or years to follow the claims.

Experts agree that more needs to be done to educate and protect the consumer rather than the industry. However, manpower, money, and legislation are the keys to protecting the half- to-three-quarters of Americans who use supplements on a regular basis.

Food First

With these risks in mind, there is a better way. For most individuals, rather than to reach for a supplement, the best plan is to think "food first" when trying to change their physique or improve their performance.

Research shows that many people—athletes included—actually do fall short on many important vitamins and minerals. And while you might assume that elite athletes have the best diets, research suggests otherwise. A 2010 study showed that many athletes are failing to meet the Estimated Average Requirement (EAR) and the RDI/A (Recommended Dietary Intake/Allowance), which respectively indicate the intake required to meet the needs of half of the population (EAR) and the intake needed to meet nearly all the needs of nearly all (97 to 98 percent) of healthy individuals (RDI/A).

Forty-eight percent of the females in the study failed to meet the EAR for folate, 24 percent for calcium, 19 for magnesium, and 4 percent for iron. For men, significant deficiencies were found in vitamin A (44 percent) vitamin C (80 percent), vitamin D (92 percent), folate (84 percent), calcium (52 percent), and magnesium (60 percent).

Without a doubt, impaired vitamin and mineral status will compromise all types of performance—sport, acting, or otherwise. Some of the deficiency signs and symptoms associated with performance have been summarized in the chart in Appendix A.

But rather than adding a supplement, the first step should be to improve your diet. It is the position of health experts, including the Academy of Nutrition and Dietetics (AND), National Athletic Trainers Association (NATA), and other groups that the best nutrition-based strategy for promoting optimal health, reducing the risk for disease, and enhancing athletic performance is to choose a variety of nutrient-rich foods. As most of the top sports nutritionists and dietitians in the country agree, it is better to get nutrients from food than from supplements.

Athletes, especially younger athletes, need first and foremost to establish good eating habits. Practicing good nutrition in the formative years can reap rewards one's entire life. The opposite is also true—emphasizing supplements can lead to later problems. According to Tavis Piattoly, MS, RD, New Orleans Pelicans Sports Nutritionist and founder of My Sports Dietitians, an online educational service and tool for high school athletes, coaches, and parents (www.mysportsdconnect. com), *"One ... very important reason to downplay supplements is that it might lead to the use of other unhealthy lifestyle behaviors including the use of all illegal substances by choice or by accident,"* as discussed earlier.

Another reason to turn to food first is that nutrition is a young science—only a century-plus young! We don't yet have a handle on all the vitamins, minerals, and compounds in every food. For example, we know that berries are a nutritious food because they have vitamins, minerals, fiber, and antioxidants. If you take a supplement with blueberry extract, you may get something healthy for you, but how do we know you're not missing something else in the actual berry that may also be good for you?

Finally, as discussed at length, supplements pose a safety issue. Although there are some laws in place, supplements are not strictly regulated. Federal and consumer groups have found that supplements can contain varying amounts of their stated ingredient, despite what the label says, may provide biologically unavailable sources of nutrients, and may contain excessive amounts of vitamins, which can exceed the upper tolerable limits (UL) set forth by the government in response to studies which have determined the highest possible safe limits for each specific vitamin and mineral.

SECTION

I

GETTING STARTED

The Legally Lean program has as its foundation five basic principles. These principles are the following:

Principle 1: "Go Hard 3: Easy 1"
Principle 2: Detox Unhealthy Habits
Principle 3: Break a Sweat
Principle 4: Connect Consciously
Principle 5: Get Lean, Get Rest

Taken together, these principles will provide you with the basic roadmap you need to follow as you work towards your personal best in health, sports, and life. Let's take an in-depth look at each one.

Principle 1: Go Hard 3: Easy 1

Research suggests that a 3:1 approach—three days of strict exercise and dieting followed by one dietary "relief" day—will keep your body metabolically fit and on track. Using this system, you will follow a relatively moderate diet of lean protein, nutrient-rich fruits and vegetables, rich sources of minerals like calcium, essential healthy fats and a limited amount of high energy carbs for three days.

Every fourth day is what I call the "relief" day. This day allows your body to recuperate, regenerate, replenish, and relax. While the program remains calorie-controlled on day four, instead of high protein, low carb snacks, you will eat additional high-energy carbs.

With the 3:1 plan, you will be following a lower-calorie diet than you were before you started the plan, so you'll decrease body fat percentage. But you will retain lean muscle, resulting in more muscle tone, faster weight loss, and a better metabolism and hormone profile.

Research supports this approach. One study had participants diet hard for three days, take one day off, and repeat this cycle again. Compared to dieters who did not take the relief day, the 3:1 dieters stimulated their metabolic rate, had a seven percent increase in total daily calorie expenditure, and increased circulating levels of leptin (the hormone that satiates you and makes you feel like you have had enough after meals).

You see, low calorie diets followed intensely without a break leave dieters hungry, glycogen depleted, discouraged, and depressed. Long term, low calorie diets actually cut metabolic rate, lowering calorie expenditure by a process called "adaptive thermogenesis." They also increase cues for hunger by increasing the hormone ghrelin and reduce the muscle-building hormone testosterone, which is important for suppressing fat production. And they increase cortisol levels, which leads to muscle breakdown, compromised immunity, and gut fat! By giving your body a break every fourth day, you will avoid these weight-loss pitfalls.

Principle 2: Detox Unhealthy Habits

The Legally Lean detox is your "rush" period—a stage of a few days to a few weeks to adjust to making significant changes to your diet, training, and/or lifestyle behaviors.

This is the most important part of your program. We all need to detox at least once in our lives to rejuvenate our nutritional spirit and our senses with delicious, clean, tasty food.

Research shows that the well-fueled dietary detox, which starts with your CORE Performance Program in Section III, is the first step toward repairing, replenishing, and rejuvenating your body. Without removing dietary toxins, your personal food addictions, and bad habits, it will be impossible to make permanent changes to your body and your life. Beginning a program without detoxing is as useless as taking a dietary supplement without changing your unhealthy eating habits.

The truth is, it can be difficult to let go of old habits. Healthy or not, they can be like old friends you've grown accustomed to. However, it's important to remove these weak links— the obstacles holding you back from being the best you can be—before you lay the foundation for new habits.

A prospective study published in the *New England Journal of Medicine* illustrates the fact that our toxic habits can influence our success. The study included 120,877 United States women and men and followed them from 1986 to 2006, assessing which lifestyle behaviors helped people maintain a healthy energy balance (calories in/calories out) and which hindered them. The findings suggest that consuming sugar-sweetened beverages, sweets, and processed foods make it harder to maintain the proper calorie balance, while eating fruits, vegetables, and whole grains makes it easier—even more reason to get rid of toxic comfort foods on a regular basis.

Reducing stress and stress related eating has also been shown to be especially important for decreasing the risks of overweight and obesity.

In a 2014 study of more than 6,000 teenage girls and boys, those who ate due to stress had a higher prevalence of overweight, obesity and abdominal obesity, binging, and rebound dieting. Stress-driven female eaters used more chocolate, sweets, light sodas, alcohol, and tobacco while stressed boys ate more sausage, chocolate, sweets, hamburgers, and pizza.

Ready, Set, Detox

When you prepare your body for your program with a detox, you are like a boxer preparing for a fight. The detox will build your body by cleansing it of harmful environmental, nutritional, and emotional toxins, and it will fuel your body for the duration of the fight.

Best of all, the detox period will also help you clear the toxins that hold you back from thinking clearly, providing you with focus, determination, and strength. You're like a cyclist who has drag and wants to cut, tighten, and clear his clothing, body, and bicycle of anything that will hold him back from moving faster. When you detox, you're like a cyclist drafting off the bike ahead of him—you're clearing your path and accelerating to get to your destination. *But be prepared.*

You might feel worse before you feel better. Headaches, nausea, and muscle pain are common when toxins are being mobilized and excreted. Sometimes cleansing with fresh foods and fluids can eliminate the buildup of years of emotional and physical residues from previous stressful events. It is critical at this initial detox stage to push through this threshold the same way a marathon runner pushes through the "wall," the point when they feel like quitting the race. For runners in the Boston marathon, the wall usually hits at the Citgo sign—the 24th mile. Just two miles to go, but it feels like an eternity. At times, your detox may feel like that, too.

But if you don't push through the "wall," the stress builds and can cause damage at the cellular level, leading to inflammation of the brain, arteries, and cells. This inflammation can permanently affect your immune system and increase blood pressure, cholesterol, and blood sugar levels. This can lead to chronic diseases like heart disease, diabetes and cancer, now reaching epidemic proportions worldwide and responsible for 70 percent of all deaths in the United States— all attributable to inflammation caused by stress.

To make the most out of this crucial stage of change, you must follow through for at least three weeks, the time it takes not only to change just one habit, but also to clear harmful toxins from your system. Stopping short of that can be more physiologically harmful to your health than never attempting to change at all.

What Is Detoxification?

Detoxification is a process that decreases negative impact of xenobiotics (aka, toxins) on the body. There are more than 100,000 toxins which can stress your system. These fall into two major groups. The first are exotoxins, which include environmental toxins such as pollution and Persistent Organic Pollutants (POPs) from your home, office, food supply, water, cleaning chemicals, pesticides, and make-up products. The second group is endotoxins, which are toxins inside the body. These include toxins that reside inside your body, such as those from recreational drugs, medications, and food additives.

How does detoxification work?

Specific foods, fluids, vitamins, and minerals can influence the detox process by activating or inhibiting the elimination of substances. Only elements that are easily dissolved in water can be effectively detoxed from the body. Toxic compounds like POPs and others are typically stored in fat and therefore are not water soluble. The goal of the detox process is to transform these toxic fat-soluble substances into less harmful water soluble substances and clear them from the body—but this requires fuel from specific foods and fluids!

Contrary to popular belief, the detoxification process requires energy. So a fasting detox is not the optimal approach and can actually be harmful and dangerous. Prolonged fasting can weaken the muscles and other organs and leave the body depleted. Your goal is to effectively get rid of the harmful stuff in your body, and you need energy from food to accomplish this.

Two Phases of Detoxification

Phase I: The Gut

Your gut is your number one defense against toxins which enter the body. The gut barrier keeps toxins from entering systemic circulation. If the toxins breach the barrier, they are "arrested" by GALT (Gut Associated Lymphoid Tissue). The gut actually generates the majority of the body's antibodies; about 70 percent of your lymphocytes surround the gut. The lymph acts as a filter to keep harmful toxins out of the body.

The major immune system in the gut is called SIGA (Secretory immunoglobins). Some research suggests that one of the reasons athletes are more prone to upper respiratory infections after competition or prolonged physical stress is because of the reduction of SIGA in the gastrointestinal tract. Important foods and/or supplements to include during this phase of detoxification are probiotics, since beneficial bacteria-probiotics boost the production of SIGA.

Probiotics are found in foods like yogurt with live active cultures, cottage cheese, and kefir, and in vegan products like kombucha, miso, tempeh, and sauerkraut. Fiber—both prebiotic fiber (which helps probiotics to colonize in the GI tract) and other soluble and insoluble fibers from vegetables, fruits, 100 percent whole grains, peas, and corn which are not digested in the gastrointestinal tract—also facilitate detoxification.

Phase II: The Liver

In Phase II of the detox process, toxins not arrested and processed by GALT and SIGA in the gut pass through to the bloodstream and are delivered via the hepatic portal vein to the liver for detoxification.

In the liver, there is a two-step process:

Step 1: Fat-soluble toxins are transformed into intermediate compounds which can be more reactive but bind more easily to nontoxic water soluble compounds in Step 2.

It is important to remember that if you cut your detox shorter than the necessary period required for complete detoxification, the compounds can stagnate and actually become more disruptive and destructive to the body. You see, you need energy, calories, and specific nutrients, vitamins, minerals and phytochemicals to drive the detox process. An uber-restrictive detox, too low in calories or at a fasting level, can be more detrimental to your health than not starting a detox at all. Moving your body through Step 2 in the liver through specific food choices and energy is essential for overall and long term good health.

Step 2: In this step, reactive intermediates and water soluble compounds make the entire package harmless and ready to be eliminated. Without optimal or complete detoxification, your body cannot efficiently remove harmful toxins and they build up in the liver.

During Phase II of the detoxification process, starting, completing and maintaining a healthy liver is crucial. Stopping midstream on a healthy detox can halt the complete passage of toxins and is contraindicated. That's why it is imperative to follow all the dietary guidelines in the detox section for a minimum of three days to two weeks for complete detoxification.

The *Legally Lean* Core Program outlined in Section III highlights the best foods for a dietary detox. These foods are anti-inflammatory, natural, organic, and plant-based, with small amounts of Omega-3-rich fish or grass-fed poultry and eggs and supplemental protein from whey or soy. The detox diet also includes anti-oxidant, phytonutrient-rich fruits and vegetables; healthy fat sources and oils such as almonds, walnuts, or pistachios; and olive or coconut oils. Beverages such as filtered water, coconut water, naturally flavored water, tea, coffee, and electrolyte fortified beverages are recommended.

Specific foods important during this step of detoxification include Brussels sprouts, garlic, onions, broccoli, cauliflower, asparagus, citrus, cocoa, wheat and oat bran, apples, grapes, cranberries, blueberries, and green tea. Moderately high protein diets, especially from plant sources, enhance the uptake enzymes which accelerate the detox process. Deficiencies in protein, and the minerals calcium and selenium can inhibit the detoxification process.

What are Persistent Organic Pollutants (POPs)?

Research suggests that low-dose pesticides and Poly-chlorinated Biphenyls (PCBs) are correlated with higher rates of obesity, unhealthy blood fat levels (dyslipidemia), and insulin resistance (aka glucose intolerance, when your body's cells cannot process insulin, the hormone that brings down blood sugars after meals, and therefore keeps them elevated). POPS have been found to contribute to adiposity and dysmetabolism, abdominal adiposity, fatty liver, insulin resistance, and endocrine disruption in women. Perfluorocarbons (PFCs), found in cosmetics, pizza boxes, popcorn bags, lipstick, computer mice, water repellents, stain repellents, and the lining on non-stick cookware have been linked to infertility and early menopause.

More information on reducing your risks can be found at http://www.natural-skincare-authority.com/cosmetic-chemicals.html , http://www.everydayexposures.com, and the Environmental Working Group: http://www.ewg.org/pbdefree.

Principle 3: Break a Sweat

No doubt about it, diet can't do it all. In addition to following your delicious Legally Lean eating plan, you will need to do some exercise if you want to burn fat, build muscle, and attain and maintain your ideal body weight and physique. Hundreds of research studies have demonstrated the physical and psychological benefits of sweating through exercise, and I can tell you that you will not reach your goals through diet alone.

Exercise helps you lose weight because it controls your appetite and allows you to expend more daily calories, tipping the balance of "calories in versus calories out" in your favor. It also builds muscle mass, which stokes your metabolism so you'll burn even more calories throughout the day, even when you're just sitting at your computer answering e-mail. And it's crucial for weight maintenance!

If you exercise hard enough to sweat, even better! Sweating accelerates the detoxification process by speeding up the clearing of toxins from your body. You'll notice changes in your appearance and physical, mental, and spiritual well-being almost immediately, because exercise encourages healthy circulation and elimination.

Any exercise you enjoy that causes you to sweat for a minimum of 30 minutes each day, whether it is stretching, Pilates, yoga, walking, running, cycling, or jogging will assist your detox by:

- Helping you breathe, exhaling carbon dioxide and reducing acidity.
- Increasing lymph flow, which creates urine and helps you to excrete toxic compounds.
- Making your gut more fit and regular.
- Increasing blood circulation.
- Improving the liver's detoxification processes.

Coach's Corner

Benefits of Sweating

- Great detoxing agent
- Rids body of wastes
- Regulates the body's temperature
- Keeps the skin clean and pliant
- Has a relaxing effect
- Gives relief from the common cold, arthritis, headaches, and hangovers
- Beneficial for mild cases of hypertension
- Draws out lactic acid
- Flushes out toxic metals.

How much is enough?

According to the Physical Activity Guidelines for Americans, issued by the U.S. Department of Health and Human Services in 2008, everybody should aim for 150 minutes per week of moderately intense aerobic activity, such as brisk walking. It's not so hard to meet that recommendation. Three 10-minute walks, five days a week, will get you there. To accelerate your progress and get in even better shape, the guidelines suggest doubling that goal to 300 minutes of weekly aerobic activity (one hour five days per week), if you can.

The American College of Sports Medicine (ACSM) recommends individuals expend 300 calories for every workout in order to promote weight loss and maintain a healthy body weight. For example, if you weigh 150 pounds, a 300-calorie workout is equivalent to a 40-minute bike ride or a 25-minute jog at a 9 minute/mile pace. More information on exercise from the ACSM at: http://acsm.org/about-acsm/media-room/news-releases/2011/08/01/acsm-issues-new-recommendations-on-quantity-and-quality-of-exercise.

Mix it up by fitting in two or more days per week of strength training, whether it's lifting weights at the gym, using resistance bands, or lifting rocks in the garden. Besides shaping and contouring your body, weight-bearing exercise increases muscle mass and bone density to help prevent bone-weakening osteoporosis, and it helps prevent age-related symptoms such as muscle stiffness and soreness. By having more muscle on board, you'll also get a metabolism boost that's especially important as you get older.

Consider this: Starting around age 25, we all begin losing one to two percent of our muscle mass per year as part of the natural aging process. By age 70, the average person will have 40 to 50 percent less muscle than they had in their twenties. As you lose muscle mass, more of the calories you consume will be stored as fat. And fat isn't benign. It produces substances known as cytokines that cannibalize muscle tissue, reducing your metabolic rate even more. But strength training can help stop this vicious cycle, or at least slow it down. If you're not comfortable using resistance bands, free weights, or weight machines on your own, and you don't have rocks or a garden, try a strength-training class at your local gym.

Break a Sweat, Change Your Mood

Another benefit of exercise is a more positive outlook. You see, there's a holistic connection between your cardiovascular, skeletal, and muscular systems, and your mind, spirit, and enthusiasm for life. In fact, regular exercise can actually save your emotional soul, providing an escape hatch from your daily stress.

Exercise can make your body feel good and feeling good increases self esteem. Therefore, exercise increases self esteem, but there's more to it than just the simplicity of this equation. It's actually a chemical reaction.

You've probably heard of the runner's high—after all, why would anyone want to run for one or 26 miles if they didn't feel good doing it? For many runners, it's more than just fun—running makes them feel darn good. They connect to God, to nature, and to the world around them when they run. And when they're finished running, they feel relaxed and energized, all in one. This is because running causes a release of endorphins, the chemicals produced when you run or perform any intense or long duration exercise.

Coach's Corner

Endorphins—Enjoying the Runner's "High"

Back in the 1970s, scientists began studying the effects of opioid (morphine-like) substances, which have a pain relieving effect on the brain. Endorphins and other similar chemicals act like neurotransmitters. Blood levels of endorphins increase to five times the body's resting level in response to exercise and rise to even higher levels in the brain. For moderate to intense aerobic exercise, the effect becomes even greater as the duration increases. So regardless of your life situation, when you complete an exercise session, you feel a sense of euphoria and exhilaration.

You also feel less pain with endorphin release, since these chemicals affect the pain receptors in your body. Endorphins may also improve appetite control and reduce anger, anxiety, tension, and confusion. And while a little is good, more is even better. The fitter you become the more sensitive you are to endorphins—an effect often referred to as the "positive addiction." How can you go wrong?

Coach's Corner

Exercise Options

Here are some of the types of exercise you can incorporate into your life:

Energy System/Four Types of Exercise:	Physical and Emotional Benefits
Cardiovascular Jogging, tennis, biking, walking, swimming, rowing, dancing, stair climbing	Increases endorphins, our built-in natural tranquilizer; strengthens the heart for emotionally depleting life circumstances; decreases risk of obesity, hypertension, diabetes, and certain forms of cancer; and eases arthritis-related symptoms.
Strength training Weight lifting, push-ups, pull-ups, chair lifts	Builds strength, builds and maintains muscle mass by releasing testosterone and growth factor (GH) in body; increases bone strength and density; empowers one with the strength to overcome personal stress, manage anger, and strengthen ego for better self esteem.
Stretching Yoga, Pilates	Increases muscle and joint flexibility; warms up body for other exercise types; increases "flexibility" with life
Leisure Activities Casual walking, golfing, fishing, gardening,	Relaxation, movements associated with activity which may stretch or strengthen specific muscle groups walking with others; emotional well-being and spirituality—being one with nature in the garden, sailing leisurely at sea, or strolling in the park or "Shinrin-Yoku" (aka Forest Bathing).

Before you begin exercising though, I have just a few words of caution.

- Always obtain a medical clearance before you start any exercise program, especially if you're more than 40 years young.

- Set small, incremental, and realistic goals.

- Watch out for all or none thinking. Depressed individuals tend to distort the big picture, over-generalizing and magnifying the negative aspects of a situation, such as sweating, heat, muscle aches, and exhaustion. There's always a remedy: water, air-conditioning, massage, and a good night's rest.

- Pick a partner—a friend, colleague, partner, or child. Even your pet can make a great training partner!

For more information on the HHS Exercise Guidelines: http://www.health.gov/PAGuidelines/

Principle 4: Connect Consciously

Connecting consciously from "farm to finish" helps reinforce and honor the commitment you've made to yourself by investing in this book and program. This means eating clean, fresh food, slowing down your eating speed, measuring your portion sizes, and tracking your progress.

Slowing down and savoring your food is an important means for enjoying the delicious foods you will be incorporating to nourish your body as the pounds melt away. It means staying connected to the environment as well as yourself.

Conscious eating (aka "mindful eating" according to The Center for Mindful Eating) is a term to describe:

> *"Awareness of our own actions, thoughts, feelings and motivations, and insight into the roots of health and contentment. It means allowing oneself to become aware of the positive and nurturing opportunities that are available through food selection and preparation; using all one's senses in choosing to eat food that is both satisfying and nourishing to your body; becoming aware of physical hunger and satiety cues to guide your decisions to begin and end eating."*

More information about the center and a free newsletter can be found at http://www.thecenterformindfuleating.org/.

According to experts on mindful eating, some strategies you can use to become more mindful of your food intake include: eating when hungry, slowing down, enjoying your food, and stopping when you're full. If you're not mindful, you become mindless according to Cornell University food behavior researcher Brian Wansink, PhD, a colleague and friend whose book, *Mindless Eating: Why We Eat More Than We Think* discusses how the size of one's plate can affect the amount of food one consumes and the resulting weight loss or gain. Wansink's website (http://mindlesseating. org/) also provides a slew of fascinating and free information.

Another great tool is TROPSTIX®, my patented eating utensil. This utensil will help you to become a more mindful eater, because it works like chopsticks you get at your favorite Asian restaurant. Without effort, it slows down the rate of your eating. With each bite, you embrace the texture, aroma, and flavor of the food, eating until you're about 80 percent full. (This is called "Hara Hachi Bu," and you will learn more about it when you read the Ground Rules in Section II).

Tracking Your Progress

Committing to your program also requires tracking your progress day by day. A food diary is a powerful tool that can help where you can slash daily calories and provide you with valuable data to fine-tune your personal weight-loss formula. Later on, you can use this information to help maintain your weight loss too.

Without a food diary, research shows that people typically think they ate half as much and exercised twice as much as they really did. Writing it down forces you to face the truth and reveals patterns and habits that may sabotage your best efforts to lose. A survey of 685 participants in the Freedom from Fat program at Kaiser Permanente in Portland, Oregon, showed that dieters who kept a food and exercise log lost 33 percent more weight in an eight-week period than those who didn't.

Keeping a food log works because it forces you to slow down and really think about your food selections. You become more aware of what you're putting in your mouth. It also reveals sneaky sources of calories and specific areas you need to prioritize, such as cutting back on added sugars, oils, or latte additions like cream and flavored syrups. If you don't keep track of what you eat, it's easy to forget that 300 calorie muffin or 500 calorie whipped cream, syrup spiked latte you scarfed down while shopping.

Tracking also helps you to determine whether you are getting most of your calories at one sitting or spreading them out throughout the day. Do you skip breakfast, then ambush the vending machine midmorning? Or mindlessly munch on junk food when you watch TV? Seeing problem behaviors in black and white can help you take responsibility for them. And, best of all, it works.

Pocket Coach©, my handheld food diary tracking system, allows you to track meal by meal your food and fluid intake relative to your program and can really help you stay on track.

Principle 5: Get Lean, Get Sleep

Rest, especially in the form of deep sleep, is essential in the detoxification process and in attaining optimal health during weight loss. The amount of rest one gets has been shown to affect energy levels, anxiousness, and decision making, metabolism, appetite, mood, and overall performance— especially in competitive sports.

Remember the *New England Journal of Medicine* study that showed that toxic food habits make it harder for people to stick with weight loss attempts, while healthy habits predicted long-term success? The same study showed that sleep duration also affects people's efforts to reach and maintain an ideal body weight. Researchers found that participants gained more weight when they slept less than six hours or more than eight hours per night. That means too little or too much sleep can both be detrimental to your efforts to lose and maintain an ideal weight.

Many factors effect deep rest, including stress, hormones, dieting, excessive exercise, diet, and the use of substances like alcohol, caffeine, and some herbs. Sadly, in response to the stresses of modern life, many people resort to over-the-counter, prescription, or illegal remedies to help them fall asleep. Do not fall into this trap! It can counteract the benefits of all your hard work on this program.

There are several safe, healthy strategies you can use to ensure a sound sleep. Non-dietary strategies include securing a dark, quiet, cool room, wearing ear plugs, and listening to soothing music or watching pleasant television programs before sleep. Also be sure to store your electronics—cell phones, notebooks and laptops—in another room.

Coach's Corner

Neurotransmitters and Sleep

Neurotransmitters are the AT&T between our minds and bodies, dictating appetite, sleep, and overall performance. Excitatory neurotransmitters like norepinephrine stimulate our bodies and minds, while inhibitory neurotransmitters like serotonin exert a calming influence. Neurotransmitters are influenced by diet and lifestyle habits. Neurotransmitters that can have a direct impact on the success of your Legally Lean program include melatonin, serotonin, and GABA.

Neurotransmitter	Relationship to Sleep/Food Sources
Melatonin	Marker of circadian rhythm; decreases body temperature.Released from pineal gland in response to darkness. Level highest at night; triggers sleep onset, decreases sleep latency. **Food Sources:** Oats, sweet corn, brown rice, Japanese radish, ginger, tomatoes, bananas, and barley.
Serotonin	Precursor to melatonin. Lack of serotonin is associated with hyperactivity, diminished tendency to fall asleep, and binge-eating. **Foods Sources:** Spinach, turkey, and bananas.
GABA (gammaaminobutyric acid)	Potent inhibitory amino acid; may be responsible for preventing sensory stimuli from reaching the cerebral cortex and interrupting sleep. Activity enhanced by barbiturates, tranquilizers, and hypnotics. **Food Sources:** Pork, beef, sesame and sunflower seeds. green, black, and oolong decaf tea.

Dietary tactics for sleeping well include avoiding alcohol and caffeine in the afternoon or late evening, since these can impact your deepest form of sleep. This sleep is called REM sleep, which stands for "rapid eye movement." This is the sleep you observe in newborns when their eyes twitch continuously. During REM sleep, your brain cells rejuvenate and your growth hormone (GH), which builds lean muscle, peaks. This leaves you refreshed and ready to start a brand new day on your program. (For additional food strategies, see Coach's Corner on **page 32**.)

Decide to Succeed

This section has taught you the overriding principles that will provide you with a template for success on your Legally Lean program. Before you go further, I would like to suggest that you commit to making Legally Lean your last diet. Why?

At some point, everyone gains a few pounds—after the holidays, on a vacation, or as a result of daily stress. This results in the need to take off a few pounds, and that can be healthfully accomplished with an approach like Legally Lean. However, gaining and losing weight repeatedly is unquestionably detrimental to your overall well-being and quality of life, and it should be avoided at all costs.

Research suggests repetitive weight cycling (repeated attempts to lose weight only to regain it) impedes permanent efforts to stay lean. I see this situation repeatedly in my athletes who need to make weight to compete. My professional boxers, wrestlers, and body builders know all too well the negative impact of weight cycling over time.

When you make dieting a lifetime habit, your body changes in response. Here are some of the changes you might see:

- More fat gain with each dieting cycle
- Fewer calories burned throughout the day
- Less satisfaction after mealtime, mostly due to lower levels of leptin, the "feeling satisfied" hormone normally produced after eating
- More hunger, possibly due to increased levels of ghrelin (the hunger hormone) and due to deprivation
- Higher levels of blood cortisol, the stress hormone produced to help you tackle your day, personal issues, and your traing sessions. More cortisol means more gut fat and more muscle breakdown.

In other words, repeated dieting and weight cycling will make you hungrier, more stressed, less lean, more fat, more frustrated, and more depressed. So it makes sense to commit to your future by following the Ground Rules in the next section and the program outlined in the rest of this book.

Make this your very last attempt to lose any significant amount of weight you may need to lose. If you fall, pick yourself up and start over again. And, at all costs, avoid a "saint or sinner" mindset. Think of your program as a journey where you grow, learn, and accept your reactions to more challenging times in life, even if that means an occasional unhealthy eating or drinking day. Remember, tomorrow is always the first day of your life. This book, the Pocket Coach©, and TropStix® Utensil emphasize the most important underlying principle: take each day at a time, each bite at a time.

SECTION

II

LEGALLY LEAN PLAYBOOK

Take Your Mark, Set, Go

Achieving the optimal physique is the culmination of proper training, adequate nutrition, hydration, and rest. The Legally Lean program keeps it simple and real. The program is built on the basics of optimal nutrition and teaches you how to fuel your body based on the foundation of exercise science. This means learning how to eat in order to maintain muscle energy and optimal acid-base conditions for the muscle to work.

In Section I, we focused on the science of losing fat verses muscle weight by selecting the healthiest foods in the best combinations at the right time, changing poor eating habits and food choices with a Detox, and the impact of training and sleep on your physique. In this section, you will find the Legally Lean Ground Rules, which are the step by step "plays" for selecting the eating plan and the food timing and combining strategies that will work best for you.

The Legally Lean Food Program starts with two basic plans: 1200 calories and 1500 calories. These plans are appropriate for healthy adults striving to reach their optimal weight in the least amount of time, athletes striving to cut weight, and others who are looking to propel their diets towards a healthier, more optimal eating regimen.

If you are a young athlete or a high school, collegiate, elite, or a professional athlete who trains multiple hours or who completes several training sessions per day, you will unquestionably require more calories. An appropriate plan for you is outlined in Section IV, Performance Eating for Athletes.

Setting the Bar

The goal of this section is to get everyone on the same nutritional page, which means consuming foods, beverages, and spices that are the best sources of vitamins, minerals, and phytonutrients to support optimal health. The recommended foods for your program can be found, in the **Legally Lean Food Bar**.

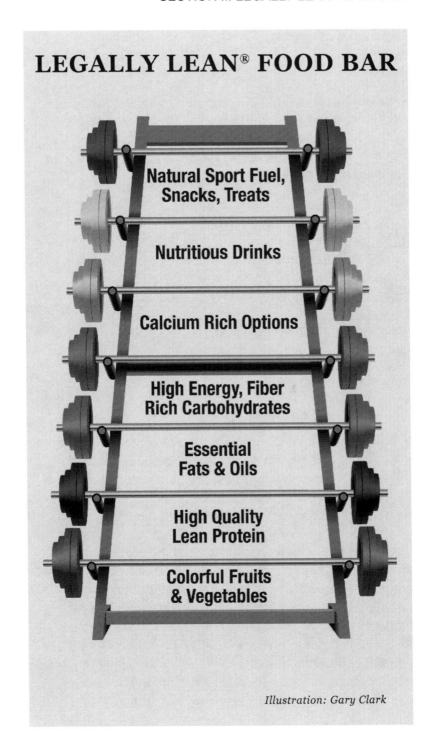

LEGALLY LEAN® FOOD BAR

Natural Sport Fuel, Snacks, Treats

Nutritious Drinks

Calcium Rich Options

High Energy, Fiber Rich Carbohydrates

Essential Fats & Oils

High Quality Lean Protein

Colorful Fruits & Vegetables

Illustration: Gary Clark

Legally Lean Ground Rules

Choosing from the options on the Legally Lean Food Bar, you will need to observe the following guidelines:

1. Choose at least one serving of a Peak Performance CORE food from each food group listed on the Bar.

Keep it simple. Try to master a few foods first, rotating the foods with different spice blends and recipes to get a phytonutrient boost along with a delicious fresh taste.

Every fourth day (recovery day) you can shop for new foods and new spices to expand your options.

Core Foods Include:

Colorful fruits and vegetables
High quality lean protein
Essential fats and oils
High energy, fiber-rich carbohydrates
Calcium-rich options
Refreshing beverages
Natural sport fuel, snacks, and treats

2. Eliminate Toxic food

This includes foods that are toxic to you and/or toxic in general. As discussed in Section I, any foods which compromise your nutritional intake or the absorption of vitamins, minerals, or phytonutrients in your food are toxic! In other words, eat clean.

Get rid of foods with added sugars. Also eliminate excessive sweets; unhealthy fats; processed, ready-to-eat packaged foods and snacks; junk foods; fried foods; and fast foods. You will also need to let go of pro-inflammatory foods such as refined (white) grains, red meats, processed meats, trans fats, and alcohol. These foods are toxic for everyone, but in addition, you will also need to identify your own *personal* potential toxic foods. Sometimes these include addictive foods like alcohol, diet sodas, and artificial sweeteners.

When trying to "eat clean," it's also best to strive for organics. Look for "Certified Organic" on the product label. According to a recent Food and Marketing Institute (FMI) survey, more consumers are spending on organics.

Why not join the crowd? I know this sounds like an expensive investment. After all, isn't one of the major grocery store chains in the organic industry nicknamed "whole pay check?"

What Does Organic Mean?

The USDA National Organic Program (NOP) defines organic as follows:

- Food produced by farmers who emphasize the use of renewable resources and the conservation of soil and water to enhance environmental quality for future generations.

- Organic meat, poultry, eggs, and dairy products come from animals that are given no antibiotics or growth hormones.

- Organic food is produced without using most conventional pesticides; fertilizers made with synthetic ingredients or sewage sludge; bioengineering; or ionizing radiation.

- Before a product can be labeled "organic," a government approved certifier inspects the farm where the food is grown to make sure the farmer is following all the rules necessary to meet USDA organic standards.

- Companies that handle or process organic food before it gets to your local supermarket or restaurant must be certified, too.

Three categories of organic:

- 100% organic means just that. One-hundred percent of the ingredients (other than water and salt) are organic.

- Organic on its own means 95 percent of the product is organic.

- "Includes organic" means 70 percent of ingredients must be organic.

Source: http://www.organic.org/home/faq
More information on Organic Agriculture at: http://www.usda.gov/wps/portal/usda/usdahome?contentidonly=true&contentid=organic-agriculture.html

Well, the notion that organic foods are always more expensive is not always true. In fact, when you compare the cost of eating foods free of unnecessary additives to the cost of health care from introducing foreign compounds to your body, you'll actually save money on medications to manage the immediate effects such as potential headaches, joint aches and discomfort, and migraines. You'll also avoid the costs associated with chronic potential issues associated with additives from Persistent Organic Pollutants (aka POPs) and others, such as metabolic disorders, diabetes, and reproductive issues (see Coach's Corner). And you may even save your life!

As the demand for organic foods and for the transparency that consumers need and want from food companies goes up, the cost will come down. Buying local organics cuts costs, as does joining a Community Supported Agriculture (CSA) or Buying Club (www. unitedbuyingclubs.com/index.htm). You can also choose in-expensive grocery store brand organics such as Publix, Kroger, Wegman's, Trader Joes, and 365 Brand. Don't be afraid to buy organic foods frozen or in bulk, both healthy options.

Coupon clipping is not just for reality shows, they can save you money too! Try www.coupons.com , www.ValPak.com, www. SmartSource.com. You can log onto the following websites which can not only help you to save but to learn how to buy, store and prepare fresh vegetables, fruits and delicious meals. The Produce for Better Foundation Organization's Fruit and Veggie More Matters Website's link to saving starts here http://www.fruit-sandveggiesmorematters.org/fruits-and-vegetables-on-a-budget or the International Food and Information Council Foundation website http://www.foodinsight.org/blogs/can-taste-and-health-really-co-exist-and-reasonable-cost%3F

If none of these stores can be found in your community, shop online! When I don't see my favorite organic foods at the right price, I Google the food and either go directly to the source or to Amazon or EBay, where you'll find deep discounts. If you need to prioritize your organic spending, according to www.organic.org, coffee, cereal, bread, and even hamburger may cost the same or even less than their conventional counterparts. Buying in season or even growing your veggies and fruits can help to save costs. Two great websites to visit for seasonal calendars, guidance and recipes are: http://www.fruitsandveggiesmorematters.org/what-fruits-and-vegetables-are-in-season and at The Plant Powered Dietitian™ Sharon Palmer's website: http://www.sharonpalmer. com/perch/resources/seasonal-produce-chart-1.pdf .

If you're on a fixed budget, then buy the organic foods that matter most: those whose conventional counterparts have the highest amounts of toxins. The Environmental Working Group (http://www.ewg.org/foodnews/) publishes the Dirty Dozen List each year to highlight foods compiled from U.S. Department of Agriculture (USDA) data on 48 fruits and veggies with pesticide residues. They also feature the Clean 15 list of fruits and vegetables of least concern.

And if none of the options listed appeal to you, grow your own! Did you know that home gardening is one of the hottest trends among 18 to 34 year olds? Even if you live in a big city apartment, you can grow your own on the window shelf and there are plenty of seeds to buy and experts to guide you with the growing process. Gardening is not only a cost savings option, it's potentially healthier, cleaner, and safer, and therapeutic too! Gardening is also a form of exercise, good for building your strength, balance and endurance. For "How-To" tips on getting started, visit http://www.fruitsandveggiesmorematters.org/starting-your-vegetable-garden

What About GMOs?

No doubt a hot topic, there are two sides to every story, and that is true for GMO (aka biotech) crops.

First of all, what are they?

According to the Council for Biotechnology Information, GMOs are: *"the process of intentionally making a copy of a gene for a desired trait from one plant or organism and using it in another plant."*

Why GMOs?

Food and nutrition expert and top sports nutritionist Leslie Bonci , MPH, RD, CSSD, LDN, author of several books (see Appendix B) shares that on the bright side, food biotechnology can help fight plant diseases; improve growth quality to ensure that the ever-growing billion-person global population will be fed in the future; provide consistent fruit quality, texture, color, and taste in order to get Americans to overcome their fruit and vegetable deficit; and reduce the amount of pesticides used for growing crops.

On the other side of the coin is the *unknown*, according to those opposed to biotech *anything* in the foods we eat. One group, the Non-GMO Project, a non-profit organization offering North America's only third-party verification and labeling for non-GMO products, points out, in the European Union (EU) GMO labeling is mandatory.

In Australia and New Zealand, all GE foods intended for sale must undergo a safety evaluation by the Food Standards Australia New Zealand (FSANZ). And, according to the website www. JustLabelIt.org, 64 countries worldwide now require labeling of Genetically Modified Foods. There are more than 60 active bills in 26 states that would require labeling or prohibit the sales of GE foods.

Bottom Legally Lean Line?

We all have the right to know what's in our foods (and supplements) and to choose the foods we want to eat. Knowing what's in the food we eat is only fair to help us make those choices. In the meantime, you can learn more about GMOs at www. GMOanswers.com and find a list of verified Non-GMO sources at: http://www.nongmoproject.org/find-non-gmo/search-participating-products/.

Additional resources: http://www.nongmoproject.org/learn-more/what-is-gmo/
Taylor, Lori. Exploring the Case Against GE Foods and Laidlaw,
Sarah. Genetically Modified/Genetically Engineered Foods: What are They?
The Integrative RDN: Dietitians in Integrative and Functional Medical Practice, Spring 2014, Volume 16, Issue 4 and http://gmoanswers.com/.

3. Select Concentrated Sources of Phytonutrients

Phytonutrients are the non-essential, biologically active, naturally occurring chemical components that provide the color, flavor, and aroma of plant-based foods. There are more than 2,000 colors, aromas, and flavors found in fruits, vegetables, whole grains, nuts, seeds, herbs, spices and beverages like tea and red wine. These compounds defend plants naturally from infections, and they can protect us, too! Phyotnutrients have a profound impact on our overall health, well-being, athletic training, and performance.

Phytonutrients contribute numerous vitamins and minerals, including antioxidants. They also protect our cells during times of oxidative stress resulting from radiation, pollution, and normal body metabolism, and they detoxify potential carcinogens—meaning they block, suppress, and even kill cancer cells. They can repair DNA damage caused by smoking and other harmful environmental exposures, and they are as effective as over the counter anti-inflammatories and anti-bacterial agents.

Specific food sources of phytonutrients include: carotenoids in carrots, green leafy vegetables, and citrus; polyphenols in apple and tea; epigallocatechin-3-gallate (EGCG) in dark chocolate and tea; allylic sulfides in onions, leeks, shallots, and garlic; indoles from cruciferous vegetables like broccoli, cauliflower, cabbage, and Brussels sprouts; and capsaicin in hot peppers. And that's just to name a few.

Choose colorful fruits and veggies; lignins from 100 percent whole grains; polyphenols from grapes and chocolate; quercetin from apples and bell peppers, etc. Eat foods raw or prepare your foods with minimal heat to preserve vitamins, minerals, and phytonutrients—steam, bake, or lightly stir fry in a small amount of virgin olive oil since some are enhanced by healthy fats like lycopene in tomatoes.

The International Food and Information Council (IFIC) has a beautiful summary of phytonutrients available FREE online titled Functional Foods at: http://www.foodinsight.org/Content/3842/ Final%20Functional%20Foods%20Backgrounder.pdf

4. Drink Up!

Fluids are as important as food when it comes to maintaining optimal health. We can last several months without some vitamins and minerals, and about eight weeks without food, but we can only last a few days without water and fluids. The importance of fluids is highlighted in the Coach's Corner on **page 136.**

To avoid dehydration, you must include a minimum of 2.7 liters of water or other fluids if you're a woman and 3.7 liters if you're a man. Lemon water, tea, coffee, filtered water, and flavored (unsweetened) natural vitamin water are all great options. If time permits, whip up your own Legally Lean Power Green Drink every morning, made with fresh wheatgrass or Moringa powder, beets, organic berries, and deep green veggies (recipe **page 186**).

Fluids have a variety of critical life functions. These include transporting blood, assisting with cellular chemical reactions for creating energy, and carrying away stressful waste products like lactic acid, which is formed during some workouts. Fluids also act as a shock absorber in joints and around the spinal cord, lubricate the digestive tract and tissues with mucus so your food flows freely down your digestive tract, and regulating your body temperature, since when you sweat, the body becomes cooler.

Since the body is roughly 60 percent fluid, you need to replenish fluids with beverages and foods on a regular basis. If you live in a hot environment, train at high altitudes, or travel frequently by plane, you'll need even more fluid. Unfortunately, few people come close to meeting their needs.

If you don't replace what you lose, it could be extra stressful for your system just to get through the day. You see, just a one percent fluid loss can make you nauseous, cause cramps, and give you a migraine headache. And if you lose more than one percent, you're at risk for dizziness, weakness, confusion, anxiety, lethargy, and even fainting. If fluid losses are not replaced, the consequences can be fatal.

In the long run, staying hydrated is more complicated than just grabbing a glass of water. Additional factors to consider when you're working on preventing dehydration include your fluid choices and the addition of ingredients like caffeine and electrolytes (minerals which help to improve fluid absorption and prevent cramping.) This topic will be continued in Sections III and IV.

5. Practice "Hara Hachi Bu"

In Japanese "Hara Hachi Bu" is a Confucian saying that means, "Eat until you are about 80 percent full." It is believed that the Okinawans of Okinawa, Japan are some of the healthiest and most prevalent centurions on the planet because of this approach to eating unlike our obese American population whose approach is "more is better".

This calorie controlled, mindful way of eating more slowly and consciously has merit. Here are three reasons why:

1. It takes 20 minutes for your body to signal to your brain that there is no more need for food.

2. Conscious eating means eating fewer total calories.

3. You'll enjoy your food more, spending time savoring the textures, flavors, and aroma.

Take it from the Okanawans who live in Japan. One of the planet's longest-lived cultures, the Okanawans eat about 20 percent fewer calories, taking in nutritious foods to balance their energy needs. Maybe that's why they have 3.5 times more centurions than the rest of Japan, one of highest rates in the world! They also suffer from fewer chronic diseases, with 59 percent less cerebral vascular disease, 59 percent less heart disease, and 69 percent less malignancy than the rest of the planet.

Some call this eating approach "calorie restriction" (CR) or eating just the amount you actually need to sustain optimal health and life.

Not to be confused with an eating disorder, calorie restriction is actually being practiced by the Okanawans. There are plenty of studies to suggest the benefits of eating just enough calories. For one thing, this approach may contribute to longer, healthier lives. There's even a society devoted to this concept at www.crsociety.org/.

As mentioned in the previous section, you can also try two strategies I created to help my clients to become more aware and slow down their eating. You can visit my website and learn more about my patented utensil called TropStix®, and you can pick up a Pocket Coach©, the food tracking pad you can take with you to mealtime. See Section I, **page 31**, for details.

6. Eat Lean Protein

Protein is essential for keeping the body healthy, strong, and looking good. Protein is a nutritional anchor when it comes to training and recovery, since when you're using more energy you require more protein to prevent the breakdown of your muscles. If you're taking boxing, martial arts, or track and field, or you play team sports such as club football, rugby, soccer, or baseball to break your sweat, no doubt you can also benefit from a moderately higher protein diet.

Some of protein's most important functions include:

- Building, maintaining, and repairing muscle;

- Regulating hormones like insulin and thyroid, which control how you process food;

- Manufacturing enzymes, which help to digest and metabolize foods;

- Building antibodies, which help protect us from disease or allergic reactions;

- Forming hemoglobin for oxygen transport around the body;

- Making muscle proteins which help muscles to contract and release upon demand;

- Maintaining the pH of the blood system for normal chemical reactions to occur;

- Transporting other chemicals, like fats, around the body; and providing an emergency fuel source when adequate carbohydrates are not available or when energy need exceeds intake.

Regardless of the food source of protein, what is most important is getting all of the essential amino acids. These nine essential amino acids are a critical part of your daily diet, because if you are deficient in one or more of the amino acids, protein will be an underperformer in the body. If you don't get enough of each of the essentials, and top your life with a little stress, you'll be more likely to get sick, lose your hair, have a poor complexion, and lose stamina.

Athletes may need up to twice as much protein as inactive men and women. If you don't have time to prepare a protein-rich meal, drink your protein or find portable foods like snack bars, puddings, or shakes that can help you meet your daily needs. Many sport drinks, bars, and shakes offer high quality protein like whey, casein, soy, egg whites, and vegan hemp, pea, and rice combos, so there is no need to stress about not being able to eat enough.

If you don't replace the protein you use in your workouts through your diet, you can lose weight. However, this type of weight loss will affect your muscle appearance. You will have the appearance of "Olive Oyl," Popeye's girlfriend whose muscles sank because she wouldn't eat her spinach. This weight loss will be even greater if you're not consuming enough total calories. It will look different from typical healthy weight loss, because in addition to losing muscle mass, you will also lose protein from your skin, hair, and immune system.

Coach's Corner

Lean Protein Options

For Poultry:
- Go cage-free, and antibiotic- and hormone-free whenever possible (see thrifty strategies for buying organic on **page 39**).
- Choose a healthy cooking method.
- Remember that grilling and blackening poultry at high temperatures results in the production of compounds which can promote the development of cardiovascular disease and cancer.
- Stick to white meat from skinless chicken or turkey.
- Bake, poach, or slow cook with mounds of veggies, and served with a side of whole grains or beans.

Eggs
- Choose cage-free.
- Choose grass fed, Omega-3 fortified.

Plant Based
- Seitan
- Lowfat almond/soy cheese
- Veggie burgers/meatless balls or ground meatless
- Dried soy or chickpeas

For Fish

• Choose Omega-3 rich salmon, sardines, and mackerel.

• Buy fish that is mercury- and polychlorinated biphenyl (PBC) free.

• Avoid swordfish and shark.

• Steam, poach, or pan "fry" at low temperatures.

• Check out the Monterey Bay Aquarium website or the Environmental Protection Agency Website for up-to-date sources of the freshest, least toxic, and environmentally sensitive farmed fishes.

If you are pregnant or considering pregnancy, the FDA suggests avoiding raw fish like sushi, swordfish, shark, mackerel, and tilefish.

Red meat

I know what you're thinking: I previously discouraged you from consuming red meat because of its potential pro-inflammatory fat content. As someone who grew up with a European mom, where red meat was the staple, I stayed strong, played sports, and grew up to be a pain-free, healthy adult, so I empathize with those of you who tend to follow the popular Paleo program, or just can't live without your red meat.

If you choose to consume red meat on special occasions, holidays, your birthday or anniversary, or just because, then:

• Choose grass-fed, antibiotic- and hormone-free if possible.

• Buy the lowest in fat and saturated fat option, like USDA lean or extra lean. In a 3.5-oz serving, lean red meat has 10 grams of fat, with 4.5 grams of saturated fat and 95 mg cholesterol or less. Examples are strip steak, shoulder steak, tenderloin steak, and t-bone steak).

• Extra lean red meat has 5 or fewer grams of total fat, with two grams of saturated fat and 95 mg cholesterol. Examples include top round steak and top sirloin steak.

Coach's Corner

Vegetarians, Protein, Optimal Health & Perfomance

For vegetarians, mastering the art of balancing plant-based foods is an essential part of attaining optimal health and sports performance. The good news is, healthy vegetarians can be assured of getting generous amounts of vitamins, minerals, phytonutrients, healthy fats, *and* protein.

One concern for stricter vegetarians is getting enough protein, especially the essential amino acids (EAA) previously discussed. The EAA are the building blocks of protein, found completely in animal products, but in more limited amounts in plant-based foods. Vegetarians also have lower levels of creatine in the body than carnivores and may benefit from taking a safe certified supplement especially if engaging in high intensity activity (See Appendix A but always check with your medical doctor first prior to taking any dietary supplement.)

Some foods might be rich in one amino acid, others in another. Therefore, variety is key within the plant kingdom. Since most athletes get stuck in training food ruts like bagels, pasta, and cereal (which, in this case, is limiting in lysine) the key is to get enough beans, nuts, and soy to "complement" or provide this missing amino acid. Soy is the only plant-based food that has all the essential amino acids.

As for vitamins and minerals, the biggest problem areas are getting enough vitamin B12, iron, calcium, and zinc. (These are abundant in meat products.) Alternative plant-based sources, fortified foods, or a supplement must be provided or deficiencies will occur and impact health performance.

Some excellent resources include my first book geared towards athletes called *The Vegetarian Sports Nutrition Guide* (Wiley, 2000) and for everyone, author/dietitian Sharon Palmer's books *The Plant Powered Diet* and *Plant Powered for Life*. Find recipes and more at her website: www. http://www.sharonpalmer. com/. The Vegetarian Resource Group is also a go-to FREE resource for everything vegetarian. http://www.vrg.org/

7. Include Healthy Fats

The healthy fats I recommend include fish oil, extra virgin olive oil, nuts and seeds, and soy. These fats include the essential Omega-3s and Omega-6s that you must get through your diet, since you can't make them on your own. The essential Omega-3 and Omega-6 have been shown to reduce both blood cholesterol levels and unhealthy LDL cholesterol levels. They are also less inflammatory than other fats.

Also, since 25 percent of the type of fat you need for your brain is DHA Omega-3 fats, it's important to get enough through your diet for brain health. In addition to using essential Omega fats in the brain, the body uses them to make hormone-like substances that regulate blood pressure, blood clot formation, blood lipids, and substances that respond to infection and injury.

Omega-3 fats are found to have many health benefits. They especially play a role in the inhibition of the inflammation associated with autoimmune diseases like arthritis, heart disease, and diabetes

Also read more about Omega-3s in Section IV, V and in Appendix A.

Coach's Corner

Meeting Your Essential Omega 3 Needs

To ensure adequate Omega-3s sources in your system, especially from the plant-based alpha linoleic acid (ALA) form, you have to do more than consume enough.

You also have to protect yourself against the following issues, which can limit the conversion of the plant-based ALA to its active form:

• Avoid excessive simple carbohydrates.

• Limit alcohol.

• Protect against vitamin and mineral deficiencies.

8. Stock Up on Wholesome Snacks & Fuel

Stock up on approved ready-to-consume energy snacks for home, in the car, or at the office to avoid excessive hunger and to use as pre- and post-workout fuel. At work, in the car, at school, in between workout sessions or classes, or eating on the fly—literally at the airport traveling—look for the following products:

- Preferably organic with a blend of high and low glycemic carbohydrates, high quality protein, healthy fats and/or fiber.

- Bars, gels, and energy chews that include natural sweeteners such as honey, beet sugar, date sugar, brown rice syrup, black strap molasses, organic corn syrup, and calorie-free stevia and monk fruit.

- Without artificial ingredients, sweeteners like aspartame and sucralose, or coloring or preservatives.

- With no more than 100 percent Daily values for vitamins and minerals

- Caffeine-free items or substances containing no more than the amount in a brewed cup of coffee, about 120mg.

- Minus artificial flavors, artificial colorings, and brominated vegetable oil (BVO). FYI—BVO is actually a flame retardant which was banned in Europe and Japan. Unfortunately, it is still included in some of the most popular sports drinks here in the United States. BVO is associated with reproductive and behavioral problems, skin lesions, memory loss, and nerve disorders.

9. Use Caffeine Wisely

Having a cup of coffee or green tea for an energy jolt might not be the worst habit, and it is welcome on the Legally Lean program since there is research to show that coffee and tea have numerous health benefits.

Caffeine is a stimulant that has been shown to improve reaction time, increase mental alertness, and reduce perceptions of fatigue. It even stimulates fat burning, causing a glycogen sparing effect. Sparing glycogen (the stored sugars in your muscles and liver) is a good thing, since with extra energy in the tank, you'll be able to go stronger and last longer—a critical component to building the time you exercise, your endurance, and your fat burn!

Caffeine may also kick up your metabolism and decrease your appetite if you tend to store fat and need to lose weight. It can also decrease your cancer risk—studies show about a three pecent risk reduction for bladder, breast, buccal and pharyngeal, colorectal, endometrial, esophageal, hepatocellular, leukemic, pancreatic, and prostate cancers in those who consumed up to several cups (3 to 6 daily), although I don't advise that as a general health recommendation because of the potential side effects for many. Studies also show a seven percent reduction in the risk of type 2 diabetes with every cup of coffee consumed daily. Caffeine can delay the onset of degenerative diseases connected with oxidative cellular stress, such as heart disease, hypertension, joint pain and headaches. And it can reduce your risk of dying from cardiovascular disease, especially if you are a woman.

Caffeine appears to improve muscle contractibility, increase work output, lengthen time to exhaustion, and reduce rates of perceived exertion both during and at the end of exercising. It may improve your ability to go longer and further by a whopping 11.2 percent. One study compared trained athletes who consumed caffeine and carbohydrate with those who consumed food-based carbs alone. Those who consumed caffeine showed a muscle recovery rate four hours after exercise 66 percent higher than those who did not consume caffeine.

Other studies have shown that caffeine use is associated with a 17 to 35 percent reduction in the DNA damage caused by free radicals, the loose oxygen molecules that destroy the body's cells, with a significant increase of 35 percent in the antioxidant *superoxide dismutase*. Caffeine has also been shown to improve cognition, your reasoning mechanism—especially important for making decisions during times of stress.

How Much Caffeine Is Too Much?

The ergogenic effect of caffeine varies between individuals, depending on numerous factors. While some individuals feel nothing on lower doses of caffeine, others who are caffeine-sensitive may suffer mental over-arousal, nervousness, heart palpitations, and elevated blood fats as a result of drinking any beverages or foods with caffeine whatsoever.

Also, if you drink caffeinated beverages on a regular basis, you're less likely to see a boost in energy levels like when you really need it, during times of stress or when dealing with fatigue. In fact, too much coffee can overtax already spent adrenal glands which have been busy producing adrenaline to "fight or flight" your daily exercise and stress.

If you cannot dream of starting your day without a cup of Joe, then my recommendation is to select healthy delivery systems like coffee and tea, which have extra health benefits. Avoid energy drinks and supplements, which in some cases have caused death. Energy drinks can be especially toxic when combined with alcohol, which has the opposite effect on the body. Often those who combine the two feel stimulated enough to drive home from a night at the club despite their level of intoxication.

If you are considering consuming caffeine for performance, it is recommended that you give it a test drive first. Research suggests that an ergogenic effect in athletes is seen at doses of one to three grams per kilogram of body weight.

That means that the 150-pound individual would need at least 68 to 204 grams to feel the benefits. Remember, if you take caffeinated beverages or products on a daily basis, they start to lose their ergogenic effectiveness, so it's best to use them on special occasions. You can also take them out on weekends and reintroduce them during the week (or vice versa).

What About Alcohol?

Alcohol provides an easy, prescription-free, and legal form of re-lief. Having a cocktail has its upside and downside, especially for those with alcohol issues. For one thing, drinking alcohol before bedtime to help with sleep actually has the opposite effect—it prevents or decreases the REM sleep your body needs to heal and repair, build muscle, and recover from a hard workout or hard day's work!

On a physical level, your muscles cannot use the calories from alcohol as a source of fuel physiologically. And at 100 calories for the average drink and up to 400 for the dressed up frozen Daiquiri, Margarita or Pina Colada, who can afford to store it as fat? In addition, while the body is processing alcohol, it limits the amount of sugar it releases into the bloodstream, which cause hypoglycemia (low blood sugar). And long-term drinking problems can lead to vitamin and mineral deficiencies, including deficiencies in B vitamins needed for energy and calcium and magnesium needed for strong bones, just to name a few.

In other words, limit alcoholic drinks to special occasions. And, if you're planning to go ahead and have a few on a special occasion, try to stay on the healthier side of indulging with the following tips:

- Drink one cup water for every alcoholic drink consumed to prevent dehydration.

- Opt for red wine or beer, which have phytonutrients that may be heart-protective.

- Consume clear alcohol like vodka, tequila, or gin to avoid excess congeners, substances responsible for hangovers.

- Mix your favorite brand (preferably clear alcohol) with healthy mixers like low-sugar juices or vitamin fortified waters, which may include antioxidants and other compounds that minimize the impact of stress.

- Take foods rich in B vitamins or take a supplement prior to or with your drink to help metabolize the booze. Examples include 100 percent whole grain snacks like pretzels, crackers, breakfast or energy bars, dried chickpeas, edamame or nuts.

- Don't skip meals to consume a liquid diet which will deplete and stress your system even more, causing you to get drunker and sicker much faster.

- Eat asparagus leaves before and after a night out on the town! Asparagus leaves contain antioxidant chemicals which may accelerate the removal of toxic liver compounds.

More on the consequences and impact of alcohol on sports performance can be found in Section IV.

10. Include Safe, Certified Supplemental Extras

As needed, recommended, and approved by your medical doctor or licensed/certified nutrition expert to select the best supplements to correct deficiencies, boost and support energy levels, enhance the detoxification process, and to reach and maintain optimal health and performance.

Priority Extras will be explored in greater detail in the A-Z Performance Food Guide in Section III and the Selected Supplement Guide in Appendix A.

Timing & Combining

Food timing and combining can make or break the success of your program. When you eat, how much you have at one sitting, the rate at which you consume your food, and the time at which you consume specific nutrients can alter strength, body composition patterns, and weight loss success. There has been extensive research looking at the timing of meals relative to hunger levels, mood, and weight loss.

The Morning Meal

Breakfast is called break-fast because it actually breaks the overnight fast. Most research demonstrates that omitting breakfast can negatively affect how we function throughout the day. Anyone who has tried to start the day without food, deal with getting kids off to school, partner and self out the door to work or contend with a difficult partner, child, co-worker, professor, or work assignment when they were hungry knows what I'm talking about. And if you've ever had the chance to watch the Hawaiian Ironman Triathlon World Championships on TV, you have witnessed the power of a morning meal. No doubt, athletes can attest to the impact the right or wrong morning food choices can make. Research suggests the morning meal will also keep you lean and fit, weighing less than those who skip!

In the morning, eat:

High quality protein, fiber-rich, low sugar, complex carbohydrate and/or a high quality fat source for better morning moods and performance. As you can see on the sample menu on **page 66**, I recommend 1 to 3 oz. from the protein list OR 1 choice from the dairy option list; PLUS 1 from the fruit or high energy carb/ whole grain list, and/or 1 from the healthy fats list.

- A single-size package of low-fat cottage cheese, Greek or Icelandic yogurts, or smoothie. Many of the products on the market are portable, easy-to-store in a mini (office or dorm) refrigerator and are tasty too! Prepare with a variety of fresh or frozen fruits or sugar free jams.

- Coffee only? Add low-fat milk, almond, flax or soy milk and make a café con leche, the Latin version of a half coffee, half-milk beverage. In just one cup of milk, you get a balance of protein, carbohydrates, and fats, as well as riboflavin (B2), vitamins A and D and calcium. Add a scoop of protein equivalent of 2 to 3 oz. of protein (about 14 to 21 grams) and blend it up for a morning coffee shake.

- More motivated? Go to the specialty food section of your grocery or to the health food or body-building store and pick up a few sport shakes and bars. These portable items can be high in protein, carbs, healthy fats or a combination of all three! If fortified, they can give you a nutritional boost to meet your needs on days that you can't find time to eat your best. Most of them do not need refrigeration and can be stored for several months.

- Really ambitious? Cook something up! Try one of my favorite recipes on **pages 183-206** or from any of my other books.

- Regardless of what you choose, choose, something—any-thing—to get your day started on the right foot.

The Midday Meal

Lunchtime meals have also been shown to affect performance on both mental tasks and on mood and energy levels for late-day workouts. Research shows that those who skip a midday meal are at risk for fatigue, anxiety, and lower levels of alertness; however, meal size is the key. On the other hand, large lunches, especially meals containing lots of calories and high energy carbohydrates may cause brain fog and lead to attention deficits and errors on normal, everyday tasks.

A larger-than-normal lunch, including heavy fatty meats, cream laden pasta dishes or fast foods, can also contribute to the afternoon dip in energy levels. Overeating at lunchtime impacts tasks which require sustained attention the most, like taking an afternoon exam or attending a long business meeting.

For midday meals:

Eat enough, but not too much. Including a morning snack can help to balance energy intake throughout the day and prevent overeating at lunchtime.

Start with at least the size of a deck of playing cards worth of protein or the equivalent (21 to 28 grams). Grilled chicken salad, canned and mercury-free water-packed tuna on salad greens, or even a six-inch turkey or sub on 100 % whole grain flat, tortilla, or roll.

Add crunchy veggies like shredded carrots, sprouts, bell peppers, onions, hot peppers, and/or leafy greens for extra fiber, antioxidants and phytonutrients.

Be consistent! Eat within the same time frame each day. Preferably eat the midday meal about 3 to 4 hours after the morning meal. If you're a night shift worker (a firefighter, police officer, nurse, or chef, for example), eat a meal before starting the shift, a snack two hours into the work "day," and a meal midway through. This will help you maintain energy levels throughout the night.

No time to eat? Stop by your local smoothie place and get a fresh fruit smoothie. To boost the protein content and satiability of the beverage, ask for extra yogurt or a protein powder scoop (both typically offered on the side). Grab a package of Omega-3 rich almonds, walnuts, or pistachios. If you need more, add a 100 % whole grain energy bar, and you're set to go!

If worse comes to worst and you're locked in your office or home bogged down with work or the flu, get a can or package of healthy, low sodium, phyto-rich soup.

If you have time, you can make a pot of one of my Legally Lean soups from the recipe section **[page 183]** and drink your lunch. Bring a portion to work with some Puppodums, traditional round Indian crisp breads or 100 % whole grain crackers, soy crisps, or rice chips and wash it all down with some bottled water, coconut water or one of my power boost beverages in the recipe section.

Snack Attacks

Nothing wrong with a little noshing in the afternoon!

The afternoon snack can also affect late afternoon cognitive performance. If you have a 4:30pm class or business meeting, a snack can have a huge impact on your energy levels, your afternoon workout, and on your mood and hunger level after work or for your evening meal. It's best to have your afternoon snack 2 to 3 hours after lunch, and for it to include approximately 100 to 300 calories.

Some examples include:

- A handful of pistachios, almonds or walnuts, dried edamame, chickpeas or whole roasted chestnuts—one of my favorites (see food lists, **pages 67-73**)
- Fresh, frozen, dried or dehydrated fruit
- Low fat dairy "options"—milk, yogurt or cheese with fresh fruit
- Portable energy bars or beverages
- Commercially available snack packs, like fruit canned in its own juice or organic baby food "pouches"
- Organic 100% whole grain high protein breakfast or energy bars
- 100 % whole grain, organic crackers or rice crackers, which are easy to store, require little preparation, and can be eaten at your desk or on the run

This is also a great time of day to get hydrated! Drink a few cups of fluid like water, bottled water or a sugar-free fruit flavored seltzer.

Evening Meal

The evening meal is critical to your body, but also to your mind, soul, and family.

Individuals who eat an evening meal feel stronger, more proficient, and more interested in life, family, and social activities than those who skip dinner. Eating a substantial night meal can also fuel early morning exercise sessions, especially when your stomach says "no" first thing in the morning.

Ideally, the evening meal should be consumed two hours before bedtime. That means if you eat at 6pm, you can go to bed as early as 8pm without affecting your sleep patterns. Eating a heavy meal that is high in calories and fat requires you to call bedtime even later. Otherwise, digestion is still at a peak and sleep can be disrupted throughout the night.

The composition of the evening meal can vary depending on your personal CORE Performance Program.

- For **Go Hard, 3 Day phase**, eat lean high quality protein and veggies.

- For "day off" high carbohydrate replenishment days or if you need to take the edge off a hectic day, or are recovering from an exhaustive run or preparing for a long morning workout, then a plate of quinoa pasta with lycopene-rich red sauce and steamed broccoli or plate of brown rice, beans, veggie soup and fruit salad or one of the recipes in the book may be your best bet. High carbohydrate meals like pasta, rice and beans, and potatoes and steamed veggies also have a calming effect and boost glycogen stores in your muscles and liver. They tend to digest faster than high protein meals and enhance the "good feeling" brain chemical called serotonin, so you may even sleep better!

So, let the games begin.
You have your Legally Lean Playbook and the ground rules to make your Core Performance Program a success. No excuses—let's play ball!

SECTION
III

CORE PERFORMANCE PLAN

Take Your Mark, Get Set, Go

Achieving your optimal physique will require your undivided attention to the Legally Lean Principles and Ground Rules outlined in the previous sections. And as we've said, you'll also need to commit to a challenging, sweaty exercise regimen and to getting adequate rest and recovery in order to reach your goals.

Now it's time to learn in more detail what you're going to eat on your plan.

The **Legally Lean Core Performance Plan** is built on a solid foundation of nutrition science. It takes into account the action and interaction of food components to help fuel your muscles, maintain cell homeostasis, and fine tune your metabolism to help you attain peak physique and performance. The Core Performance Plan is intended for healthy adult men and women interested in a healthy, calorie controlled, fast-working plan.

This plan will work if you want to:
- Lower body weight, body fat, blood fats, blood sugars, and blood pressure;
- Reduce aches and pains associated with excess body weight and poor dietary choices;
- Detox after an alcohol or refined carbohydrate binge or wild vacation;
- Prepare for a special event like an upcoming reunion, wedding, or graduation;
- Lose weight for a movie or television role;
- Or for athletes attempting to make weight to compete or to gain a competitive edge in their sport.

The **Core Performance Plan** is not intended for boys or girls under 18 years of age, pregnant women, or breastfeeding women (who generally have higher calorie requirements even when trying to lose baby weight), or anyone with a medical condition or psychiatric disorder. It is also not intended for serious athletes unless they need to "make weight" for a sports competition such as wrestling or boxing which requires a specific fighting weight.

The goal is not to stay on the **Core Performance Plan** indefinitely, but rather to use the program to jump start your weight loss and establish healthier eating habits.

You can also use the program as a springboard for launching a new health kick, regardless of your ultimate eating plan. You can think of the **Core** as a dietary base camp when you've gotten off track and need to detox from a night out on the town or a vacation.

Setting the Bar

The Legally Lean program has two **Core Plan** options: 1200 calories for women and 1500 calories for men. Women can also follow the higher calorie men's program if they are already consistently consuming at least 500 calories more a day (2000 calories), rather than taking their calories down to 1200.

On the **Core Plan**, you can expect to lose at least one to two pounds per week. Weight loss rate depends on several factors, including the quality and quantity of your current diet and exercise program, your commitment level, and how closely you stick to the Principles and Ground Rules outlined in the previous sections.

The maximum weight you can expect to lose is three to five pounds each week. The amount of weight loss depends upon how different your current diet, lifestyle habits, and exercise program are from the Core Plan. In other words, the worse off you are—the worse you eat and the less exercise you do—the more you can expect to lose.

For example, if you regularly consume red meat; whole fat milk and cheese; fried food; refined carbohydrates such as bread, cereals, crackers, cookies, and cakes; sugary beverages and alcohol; and add extra oils, dressings, sauces, sugar, and cream to your meals, you will lose more than someone who already exercises, eats a plant-based, high vegetable, fruit and whole grains diet. Bottom line: the more you need to change, the more you will lose.

Your weight loss will also be dependent on how well you eat and do not restrict on the program. Research shows that restrictive dieters stop losing weight and plateau at some point, due to the law of metabolic efficiency discussed in Section I. On restrictive diets, your body shuts down.

The goal of the **Core Plan** is to preserve lean muscle in order for your body to continue to burn off the fat! This means eating small meals every two to three hours and including all the foods from the **Legally Lean Food Bar** (*see diagram on page 37*). Using the Legally Lean Food Bar on page 37, you will consume the following (per day):
- 2 or more cups of high fiber, low calorie veggies like greens, tomatoes, onions, mushrooms, cucumber, broccoli, or asparagus

- 2 cups of fruit
- 1 to 3 ounces of lean, high-quality protein
- High energy, fiber-rich carbs like 100 percent whole grains, brown rice, whole grain pasta, quinoa, beans, peas, and corn
- Essential fats and oils from nut butters, extra virgin olive oil, avocado, and coconut
- Keep high calorie, low fiber carbs and extra fats to a minimum.

The foods should be consumed with unsweetened, calorie-free, nutritious beverages and naturally sourced sport drinks, sport bars, and shakes as needed for exercise.

Following the **Core Program** also means going all out, following your plan to a "T" for three days—sticking as closely as you can to the food groups, portion sizes, and menus— then following with one "change-it-up" day, a less intense, higher carbohydrate, light exercise day to recover from your hard three-day effort and to replenish your muscles and mind.

Exercise

I recommend exercising in the morning before your day (or anyone else's day) begins. This way you have no excuse not to exercise. If you like, you can also include a second workout later in the day, choosing exercises that complement the morning workout.

That means that if you ran in the morning, do strength training, TRX or Cross Fit training, yoga, or a dance class in the evening. However, a consistent, rigorous exercise program *any time* of day is always acceptable if that's the only time you have to exercise. As long as you get the job done, that's what counts.

As for the type of exercise to choose, that's up to you. Make it something that you like to do, and make sure that you break a sweat! The rest of the exercise advice, I will leave to your certified personal trainer.

Medical Check Up

Last but not least, before you officially start, get a medical checkup if you haven't had one in the past year, especially if you are 40 years old or older. Request a baseline blood test called a CBC (complete blood count), which is a measure of your immune status including hemoglobin, hematocrit, and red and white blood cells.

Also be sure to ask for a cholesterol profile and blood sugars, liver and kidney enzymes, vitamin D, and a urine and stool analysis. If you are female, be sure to visit your gynecologist and include a mammogram, regardless of your life stage. If you are over 50, please get a colonoscopy, which is a test that has been shown to save many lives.

At a minimum, your checkup will give you a benchmark to let you know how you stand health-wise. You can also use the results as a wakeup call—the impetus for change that gets you motivated to start your program. Then follow up with your medical doctor about 9 to 12 weeks after you start the program (to give your body enough time to show blood and physical changes) and celebrate your accomplishments!

Food Servings Daily

	Women - 1200 calories	Men - 1500 calories
Vegetables	3 cups	2 cups (can add extra cup if desired)
Fruits	2 cups (4 pieces)	2 cups (4 pieces)
Dairy/Dairy Options	2 cups each	2 cups each
High energy carbohydrates: 100 percent whole grains, brown rice, oats, potato, high fiber bread or cereals	1/2 cup (size of 1/2 a tennis ball)	1 cup (size of 1 tennis ball)
High carbohydrate veggies or legumes: peas, corn, squash, yuca, plantain, beans	1/2 cup (size of 1/2 a tennis ball)	1 cup (size of 1 tennis ball)
High quality lean protein	size of 2 decks of cards— (56 grams protein)	size of 3 decks of cards—(63 grams protein)
Healthy Fats	3 tsp. healthy fats— size of (1/2 shot glass)	4 tsp. healthy fat— (size of 1/2 shot) glass. Plus no more than another drop of additional fat
Beverages (IOM Rec'd Minimum)	9 cups fluids (2.7 liters)	13 cups fluids (3.7 liters)
Snack Options:	100 calories (25 grams) protein for 3 "hard days" or 100 calories (25 grams) carbs for Recovery Day (every 4th day)	100 -150 calories (25 grams) protein for 3 "hard days" or 100-150 calories (25 grams) carbs for Recovery Day (every 4th day)
Core Program Nutrition Composition:	1200 calories Go Hard 3 Days (high protein): 144 grams carbs (46%); 115 grams protein (36%); 25 grams fat (18%) High Carb Recovery Day: 169 grams carbs (54%); 90 grams protein (29%); 25 grams fat (17%)	1500 calories Go Hard 3 Days (high protein): 164 grams carbs (44%); 117 grams protein (31%); 42 grams fat (25%) High Carb Recovery Day: 189 carbs (50%); 92 grams protein (25%); 42 grams fat (25%)

On the Menu

The next step is translating the science into actual food!
Here are some examples of menus that fit the above guidelines:

Pre-exercise (less than 1 hour before):

8 oz. hot/cold beverage—water with lemon, tea, coffee;
Pre-workout beet juice or powder in water 30 minutes before for
natural nitrate boost!

Pre-exercise (more than 1 hour before):

½ sport or breakfast bar and 16-20 oz. green tea/water

During exercise: less than 1 hour: water/electrolytes; **more
than 1 hour +:** natural sports drink, low sugar coconut water,
organic energy chews or gel as needed

Post-workout: 100-150 calories in recovery shake OR bar with
both high quality protein and carb; low sugar sports or coconut
water or sugar-free green tea add electrolytes, Moringa powder
OR wheatgrass greens powder if desired

Post-exercise:

See Performance Nutrition, Section IV for more specific fueling
guidelines if you exercise longer than one hour.

Breakfast Options (Choose One):

* Beverage: 1 cup coffee, green tea, hot water with lemon or
  veggie juice

* Protein smoothie made with 1 cup fresh fruit and 1 cup low fat
  "milk" (lactose-free, almond, flax, soy or rice milk), plain, 0%
  fat Greek or Icelandic yogurt, or high quality protein powder

* 1 Egg/1 cup egg white omelette with mushrooms, tomatoes,
  spinach, and onions, 1 cup "milk" and 1 cup fruit

* 0% plain Greek or Icelandic yogurt with fresh berries and ¼
  cup 100% high fiber cereal

* 1 serving 100% whole grain cooked cereal with 1 scoop
  protein powder (7-15 grams), 1 cup "milk", ½ banana

Mid-Morning Snack Options (Choose One):

* 15 gram protein low sugar shake/bar, 100-150 calories
* 12 almonds with fresh apple
* ¼ cup dried soy or chickpeas with apple

- 1 tbls. nut butter or 2 tbls. low fat nut butter with piece of fruit
- 1 oz. lowfat cheese or 2 oz. nonfat cheese with fresh fruit
- 0% fat Greek or Icelandic plain yogurt with berries

Lunch Suggestion:

1 cup deep green veggie salad,
+ 2 tsp. olive oil/balsamic dressing
+ 4 oz. lean protein—chicken, turkey, veggie burger, tofu, nonfat cheese, almond, soy or feta cheese
+ ½ cup fresh fruit—berries, mango, kiwi, watermelon, pineapple, citrus sections
+ rice crackers or slice of 100% whole grain bread or ¼ cup beans on salad or side

Afternoon Snack Options (Choose One):

- 15 grams shake/bar, 100-150 calories
- Baby carrots with ¼ cup hummus
- Fresh veggie/fruit juice blend with 7-15 grams unflavored protein powder
- or snack choice from morning snack options

Dinner:

1 cup deep green salad with mixed vegetables
2 tsp. extra virgin olive oil
4 oz. chicken, turkey, game—organic, meat 1 x week
1 cup steamed broccoli, Brussels sprouts, asparagus or greens
½ cup brown rice, whole grain pasta, sweet potato, winter squash/pumpkin or ¼ cup beans, hummus, plain lentils, in soup or dip

Snack: 2 hours or more before bed

- 1 cup of "milk"
- 0 % plain Greek or Icelandic yogurt
- 6 almonds or 8 pistachio nuts

Legally Lean Grocery List

(Updated versions available at www.LegallyLean.com)
Each item equals <u>one serving</u> unless otherwise indicated.

High Quality Protein (Women: 8 oz. daily; Men: 9 oz. daily)
Animal- or plant-based, lean cut, grass fed.

- 1 egg or 5 egg whites (cage free)
- 1 oz. chicken, turkey, lean meat, game (venison, bison, ostrich) preferably free range, organic, antibiotic-free
- Fish: Pacific halibut, herring, catfish, salmon (Alaska Wild), arctic char, barramundi, mussels, sardines
- 1 oz. low fat or nonfat cheese
- ¼ cup cottage cheese

Vegetarian Protein

- Veggie burger (one is usually equal to 2-3 protein servings, 18-21 grams)
- ½ cup black soybean tofu (usually equal to 1 protein serving)
- 2 oz. low fat almond or soy cheese (2 protein servings)
- 3 oz. seitan (usually equal to 2-3 protein servings, 18 grams)
- 3 oz. tempeh (usually equal to 2 protein servings, 16 grams and 1 fat serving)

High Protein Snacks

- Organic beef, turkey, or vegetarian jerky
- ¼ cup edamame goji blend (equals 1 protein and 1 fruit)
- Dried chickpeas
- Dried soynuts
- Organic dried pea snack

High Protein Sport Fuel
Includes shakes, bars, and powders. Check labels carefully.

- 21 grams protein = 3 protein servings
- Look for: less than 8 grams sugar/serving; less than 5 grams fat/serving
- Whey isolate, egg white, soy, or veggie blend—pea, hemp, rice powder

Calcium-Rich Options
(Dairy or Dairy Alternatives, Organic Preferred) (2 cups daily)

- Low-fat nonfat organic milk, almond, soy, hemp or flax milk (unsweetened)

- 6 oz. plain 0% or 1% Greek or Icelandic yogurt
- Frozen desserts—low or nonfat with live active cultures preferred
- 2 oz. low/nonfat almond, soy, or dairy cheese
- 3 tbls. lowfat sour cream

Healthy Fats (Women: 3 tsp./15 grams; Men: 4 tsp./20 grams)
(1 serving =)

- 8 olives
- 16 pistachios
- 6 almonds (23= 3 servings)
- Tiger nuts (20 = 1 fat, ½ high carb serving)
- 2 Brazil nuts
- 4 walnut halves
- 10 peanuts
- 5 hazelnuts
- 1 tbls. sesame, pumpkin or sunflower seeds
- 3 tbls. coconut
- 2 tsp. tahini
- ½ oz. dark chocolate
- 2 tbls. ground flaxseed
- 1 tbls. chia
- 1 tbls. hemp seed
- 1 tsp. almond or other nut butter
- 1 tbls. lowfat peanut or soy butter
- 1/$_{8th}$ (3 tbls) avocado
- 2 tsp. natural spreads
- 1 tbls. organic salad dressing (low sodium)
- 1 tsp. olive, coconut, flax, grape seed, almond oil (cold pressed, organic preferred)
- 1 tsp. butter
- 3 spritzes organic cooking spray

High Carb Foods
(Women: 1 cup (2 servings) day; Men: 2 cups (4 servings) day)

- 100% whole grains (pasta, brown rice, amaranth, millet, wheat berries). Look for organic, more than 5 grams fiber per serving, and less than 8 grams/2 tsp. sugar per serving.

- ½ cup cooked quinoa cereal or pasta
- ½ cup cooked oats/oatmeal
- 1/3 cup dry quinoa flakes cereal
- ½ cup cooked brown, black or wild rice
- 100% whole grain wrap

High Carb Vegetables
(fresh, frozen, dehydrated, or BPA-free canned)

- 1 baked potato (sweet, purple, white) (= 2 servings or 1 cup)
- ½ cup peas, corn, lentils
- 1 cup acorn, butternut, or winter squash
- 1 artichoke
- ½ cup beets
- ½ cup soup (black bean, pea soup, or low-sodium corn chowder)
- ½ cup dasheen (taro)
- ½ cup plantain
- Dried or sprouted chickpeas
- ¼ cup edamame
- 1/3 cup lowfat/nonfat refried bean dip
- 1/3 cup lowfat/nonfat hummus dip

High Carb Energy Snacks:

- 1 organic baby food "pouch" sweet potato, corn, and apple organic baby food
- 3 cups air blown organic popcorn or popped sorghum
- ½ cup whole chestnuts
- ¼ cup dried soybeans
- 10-15 baked tortilla or potato chips
- 1 oz. soy crisps
- 1 brown rice cake
- 8 rice crackers

Fruits (2 cups/4 servings each for both men and women)
Includes whole fruits, fresh, frozen, canned, dehydrated, juiced.

Organic preferred. Dried is okay as a treat, but is high in sugar.

- 1 apple
- 4 apricots
- ½ banana
- ½ black sapote (equals 2 fruit servings)
- ¾ cup blueberries or blackberries
- 1 carambola (star fruit)
- ½ grapefruit
- 15 grapes
- 1 guava
- 1 kiwi
- 10 litchi
- ½ cup mamey
- ½ mango
- 1 nectarine
- 1 orange
- 1 cup papaya
- 1 peach
- ¾ cup pineapple
- 2 plums
- 1 cup raspberries
- 1 ¼ cup strawberries
- watermelon

Dried Fruit

- ½ oz. goji berries
- ½ oz. mulberries
- 2 figs
- 3 dates
- 2 prunes
- 1 oz. raisins
- 1 oz. persimmons
- 1 tbls. dried unsweetened cranberries

Fruit Juices

- ½ cup tart cherry juice
- 1 cup low sugar 100% juice

Fruit Snacks

- Dried organic fruit bar (equals 2 fruits)
- Organic high fiber bar with 14 grams fiber (equals 2 fruits)
- Dried fruit "leather"
- 1 oz. baked apple chips
- 1 package organic energy chews (equals 2 fruit servings)
- 1 organic baby fruit/veg puree pouch (carrot, squash, or apple)

Vegetables
(Women: 3 cups; Men: 2+ cups) Includes whole vegetables, fresh, frozen, BPA-free canned, dehydrated, or juiced. Organic preferred.

- Arugula, lettuce
- Asparagus, broccoli, Brussels sprouts, cauliflower, cabbage, cucumber, celery, carrots
- Bell peppers (red, yellow, orange, green)
- Chayote, eggplant, jicama
- Greens (beet, dandelion, kale, mustard, turnip)
- Onion, garlic, leeks, scallions, shallots
- Mushrooms (all varieties)
- Radishes
- Squash (zucchini and yellow)
- Spinach
- Tomatoes
- Water chestnuts

Beverages
(Women: 2.7 liters/9 cups+ per day; Men: 3.7 liters/13 cups+ per day)

- Bottled water
- Coconut water (1 serving = 1 fruit)
- Sparkling water
- Naturally-flavored sparkling water
- Tea
- Coffee
- Hot cocoa (unsweetened)
- Naturally-flavored unsweetened sports drinks

Seasonings
Use as desired—these are encouraged! Fresh is best.

- Parsley
- Basil
- Caraway
- Celery seed
- Chives
- Cilantro
- Cinnamon
- Cumin
- Curcumin
- Dill
- Fennel
- Garlic
- Apple, balsamic, and rice vinegar

- Ginger
- Hot pepper
- Onion
- Salsa
- Tumeric

From the Lab to the Table
The A-Z Legally Lean Food Reference Guide provides some additional scientific insight on the ergogenic, fat burning, and nutritious properties of selected foods that are recommended on the grocery lists. These foods will add extra value to your diet and give you energy. They will also enhance your training, performance, and recovery and help you reach your optimal health and desired weight.

The foods on this list are good sources of one or more of the following:

- vitamins, minerals, and compounds or healthy fats which synergistically work together in food to promote health and training benefits;

- ergogenic compounds which accelerate the rate of weight and/or fat loss. These are potentially thermogenic and lipolytic, helping you to churn more calories and break down more fat naturally; and

- antioxidants, antimicrobiasl, antifungals, anti-inflammatories, immune-building constituents, which means a healthier you for life!

For example, for athletes or others "heated up" by their new intense exercise regimen, some of the foods (like ginger and hot peppers) will naturally stimulate your body to cool off. Unlike caffeine, which stimulates your heart, these spices stimulate your circulation and help to raise body temperature. This means if you are training in a hot climate, the increase in body temperature can make you feel cooler by causing you to sweat (which cools the body when the perspiration evaporates).

As scientific research continues to explore and discover additional food compounds with health benefits, this list will be updated too at the book's website: www.LegallyLean.com. For now, a great website to visit for additional information on Functional Foods and other cutting edge food news is at the International Food Information Council Foundation http://FoodInsight.org. For the latest nutrition and grocery news visit: Supermarket Savvy website: http://www.supermarketsavvy.com/ or Phil Lempert, THE Supermarket Guru® for research, product reviews, newsletter at: http://www.supermarketguru.com/.

Almonds
Super Nut with fewer calories! As noted in the *American Journal of Clinical Nutrition*, almonds have just 129 calories/1 oz.—20 percent fewer calories than originally thought. Good source of vitamins B2 (riboflavin) and vitamin E, calcium, potassium, magnesium, manganese, copper, fiber, and Omega-3. In studies, dieters who include almonds have lost more weight and waist inches and seen a drop in systolic (top number) blood pressure.

Anise
Licorice-flavored, star anise is a good source of minerals, potassium, iron, and calcium. Contains "shikimic acid," a precursor to "oseltamivir," an antiviral medication that is marketed as Tamiflu. Combined with quercetin, has immune building properties and is also antifungal, antibacterial, and antioxidant. (23 calories in 1 Tbls.)

Apples
Eaten with skin, apples contain the compound quercetin, which may improve athletic endurance, decrease illness, and reduce inflammation.

Arctic char

Fish ranked high in sustainable fish reports. 154 calories per 3 ½ ounces. Great source of protein and contains 75 percent of the recommended Omega-3.

Aronia Berry (aka chokeberry)

Tart astringent berry, high in antioxidants and phytonutrients called "anthocyanins" like you find in berries (like blueberries and goji berries) including quercetin, epicatechin, peonidin, petunidin. Incorporated into many shelved grocery products including wine, jam, juice, tea, salsa, ice cream, and candy, like gummies.

Artichoke

Just 64 calories per serving. Good source of folate, dietary fiber, and vitamins C and K. Contains the prebiotic inulin, which enhances gut health, as well as apigenin-7-rutinoside and narirutin; compounds which are antioxidants. Contains compounds "cynarin and cyaniding" which may stimulate vascular Nitrous Oxide (NO) production **(see pages 193 and 224)** which can reduce blood cholesterol levels and improve immune response.

Arugula (also collard and mustard greens)

Deep green veggie, good source of calcium, vitamin A, and folate.

Asparagus

Contains vitamin C, folate, and the antioxidant glutathione. A *Journal of Food Science* study found that extracts from leaves and shoots boost enzymes that metabolize alcohol. Planning to indulge? Include fresh or juiced before and after drinking bout!

Avocado

Contains healthy anti-inflammatory fats; vitamin B6; folic acid; vitamins A, C, B1, and B3; and the minerals iron, zinc, and copper. Contains high levels of lutein and glutathione for detoxification and phytosterol for cholesterol reduction.

Basil

Contains vitamins A and K and minerals manganese and copper. Anti-inflammatory, antiseptic, preservative, slight sedative, digestive regulator and diuretic. Contains "Eugenol" compound which blocks COX enzyme responsible for inflammation.

Bay Leaf

Contains vitamin A and minerals potassium and calcium. Inhibits colon cancer cell growth. Is a stimulant in sprain healing.

Black Pepper

Antioxidant. The compound "Piper Nigrum" stimulates metabolism and increases nutrient absorption. Is anti-gas and diuretic. Induces sweating, which cools the body. Antibacterial may protect against colon cancer, anti-inflammatory. Contains quercetin, vitamin K, and the minerals manganese, copper, and potassium.

Beets/Beetroot Juice

Natural source of nitrate. Consumed immediately before, during, and after long duration exercise like cycling and running, may enhance performance in four to 30 minute sessions by increasing vasodilation (blood flow) and muscular sugar uptake and reducing blood pressure and the oxygen cost of training. While there is a possibility that uncontrolled high doses of nitrate (such as salts from processed meats like hot dogs) may be harmful to health, natural food sources are most likely to promote health. Nitrates are also found naturally in spinach, lettuce, and celery.

Bell Pepper

Rich in antioxidants, B6 (for protein metabolism), and folate. From tart to sweet, green, orange, yellow and red, compounds/enzymes cysteine S-conjugate beta-lyases may prevent cancer growth.

Black Sapote

Unusually rich black, pudding-like fruit rich in vitamins A, C, and potassium.134 calories for almost a ½ cup. Great as a low-cal chocolate or ice cream substitute!

Blackstrap Molasses

Great nondairy source of calcium. 2 tbls. = 350-400 mg!

Black Tea

Compound Flavonol- 3- glycosides may reduce food intake, body weight, and blood fat levels.

Brewer's Yeast

80 calories for 3 tbls., 9 grams protein per serving. Deactivated yeast powder is a great source of B vitamins and is rich

in selenium, molybdenum, zinc, and phosphorus. It is delicious sprinkled on veggie dishes, soups, and grains.

Brazil Nuts
In 2 nuts, you get the DV for the mineral selenium, critical for thyroid and immune function.

Callaloo
This "Kale a la Caribbean" is an excellent source of vitamin A and calcium. Add to stews, brown rice dishes, and pasta.

Carambola
Star fruit contains just 42 calories and has 3 grams of fiber, antioxidants, vitamins A and C, and minerals potassium, magnesium, and phosphorus.

Cassava (Yuca)
High energy, potato-like Latin American staple starch. Contains vitamins B1 and C and minerals potassium, iron, and magnesium. Great comfort and filler food!

Chayote (Christophene, Cho-Cho)
Low calorie Caribbean staple. A great meal "volume" builder without the excess high energy carb calories; great for stuffing and baked products. Contains vitamin C and potassium.

Cherimoya (Custard Apple)
64 calories and 2 grams of fiber per fruit. Contains vitamin C and minerals calcium and phosphorus. A delicious treat when pureed and added to morning smoothie or frozen like ice cream!

Chestnuts
Lowfat, high carb, high fiber, "non nut" snack. Can be added to stuffing, soups, salads, and veggies dishes. Provides 21 percent DV of vitamin B6, 15 percent DV of folate, and 22 percent DV of copper.

Chia Seeds
"Salvia Hispanica" phenolic compounds help maintain

healthy blood fats and sugars. High in protein, Omega-3 & -6, antioxidants, and calcium.

Chili Pepper

The "hottest" veggie on the block, this low calorie metabolic booster varies in heat, depending on the capsaicin level; capsaicin's "capsiates" may decrease body weight by stimulating thermogenisis; may enhance fat breakdown; spares muscle glycogen to increase endurance; and also contains vitamins A and C. See salsa recipes!

Chocolate

Cocoa powder is flavonol rich, so it can improve blood flow and aid endothelial function, which is a measure of blood vessel health. 200 mg/day are needed, and can be found in 1 ¾ tbls. cocoa powder (20 calories), ½ oz. baking chocolate (70 calories), or 2 oz. dark chocolate (320 calories).

Cinnamon

Antioxidant, anti-inflammatory, anti-cancer, and anti-diabetic. "Cinnamaldehyde" may decrease muscle soreness.

Coconut Water

Natural sports drink and a great source of electrolytes, potassium, and sodium. Increases bioactive enzymes which aid in metabolism and digestion. Anti-cancer, antithrombotic.

Coffee/Caffeine

Energy boosting. Research suggests it improves strength and endurance, reduces rates of perceived effort, and improves hydration and recovery. May positively affect cognitive performance, mobilize fat, and spare glycogen from muscles during exercise. Increase intestinal absorption and oxidation of carbohydrates to speed rate of glycogen resynthesis during recovery. May also reduce perceived exertion and pain of training!

Cranberries

Antibacterial "proanthocyanins" may prevent (not treat) urinary tract infections (UTI) by preventing bacterial adhesion. Anticancer: may reduce esophageal and breast cancer growth. In a study, adult consumers were less likely to be overweight/obese despite eating more calories than noneaters.

Cruciferous Vegetables
(Broccoli, Cauliflower, Cabbage, Brussels Sprouts, Kale)
Contains Isothocynate compounds which are anti-inflammatory and reduce muscle damage. High in antioxidants, fiber, vitamins, and minerals.

Cumin
Antimicrobial, anti-inflammatory, immune booster, antioxidant, antiseptic. Contains the minerals calcium and potassium.

Curcumin (Tumeric)
Spice flavor and natural coloring compound; antioxidant. A study shows it may reduce toxic effects of environmental stress on the brain in endurance trained athletes. Prevents glutathione depletion and maintains liver antioxidant status. May also detoxify heavy metal toxicities from arsenic, cadmium, lead, and mercury.

Dill
Contains the minerals potassium, calcium, and magnesium. Diuretic.

Dasheen (Taro)
The "spiritual" tuber in Asian culture, this starchy comfort veggie has 94 calories/1/2 cup and contains vitamin B6 and potassium. The leaves are high in vitamins A, C, and folate and minerals potassium and calcium.

Garbanzo beans (Chickpeas)
Not just for "chicks," these are anticarcinogenic and rich in protein, fiber, B vitamins, folate, essential fats, calcium, phosphorus, and potassium.

Garlic
Organo sulphur compounds boost immune system and reduce platelet aggregation.

Ginger
Gingerol compounds may reduce muscle soreness, headaches, nausea, and motion sickness and combat gas. Contains minerals

potassium, magnesium, and phosphorus.Peeled, grated, sliced, or minced and added to any dish gives it a POW factor!

Goji Berries

Antioxidant-rich dried fruit, ¼ cup has 90 cal. and 4 grams protein and contains vitamins A (180% DV), C (30%), and iron (15%).

Green Tea

Epigallocatechin-3-gallate (EGCG) antioxidant, anticarcinogenic, anti-inflammatory, metabolic booster. May reduce body weight and prevent weight gain.

Guava

Tropical fruit with 46 calories and 5 grams of fiber. Great source of vitamins A and C and the compound lycopene. Natural laxative. Can be eaten raw, added to smoothies and baked dishes, or used as a topping for main courses.

Jicama

This crunchy vegetable crudité addition is perfect for soups, stews, salads, or straight up. Good source of vitamin C, potassium, and phosphorus. Contains 23 calories and 3 grams of fiber.

Key Lime

Florida native lime. Contains 2 grams fiber and is rich in vitamin C, potassium, and calcium.

Kiwi

90 calorie nutritional bargain, one of the most nutritious fruits, with 5 grams of fiber, more potassium than a banana and two times the vitamin C of orange. Also contains folate, vitamin E, magnesium, and copper.

Lemongrass

Its "Citral" compound is antimicrobial and antifungal. Contains B vitamins and folate.

Lychees

China native, just 63 calories for 10 fresh. Contains vitamin C and potassium.

Mamey

Cultivated in Panama since 1500s, this is my personal favorite snack. It keeps the body and gut energized. Contains 51 calories and 3 grams of fiber in ½ cup. Rich in vitamin C and A, B6, folate, magnesium, calcium, copper, and iron. Delicious straight up scooped from the shell or added to shakes/smoothies.

Mango

An India native, this 6,000 year old "love" fruit is both sweet and sour. Low in calories, at just 67 per half fruit. High in vitamins A and C and contains potassium, calcium, and phosphorus.

Mint

Stimulates the body naturally. Antiseptic. Peppermint relaxes bronchial smooth muscles, increasing ventilation and brain oxygen. Reduces blood lactate. Contains the minerals calcium, potassium, and magnesium.

Moringa (Plant or Powder)

Plant native to India, powdered. Great source of calcium, potassium, and iron. Provides a boost of B vitamins. Can be added to smoothies, shakes, juices, and sauces.

Mulberries

Dried fruit is just 43 calories for 3 ½ oz. Anti-inflammatory and anticarcinogenic. Rich in B vitamins, iron (23% RDI), vitamin K, and magnesium.

Okra

Known as the "godfather" of vegetables, and a staple in the African culture, this low calorie vegetable (26 calories for each ½ cup), has 2 grams of fiber, is a great source of vitamin C, and is a good source of magnesium. Eat fresh, cooked, or grilled.

Oregano

Digestive aid. Eases migraines and motion sickness. Contains vitamin A, calcium, potassium, and magnesium.

Mushrooms

One of the most nutrient-dense, lowest calorie, and versatile vegetables, mushrooms are a rich source of B vitamins, vitamin D, selenium, copper, and potassium. Mushrooms are one of the few natural sources of umami, the fifth basic taste after sweet, salty, bitter, and sour. The darker the mushroom, the more umami it contains. Mushrooms are also phytonutrient rich in Beta-glucans, which have been shown to have immunity-stimulating effects and contribute to resistance against allergies and may also participate in fat and sugar metabolism. The Beta-glucans contained in oyster, shiitake, and split gill mushrooms are considered to be the most effective. They also contain a compound called "ergothioneine," a naturally occurring antioxidant that may also help protect the body's cells against cancer.

Papaya (Paw-Paw)
Low calorie, colorful nutritional bargain (30 calories/2 grams fiber) for ¼ of a medium, Bromelain/papain enzyme rich fruit (see pineapple). Great straight up, in smoothies, added to main dishes, and in soups, stews, yogurt, or salads. Contains vitamin C and potassium.

Parsley
Natural body stimulant. Contains vitamins A and C and minerals calcium, potassium, and phosphorus.

Passion Fruit
Brazil native contains a small amount of protein and is loaded with fiber! Excellent source of vitamins A, and C and potassium. Scoop it with a spoon or add it to smoothies, yogurt, sauces, or dressings.

Peas
Almost the perfect legume. Low fat, high fiber. Great source of vitamins C, K, and Bs and minerals iron, potassium, zinc, and manganese.

Pineapple
Contains "Bromelain," a digestive enzyme. Anti-inflammatory, accelerates recovery, reduces muscle soreness. Good source of vitamin C, folate, and potassium.

Pistachios
One of the lowest calorie nuts per serving. May lower blood

fats. Excellent source of healthy essential Omega-3 fats, antioxidants, vitamin E, copper, manganese, potassium, calcium, iron, magnesium, zinc, selenium, and several phytonutrients.

Plantains
Favorite Latin comfort food, cousin to banana. Must be cooked; boiled is best. Good source of vitamin C and B6 and minerals potassium and magnesium.

Potatoes
White, sweet, purple, all power-packed with potassium, vitamin C, B6, B3, iron, phosphorus, copper and fiber. Great to eat cold/hot, any way and time of day!

Probiotics
Gut and overall health booster. Lactobacillus may enhance immune system and decrease illness in the exercise-stressed. May decrease the severity and duration of upper respiratory tract infections (URTI).

Rosemary
Natural body stimulant. Stimulates perspiration. Gas reliever. Contains the minerals calcium, potassium, and magnesium.

Saffron
Digestive aid and gas reliever. Contains the minerals potassium and phosphorus.

Sapodilla
Tropical 141-calorie, high fiber (9 grams) fruit. A sweet treat and a natural dessert option. Good source of vitamins A and C and minerals potassium, calcium, and folate.

Spaghetti Squash
Cooks up like spaghetti with only one-quarter of the calories. High in fiber and a good source of vitamins A, C, B6, and K and folate and flavanoid compounds.

Sudauchi Fruit Peel/Raw
With just 68 calories, this small, round, green citrus fruit native to Japan has been shown to significantly decrease body weight,

waist circumference and blood triglyceride levels (in those with levels of 120 mg/dL or more).

Tart Cherries

Antioxidant, anti-inflammatory compounds may reduce muscle damage and oxidative stress following exercise. High in melatonin, which may also help with sleep. Eat fresh, frozen, or juiced.

Thyme

Diuretic. Stimulates perspiration and relieves gas. Contains vitamin A and the minerals calcium, potassium, iron, magnesium, and phosphorus.

Tiger Nuts

Low fat nut with 70 calories and 3.5 grams of fat for 20 nuts. Really a tuber! Great for a snack and can be used to lower the calorie density of traditional trail mix. Contains the minerals potassium and magnesium.

Watercress

Part of mustard greens, cabbage, and arugula family, only 11 calories per ½ cup, high in vitamin C (72% RDA), vitamin K, phytonutrients, beta carotene, B vitamins, minerals. Research suggests may increase protection against exercise-induced oxidative stress.

Watermelon

L-Citruline compound may reduce muscle soreness after exercise.

Wheat grass

Natural source of vitamins and minerals, with 100% of necessary vitamin K. Organic powder form can be added to smoothies, shakes, juices, and sauces.

SECTION

IV

PERFORMANCE NUTRITION FOR ATHLETES

In this section, you will find the latest information on the following areas:

Food for Fuel
Body Composition
Performance Nutrition Formulas
Nutrition Periodization
Workout Meal Planning
Competition Menus
Gut Distress
Overtraining Syndrome

Muscle Fuel

As a serious athlete, you are asking your body to do a lot. And just like a race car needs the correct type of fuel to maximize its effectiveness, so does an athlete. You need to understand and think about what you are putting in your body if you want it to reach optimal performance.

To be successful in sports, your body must be continuously suplied with food energy, called calories. If calorie intake exceeds needs, you'll gain weight and body fat, which will make you feel heavy and train and compete more slowly. It will also increase your risk for injury. If calorie intake does not meet demands, you won't be able to maintain your muscle mass and speed, and your recovery will be slow and incomplete.

Your body must be supplied with a continuous flow of energy from food to perform all of its functions. Eating a clean diet fuels your muscles, builds new tissue, preserves lean muscle mass, optimizes bone strength, repairs existing cells, maximizes oxygen transport, maintains fluid and electrolyte balance, and regulates metabolic processes every minute of every day!

Three Energy Systems

Any time you ask your body to generate power for exercise, your body relies on ATP (adenosine triphosphate) found within your cells' mitochondria. This is the energy powerhouse of all the body's cells, especially muscle. Although ATP is the main currency for energy in the body, the body is not actually capable of storing very much of it. In fact, you only have about 3 ounces of stored ATP, enough energy for several seconds of exercise at any one time. Therefore, ATP must be continually resynthesized to provide a constant energy source during exercise.

With ATP as fuel, the body utilizes three metabolic systems to provide the energy you need. Two (the *Immediate Energy System* and the *Glycolytic Energy System*) are devoted to high intensity activities like all-out sprinting, weight lifting, boxing, martial arts, tennis and intermittent high intensity team sports like football and soccer. The third energy system (*aerobic metabolism*) fuels moderately paced endurance sports like distance running, swimming, or cycling.

You use all three of these systems at some point during your training, regardless of your sport. However, how much you use each system, as well as the amount of calories and fat you use with each session, depends on the duration, intensity, type, and frequency of your workouts. It also varies with your diet, fitness, stress level, sleep status, age, gender, and genetics. Let me walk you through each one.

System 1: The Immediate Energy System (or ATP-CP)

The Immediate Energy System fuels all-out energy bursts that occur for less than six seconds, like lifting weights in the gym at 100 percent of your maximum effort. This system relies on ATP, the simplest but highest form of energy stored in all cells of the body. Structurally, ATP is directly affected by the consumption of carbohydrates, since carbohydrates are the source of ribose, one of ATP's building blocks.

This system also relies on creatine phosphate (CP), which is stored throughout the body, about 95 percent of it in muscle. Creatine helps to replenish ATP when energy bursts of a few seconds are required repeatedly. It is manufactured in the body from three amino acids: arginine, glycine, and methionine. Creatine also comes from foods like soy, fish, eggs, and meat. Since creatine is the only fuel source that can keep up with very high intensity needs, it has the ability to regenerate ATP for repeated all out bursts.

System 2: The Glycolytic Energy System

The Glycolytic Energy System supplies the fuel you need for longer sessions of intermittent high intensity exercise, such as dance sequences, soccer drills, and tennis volleys. This system burns carbohydrates at a very high intensity at the cellular level. The amount of ATP available in this system is relatively small, available for all-out efforts lasting up from 60 to 120 seconds. Examples are the 400-meter sprint, three minutes in the boxing ring, or a cheerleading dance sequence. The Glycolytic Energy System relies on the stored form of carbohydrate, called glycogen. This is found in muscles and the liver.

To make this system work, B vitamins are also required. Anything that depletes B vitamins (such as under-eating, a B vitamin-deficient diet, drinking too much alcohol, or taking medications that interfere with B vitamin absorption) has the potential to decrease your energy levels.

Without adequate dietary carbohydrates, glycogen becomes depleted. Like a car running out of gas, you won't be able to push forward and get into the fat burning zone, System 3, Aerobic Metabolism.

Coach's Corner

Why Lactic Acid Rocks!

When exercise continues above the call of duty, at intensities beyond the body's ability to supply oxygen (as in System 3—Aerobic Metabolism), a compound called *pyruvate* which normally generates aerobic energy is temporarily converted into lactate, aka *lactic acid*, which enables glucose (sugar) to be used for 1 to 3 minutes of high intensity anaerobic energy but at a cost.

If muscles don't keep up with the production of lactic acid, its acidic sidekick, hydrogen, accumulates in the blood. Hydrogen increases the acidity of muscles, interferes with electrical impulses to nerves and muscles, and impairs muscle contractions, and consequently causes muscle burning and fatigue. While it's intended to be a physiological lifesaver, protecting us from overstraining by slowing down our pace to a point where we can start to work aerobically, it's that burning muscle pain and inability to keep up that gives lactic acid bad press.

And while lactic acid is often blamed for muscle soreness and burning pain, it's not to blame. It's the acidic hydrogen! As for the lingering stinging muscle pain which often peaks at 24-72 hours after a hard workout session (aka DOMS, or delayed onset muscle soreness) it's more likely due to "micro tears" in the muscles, the normal physiological consequence of eccentric training which most likely occurs when muscles are stretched to their max, like your quad muscles are in downhill running.

The good news is that lactic acid is really the good guy, a sustainable energy source. It can be recycled—removed from the muscle, transported into the bloodstream, and converted to glycogen for use as energy in muscle tissue, the liver, or the brain. The conversion of lactic acid to glycogen occurs in the liver and, to some extent, in the muscles, particularly among trained athletes. More training = more efficient use of lactic acid. In other words, you become a better recycler, adapting more quickly to training at higher levels of exercise.

Without the production of lactic acid, this system would shut down. That's when lactic acid should get a good rap, but its good side is often overlooked.

System 3: Aerobic Metabolism

Aerobic Metabolism is the longest lasting energy system, fueling workouts that last longer than several minutes. Even if you're a gym rat (as opposed to being a runner like me), you will tap into this energy system if you combine multiple workout sessions back to back, like circuit training plus a five-mile run or a 20-minute warm-up bike ride followed by your favorite dance workout. Think of the aerobic system as your backbone for training, ultimately priming your system to burn more fat for all workouts.

The aerobic system relies on the breakdown of all nutrients—carbohydrates, protein, and fat stored in the body—to provide energy. Without a balanced diet of carbohydrates, protein, and fat, you can't effectively train. And effective training is the key to making improvements in strength, agility, and speed.

The more fit you are, the more fats you use. You see fitter men and women store more fats in their muscles (called "intramuscular triglycerides"). The more time you spend building your aerobic, fat burning base, the more fat burning enzymes you make and the more efficient your mitochondria are. These are the aerobic powerhouses that burn the fats you have locally and make more readily available in muscles to burn!

All Systems Go!

Just to recap, at the beginning of your workout, ATP is produced during the first few seconds as you get started. As your session continues, System 2 kicks in, and you break down sugars and muscle carbs and keep going—if you have replenished with enough carbs after your last training session.

If you keep your high-intensity training going for a Cross Fit, circuit, interval, track, or cycling sprint session, or even a series of high-power moves in basketball, football, or soccer, then you'll continue to rely on carbs, and then lactic acid, to regenerate more carb fuel for exercising at high intensity (see Coach's Corner on Lactic Acid on **pages 88-89**). If you don't replenish, and want to continue training or competing, you'll run out of fuel and eventually collapse. If you follow my Fat Burning Fuel recommendations in the next section of this chapter, you'll be able to push further and longer, stay energized and alert, and rely more on System 3, burning fat as your muscles preferred energy source for your workout session.

Fat Burning Fuel

The intensity and duration of your training will determine the relative rates of carbs, protein, and especially fat you burn for exercise. While the high-intensity Systems 1 and 2 are dependent on breaking down carbohydrate for energy, carbohydrate can also be created from specific amino acids, primarily alanine and the branched-chain amino acids (BCAA). Using these building blocks, your body can make new sugars through a process called "gluconeogenesis," which literally means "generation of new sugars."

How does dietary protein fit into the energy mix? The truth is, there is no easy answer. Unless you are under-eating, overtraining, or interested in building muscle mass, you can generally meet your daily protein needs through food and won't need supplemental protein. That's because when compared with carbohydrates and fats, protein generally provides less than 10 percent of the total fuel used for exercise, so it's not a major player for individual training sessions.

However, protein—or more importantly, its building blocks, like branched chain amino acids (BCAA), essential amino acids (EAA), and conditionally essential amino acids (CEAA)—may have a critical role in muscle synthesis (called anabolism). These amino acids are also key in preventing muscle breakdown ("catabolism"), boosting immune function, ensuring complete recovery, and of course, growth in the younger athlete. Supplementing these amino acids within or in addition to your healthy Legally Lean program may have some merit, depending on your goals.

Effect of Training

Your diet, training, and fitness level—in other words, your dietary composition (how much or little fat and carbohydrate) and when you consume your meals and snacks relative to the amount and type of training you are doing—will also determine how fat-efficient you are. Some experts suggest eliminating pre-workout snacks and including a caffeinated drink to accelerate fat use for fuel during exercise. You'll also hear other experts recommending proportionately high fat diets, above 30 percent total calories to encourage more fat use and more glycogen sparing. As you can imagine, there are pros and cons to this approach, given that in the short run, fats cannot be used for high intensity exercise or competition and long term, some high fat diets may contribute to high blood fats and an increased risk for heart disease and cancer.

Even if your sport involves mainly efforts at high intensity, all-out exertion, you can still benefit from training in a fat-burning zone. That's because it lowers your respiratory exchange ratio (RER), a measure of the amount of CO_2 produced divided by the amount of O_2 consumed. Lowering RER lowers blood lactic acid levels, so you don't physically "burn" so much. It also lowers stress hormone levels, which will spare muscle glycogen. In addition to strengthening your heart and improving oxygen delivery to muscles, aerobic training increases the number of mitochondria and the circulating evels of fat-burning enzymes involved in ATP synthesis, enabling you to burn more fat!

Body Composition

As a competitive athlete, you need to know more than what the bathroom scale tells you. That's why I often discourage my athletes from weighing themselves daily. Heights and weights and the commonly used Body Mass Index (BMI, see Coaches Corner) only tell part of the story since a weight reflects total mass. Total weight mass is affected by meals and fluid intake, but overlooks what the weight represents—whether it's fat, muscle, or fluids. In other words, scales may provide a measure of total weight, but they do not reveal the lean-to-fat ratio of that weight. Body composition is a better measure, because it helps you understand the different components that make up your weight.

Coach's Corner

Body Mass Index

One measurement that is used to assess "weight for height" is called the Body Mass Index (BMI). BMI is calculated by dividing your weight in pounds (lbs.) by height in inches (in) squared and multiplying by a conversion factor of 703. It is a tool the medical community uses to classify individuals as overweight or obese. It is also a predictor of cardiovascular disease and Type II Diabetes. A free online BMI calculator can be found at: http://www.cdc.gov/healthyweight/assessing/bmi/adult_bmi/english_bmi_calculator/bmi_calculator.html.

According to the Centers for Disease Control (CDC), the weight status categories associated with a BMI are as follows:

BMI	Weight Status
Below 18.5	Underweight
18.5 – 24.9	Normal
25.0 – 29.9	Overweight
30.0 and Above	Obese

The problem is, BMI does not look at the ratio of fat to lean mass. Therefore, a lean, heavier-than-normal-weight athlete, who has a lot of muscle mass, can appear to be excessively heavy for their height and classified as overweight or obese using the BMI criteria.

For example, in one study with 85 football players from Division I schools, measurements were taken (by position) for height, weight, waist circumference, and percent of body fat over a two week period following football season. When analyzed as a whole, 35 percent of the players were considered obese! When body fat percentage and waist circumference measurements (another measure of body fatness and obesity) were included, only 17.6 percent had a body fat percentage greater than 25 percent, the cut-off that increases risk for heart disease. By position, only offensive linemen had a mean percent body fat greater than 25 percent. Therefore, while BMI is useful for measuring the risk of disease based on weight for the average person for football players and other large muscle dense athletes, it is certainly not the best or most accurate tool.

More information on BMI at the Centers for Disease Control (CDC) website: http://www.cdc.gov/healthyweight/assessing/bmi/adult_bmi/index.html?s_cid=tw_ob064.

Muscle or Fat?

It's important to know how your diet and training are affecting the amount of body fat and lean muscle mass you have to understand how that distribution helps or hinders your performance. Tracking your body composition also helps you to determine how much and what percentages of carbs, protein, and fat you need in your diet to attain and maintain optimal performance.

Body composition can help you to determine if you are a good fit for your desired sport or position on that sport team, or if you might be more suitable for another sport, especially if you are considering multi-lettering in high school or college. That's because for some sport and position specific athletes, like football linemen, distance swimmers, and sumo wrestlers, body fat is an asset, while a leaner physique has an advantage in running, diving, and gymnastics.

As a competitive or professional athlete, keeping track of your body composition is a mandatory part of a performance nutrition program, because you will need to modify your diet as your composition changes. If you are uncomfortable tracking these numbers, the best bet is to hire a certified personal trainer, coach, sports dietitian (RD, CSSD), physiologist, or ISAK certified anthropometrist who can take and track these measurements for you.

This section will provide an overview of methods used to test body composition. Understand that none of the methods for determining body composition is foolproof or precise. All the methods (including the gold standard of underwater weighing) have a margin of error. This is because the reference values used are based on data collected decades ago using cadavers—the "deceased" that represented neither athletes nor a good cross section of racial groups. The best anyone can do is to provide relative measurements of body fat and lean muscle mass.

Measuring Body Fat

There are several ways to measure body fat. Unfortunately, the most accurate methods are expensive and tend to be inaccessible to most athletes. These methods include underwater weighing, BODPOD, and Dual Energy X-ray Absorptiometry (DEXA). These devices are typically found in clinical settings, in research laboratories, or at professional training camps.

When underwater weighing is used, an athlete is submerged in a large tank of water, and based on specific formulas, their ratio of lean tissue (dense) to fat tissue (less dense) is measured. The more body fat a person has, the less they will weigh underwater. While this method is accurate, it is not always practical, since it is not widely available and is not suitable for athletes who have a fear of being underwater.

The BODPOD is a more sophisticated method that uses the same principle and formulas used with underwater weighing, except with air displacement. Used at the NFL Combine, some universities, and the professional level, the BODPOD looks like an oversized egg that a player can step into and sit down while keeping their head outside the unit. Their body fat is calculated in just a few minutes. The BODPOD is as accurate as underwater weighing and is a more practical way of measuring body fat for large groups of players in just a few minutes per person.

A more expensive, but gold standard, method for taking body fat measurement is called Dual Energy X-ray Absorptiometry (DEXA). Found in exercise physiology departments and clinical settings, the DEXA is a noninvasive, accurate, but expensive means of measuring body fat and lean tissue. DEXA is also used to determine bone density, a measure which is used frequently with non-menstruating female athletes and peri- and post-menopausal women, and mature men to determine the impact of aging, diet, hormones, and genetics on bone strength.

If you ever have the chance to get your body fat measured in one of these ways, take advantage of it. At least you will have a standard to measure yourself against when you use the less accurate but more practical and less expensive methods. Many university exercise physiology and/or kinesiology departments conduct studies that often include free assessments for participants. These studies are more often than not posted on university websites or on campuses.

Practical Strategies for Determining Body Composition

More popular, practical, and less expensive devices used to measure body fat measurement include anthropometry and Bioelectrical Impedance Analysis (BIA). Anthropometric methods measure various parameters around the body, such as taking the circumference of your waist or measuring the thickness of your skinfolds.

A skinfold measurement is typically taken by a trained expert with a piece of equipment called a skinfold caliper. The skinfold caliper is used to "pinch" (i.e., scientifically grab) fat tight below the skin at specific sites around the body, including the triceps, subscapular (back), abdomen, suprailleum, iliac crest, thigh, calf, bicep, and chest. The fat below the skin is called subcutaneous fat and makes up about 50 percent of the fat in your body.

The numbers from the various measurements are added together to get a total. Then experts plug this number into a formula to get a benchmark measurement of where the athlete is preseason, to track an athlete's progress, to see if the athlete fits into the position for their sport, and sometimes to compare them to other athletes within that position to see if the range is optimal for performance.

The advantage of using a skin fold caliper to measure body fat is that you get the individual measurements for different sites and can assess how a diet and training program is impacting different parts of your body. However, there can be disadvantages. Both the accuracy of the tester and the validity of the formula that the tester uses can vary, and there can be inconsistency in measurements between testers if you obtain measurements from different individuals. Some experts also suggest that not all formulas are created equal.

Another inexpensive body fat analyzing device is the BIA. You have probably either heard of or seen a piece of equipment that incorporates a BIA function. BIA come in hand held devices, built into your bathroom scale, or hooked up to a machine by electrodes attached to your body. It's a measurement that's based on the conduction of a very low level, safe electrical current through the body. Since fat does not conduct electricity and water does, BIA can detect how much fat your body has. BIA also measures total weight, muscle mass, water, and bone mass.

These methods are inexpensive, quick, and noninvasive and used by most strength coaches, athletic trainers, and sports dietitians/ nutritionists worldwide. With both of these methods, the body fat percentage is taken by measuring body density, not percentage, and then calculating the percentage using one of several formulas. However, you might want to think twice about taking the actual body fat percentage number too seriously since both BIA and skin-fold measurement have their shortcomings.

BIA is affected by hydration levels, food intake, skin temperature, and other factors. That means that there is a lot of room for errors, especially with athletes, for whom water balance is such an issue. BIA scales themselves can also vary, with an over-prediction of percentage of body fat in several systems. There has also been conflicting data with its application to different cultures.

While BIA is a very practical tool, it has been shown to be less accurate than skinfold measurement and has been shown to over-predict percent of body fat in some groups. In one study, where skinfolds and BIA were compared in football players, there was a significant difference in percentage of body fat between Caucasian and African Americans. The mean Caucasian percentage of fat was 18.1 +/- 6.1 percent (4.7 to 31.3 percent), while in the African Americans, the mean was 15.2 percent (5.6-27.3 percent).

Researchers suggested that not only does the BIA over-predict percentage of fat in college football players, but that in African Americans, BIA is even less accurate than skinfolds. On an individual basis, BIA predicted only 36 percent of African Americans and 60 percent of Caucasians within 3.3 percent of their underwater weighing value.

In summary, with an accurate tester and the right formula, skinfold measurement is your best bet for measuring body fat. Eighty-nine percent of the time, skinfold measurement predicts body composition within 3.3 percent of underwater weighing. BIA only predicts within that range 51 percent of the time.

Coach's Corner

Measuring Your Own Body Composition

If you do plan to take your own measurements and calculate your body fat percentage, you will need to equip yourself with the following:

Scale
If you purchase a scale with a BIA device, you should weigh yourself at the same time during the day and not exercise before nor eat or drink for the previous 12 hours. This may yield a more accurate result.

Tape measure
Purchase a cloth tape measure with a spring tension device to keep human error to a minimum.

Calculator
Math wizard or not, the formulas are easier to calculate with a device. You can use your cell phone calculator, too.

DIY Body Composition Testing
While not foolproof, here is one way you can guestimate your body fat percentage on your own.

1. Calculating your body fat percentage from your BMI
Once you know your BMI (see appendix or online), you can calculate your body fat percentage from your BMI. Use the following formula:

% body fat percentage = (1.20 x BMI) + (0.23 x age) - (10.8 x gender) - 5.4

Use for male gender = 1, for female gender =0.

For example if your BMI is 28 and your age is 21, and you are a male, the formula becomes:
BF percentage= (1.20 x 28) + (0.23 x 21) − (10.8 x 1) − 5.4.
BF percentage = 22.23 percent.

In my opinion, while it does not appear to be the most accurate method of calculating body fat percentage, it is one quick way you can calculate your body fat percent at home. According to the researchers Deurenberg et al published in the *British Journal of Nutrition*, *"The prediction error is comparable to the prediction error obtained with other methods of estimating BF percentage, such as skinfold thickness measurements or bioelectrical impedance."*

 Coach's Corner

What is a Good Target Body Fat Percentage?

In my practice, I target body fat goals based on a few reference points.

1. Normal and healthy ranges (see chart) to attain and maintain optimal training and performance.

2. The range that sustains and maintains menstruation in women.

3. History of the range in which the athlete has achieved peak performance.

4. Range of normal and elite, sport-specific, position-specific percentage body fat.

	Normal	Desired	Minimal Adults	Minimal Adolescents
Males			5%	7%
Athletes	5-16%	6-12%		
Nonathletes	10-22%	12-16%		
Females			12%	14%
Athletes	11-28%	12-18%		
Nonathletes	20-32%	18-24%		

Losing Weight and Lowering Body Fat

Now that you know your body fat percentage, what if you want to lower it? It helps to have an idea of what weight you would need to reach in order to achieve your desired body fat percentage. Fortunately, there is a formula for determining how much you would weigh if you were at your goal for percent body fat. Here is how the formula works. Let's take, for example, an athlete who weighs 190 with 15 percent body fat, and who wants to be at 10 percent body fat.

Target Body Weight = $\dfrac{\text{Fat Free Mass (FFM)}}{\dfrac{1-(\text{desired \% fat})}{100}}$

1) Calculate Fat Free Mass.

Fat Free Mass = 190 x 0.15 = 28.5 pounds fat

Body Weight − Fat Mass = Fat Free Mass (FFM)

Take 190 pounds − 28.5 = 161.5 pounds Fat Free Mass

2) Take Fat Free Mass of 161.5 and divide by (1 − .10). This equals your Goal Weight.

Fat Free Mass 161.5/ (1 − 10%) = _____ Goal Weight (use 1- .10 =0 .9).

Fat Free Mass 161.5/0.9 = _____ pounds Goal Weight.

Goal weight = 179 pounds.

In other words, in order to reach their goal of 10 percent body fat, this athlete would need to target a goal weight of approximately 179 pounds.

Now Take Yourself.

Target Body Weight $= \dfrac{\text{Fat Free Mass (FFM)}}{\text{1-(desired \% fat)}}$
$$\text{100}$$

1) Calculate Fat Free Mass.

Fat Free Mass = your weight x your body fat = _____ pounds fat.

(_____Percent Body Fat x _____Body Weight = _____Fat Mass (or take number from body comp formulas in previous section).

Body Weight – Fat Mass = Fat Free Mass (FFM).

Take your weight pounds – _____Fat Free Mass = _____pounds fat free mass.

2) Take Fat Free Mass _____ and divide by (1 – __goal % fat) = _____Goal Weight.

Goal Weight in pounds = _____.

How Many Calories Do You Need?

As you can imagine, the number of calories needed to attain and maintain a desired weight varies greatly among athletes. For example, a 220-pound high school football player who is still growing may require between 4,000 and 5,000 calories a day during the playing season, while his 45-year-old, 140-pound mom who is a triathlete may need to eat fewer than half of those calories or run the risk of gaining weight!

The same could be said about calorie needs varying for the same individual. If the football player is in season, his needs will be very different from when he is in preseason or when he is sidelined with an injury. When his mom is recreationally training, her needs will be very different from when she is competing in the Hawaiian Ironman World Championships. Suffice to say, when calculating your calorie needs, several factors need to be considered, such as your training level, specific sport and goals, age, gender, diet and health history, and of course, genetics.

We'll talk more about how to calculate exactly how many calories you will need to maintain, lose, or gain weight later in this section. But the first basic fact to know is that most athletes need a lot of calories—more calories than non-athletes or those just getting started using the Legally Lean Core Performance Plan of 1200 to 1500 calories outlined in Section II.

Secondly, be aware that the large number of factors determining calorie needs from day to day mean that it is not an exact science. Unless you are measured in a research study in a clinical setting and monitored 24/7, calculating your energy formula is like using "MapQuest." It's really just a start for determining where you need to go.

To really discover how many calories you need, in addition to using the formula below, it's best to track how much you eat and train with my Pocket Coach© or your favorite online food tracking program and comparing that information with body composition measurements and the feedback from your performance, energy levels, and overall health. In this way, you can determine if the calorie level you're consuming is adequate to sustain, maintain, and accelerate your physique toning and training progress.

Your Calorie Formula

To calculate total calories required daily for your weight (or goal weight), training, and metabolism, you need to use three factors:

1. Basal Metabolic Rate (BMR). This is the rate your body burns calories at rest.

2. Energy Expended for Physical Activity (EEPA). This includes everything from sitting in class to sports practice and even sleep.

3. The Specific Dynamic Action of Food (SDA). This reflects the number of calories you use to digest and metabolize protein, carbohydrates, and fats in your body.

The tricky part about calculating daily calorie needs is that there is no perfect formula. All three of these factors are influenced by numerous variables that change on a daily, monthly, and seasonal basis. Some of these factors have been outlined in the Coach's Corner.

Coach's Corner

Factors Which Influence Daily Calorie Needs

Components of Formula	Influences on Expenditure of Calories
BMR (Basal Metabolic Rate)	Genetics (40 percent), weight, size, age, health, body composition, exercise level, diet
EEPA (Energy Expended for Physical Activity)	Weight, body composition, muscle fiber, training intensity and duration, diet
SDA (Specific Dynamic Action of Food aka TEF Thermic Effect of Food)	Weight, size, diet composition, health

Needless to say, calculating energy needs can become very complicated, so I will try to make it as simple as possible for you.

Step One: First, calculate your BMR. This is the minimal number of calories your body needs just for daily survival. I recommend using the Cunningham formula, because it is designed especially for athletes and takes into consideration lean muscle mass. Here is the formula:

BMR (calories/day) = 500 + (22 x Lean Body Mass in kilograms)

To calculate kilograms of body weight, take your weight in pounds and divide by 2.2.

My weight in pounds =_____ / 2.2 =_____kg.

Then, just like you did in the previous section on body composition, you take your weight and multiply that by your body fat percentage to get pounds of fat. (In this case, it is kilograms of fat).

So, for example, if a 175-pound (79.5kg) athlete has 10 percent body fat, his kilograms of fat would be calculated like this:

Weight = 79.5 x .10 = 7.9 kilograms fat.

Now try it with your own numbers.

My kilograms weight _____x my percent body fat _____= kilograms fat weight.

Now to get lean body mass, you take total weight and subtract fat weight.

In this athlete's case, it looks like this: 79.5 − 7.9 = 71.6 lean body mass.

Use the space below to figure out your own lean body mass.

Your kilograms weight_____ - your kilograms fat weight_____= lean body mass _____.

The next step is to calculate BMR. With our hypothetical athlete, the calculation would be the following: 500 + (22 x 71.6kg LBM) = 2075 calories.

Now, to calculate your own BMR, take 500 + (22 x _____your lean body mass) = _____calories.

Another very simple method for calculating BMR calories that doesn't use body composition measurements for each gender is the following:

Men = 1.0 x body weight (kilograms) x 24 hours

Therefore, for the 175 pound (79.5kg) athlete, the formula is:

BMR = 1 x 79.5kg x 24 =1908 BMR calories.

Women= 0.9 x body weight (kilograms) x 24 hours

So for the 140 pound (63.6kg) female athlete, the formula is:

BMR = 0.9 x 63.6kg x 24 = 1374 calories.

Try this formula with your own numbers.

BMR = _____ factor x _____your weight (kg) x 24 hours.

When you compare the results, you can see that using the Cunningham equation provides a higher number of calories for the male athlete than the gender-specific formula does. The higher result is probably a more accurate prediction of his BMR needs, since it takes into consideration not only body weight, but also the composition of that weight.

Step Two: Next calculate your EEPA—Energy Expended for Physical Activity. To do that, you can either add together all the calories you expend in a day by logging onto a website which provides calorie expenditure online (there are several, including one from the CDC which lists expenditure by minute according to exercise intensity at http://www.cdc.gov/nccdphp/dnpa/physical/pdf/PA_Intensity_table_2_1.pdf or one that provides specific expenditure for calories spent for different weights http://www.nutribase.com/exercala.htm). Or, for a shortcut with an online calculator, for example, try http://www.exrx.net/Calculators/Calories.html.

Alternatively, you can calculate your EEPA on your own by multiplying your BMR by the activity factor that matches your training level best. (Most serious athletes in training have a factor between 1.550 and 1.9 depending on training phase of the year.)

Here are the factors:

1.200 = sedentary
(little or no exercise)

1.375 = lightly active
(about 30 minutes of moderate training, 1 to 3 days/week)

1.550 = moderately active
(45 minutes of moderate training, 3 to 5 days/week)

1.725 = very active
(training for 1 hour, 6 to 7 days/week)

1.900 = extra active
(very hard training, including weight lifting, 2-3 days/week)

Therefore, EEPA based on 175-pound athlete and hard training would be the following:

2075 calories x 1.9= 3942 Total Calories, BMR and EEPA.

Step Three: Multiply the total of BMR and EEPA (from Step Two) by 10 percent, for the specific dynamic action of food (SDA). This accounts for the energy spent on digestion and metabolism.

Example: The SDA equals 3942 x 0.1 = 394 calories.

Step Four: Add the total from Step 2 to the total from Step 3 to get the total number of calories you need to maintain your present weight.

Example: 3942 + 394 = 4336 calories.

Based on this example, the *total* daily calorie needs daily are 4,336.

Now do the math for yourself.

If the same athlete was injured and not training, the activity factor would be much lower at 1.2; the calories expended for BMR and EEPA would be lower at 2,498 calories; the SDA would be lower at 249 calories; and the total calories needed would be 2,739 calories. That's a decrease of over 1/3 from when the same athlete was training intensely.

You can see then how easy it is how an athlete who takes a few days rest or becomes injured, and continues to eat as much as he or she normally does during training, can gain weight and fat. The extra weight typically starts a vicious cycle of overuse injuries and poor recovery, and optimal training cannot resume.

Losses and Gains

In an effort to maximize performance or to meet weight criteria determined by specific sports (cutting weight for wrestling, boxing, sailing, or rowing or reaching a higher weight for power lifting, football, or baseball), many athletes take drastic measures and supplements to lose or gain weight. As discussed in this book's Introduction, this can lead to detrimental consequences and even death.

Although attaining a lean, light physique may sometimes be appropriate, and can be a legitimate way to enhance sports performance and build one's self esteem, research has suggested that drastic weight-reduction or weight-gain programs may involve elements of risk, especially when the weight gain or loss is expected in an unrealistically short amount of time. This can wreak hormonal, metabolic, emotional, and physiological havoc on an athlete's body. For some young athletes, achievement of an unrealistically low weight (or conversely, a high weight with the use of weight gainer or other supplements) can jeopardize growth and development.

The goal weight of an athlete should ultimately be based on optimizing health and performance and should be based on the athlete's weight and body composition when they had their best previous performance. According to the Academy of Nutrition and Dietetics (AND) and the National Athletic Trainers Association (NATA), adequate time should be allowed for a slow, steady weight loss of approximately one to two pounds each week over several weeks. Weight loss should be achieved during off season or preseason when competition is not a priority.

The NATA suggests the following weight loss and weight management strategies for participation in all sports and physical activities.

- Recommendations for the lowest safe weight should be calculated at no lower than the weight determined by the reference body fat composition delineated by sex and age (see previous section on body composition). The lowest safe weight can also be defined as the lowest weight sanctioned by the governing body at which a competitor may compete.

- When no standard exists, athletes are advised to remain above a certain minimal body fat. The highest safe weight should be calculated using a value at the highest end of the range satisfactory for health: 10-22 percent body fat in males and 20-32 percent in females.

Coach's Corner

Tips for Weight gain and Loss

Tips for Weight Loss

To lose one pound per week, deduct between 250 and 500 calories daily. Here are some easy ways to hit that target:

- Substitute a cup of high fiber veggies at each meal in lieu of high energy carbs like pasta, rice, and beans. For instance, spaghetti squash has ¼ of the calories of wheat spaghetti.

- Cut back on sport shakes and bars. Most athletes overconsume protein which is not generally used as an energy source for exercise. Therefore the excess is stored as fat.

- Reduce excess snack calories especially from whole milk dairy products like cheese and yogurt, high fat nut-based energy and breakfast bars, or chips and crackers. Substitute dried chickpeas, dried soynuts and low fat nut butter spreads instead of tree nuts and nut butters.

- Cut back on the unnecessary extras such as condiments like mayo, oil, salad dressing, sauces and added sugars found in sport drinks, fruit juices and carbonated beverages.

- Cut back or quit alcoholic drinks. Each beer is the caloric equivalent of eating two slices of bread, each glass of wine is like eating the caloric equivalent of two fruits and a shot of hard alcohol is like having two pats of butter! Alcohol is metabolized to fat and compounds which compromise your ability to use fat as an energy source for exercise. Alcohol CANNOT fuel muscles. There is no place for alcohol in a performance eating program.

To gain a pound of lean muscle per week, start with a minimum addition of 250 to 500 calories daily.

Try the following:

- Eat five to six meals daily. Try three main meals and 2-3 snacks including high-quality protein and high-energy carbs.

- Switch from nonfat and low fat to full fat foods such as whole milk, yogurt, butter, salad dressings and nut butters.

- Add a glass of whole milk to meals and snacks. If lactose intolerance is an issue, try whole almond, hemp, flax, soy or rice milk.

- Don't drink at mealtime until you finish eating, since beverages can be filling.

- Replace low-calorie beverages with 100% fruit or fruit/ veggie juice blends, sports drinks, and yogurt shakes.

- Add the equivalent of about 3 to 4 oz. (21 to 28 grams protein), the size of an additional deck of cards of lean protein at each main meal, breakfast, lunch and dinner.

- Double your portion sizes from the High Energy Carb Core Food Group options, like 100 percent whole grain pasta, brown rice, bread, cereals, crackers, beans, peas, and potatoes.

- Snack between meals on healthy, high calorie choices like nuts, trail mix, dried fruit and nut butter sandwiches.

- Use higher calorie food options in each group at every meal. For example, try granola instead of plain cereal, whole grain muffins or waffles instead of toast, and pan fried meats, poultry or fish cooked in olive oil instead of grilled dry without oil.

- Eat a pre-workout snack with protein and carbohy-drates. A quick metabolizing sport or breakfast bar 45 minutes to one hour before the workout to avoid any gut distress (see **pages 144-146**).

- After workouts have a recovery snack, meal, bar or shake. Get at least 0.1 grams protein per pound body weight (20 grams for the 200 pound athlete), with a good source of carbohydrate (about ½ gram per pound body weight, 100 grams for the 200 pound athlete). That's about a 400 to 500 calorie snack, bar, shake or meal after workouts. Good choices are a recovery shake, a fruit smoothie with powder whey protein, or a six-inch lean meat/turkey/chicken/fish sub.

Setting the Bar for Athletes

Using the Legally Lean Principles and Play Book Ground Rules for your program, your Legally Lean Athlete's Food Bar kicks the Core Performance Plan up a calorie notch to meet daily energy needs
(See next page.)

Legally Lean® Food Groups and Servings
Nutrient Composition of Performance Eating Plans

Food Group	Pro (Gms)	Carb (Gms)	Fat (Gms)
Milk or non "Milk" options ~80-100 calories/serving	8	12	varies
Fruits ~60 calories/serving	0	15	0
Vegetables ~50 calories/cup	4	10	varies
Grains/High Carb Veggies ~80-100 calories/serving	3	15	varies
Protein/Animal Protein Options ~55-75 calories/serving	7-10	0	varies
Fats and Oils ~45 calories/serving	0	0	5
Total Calories*: Grams(g)/Percent% calories from: Carbohydrates Protein Fat			

* Approximate calories based on The American Diabetic/Dietetic Association exchanges using the Compu-Cal/pro Nutrition Assesment Computer

Energy (Calorie) Levels*

1800	2000	2400	3000	3500	4000	5000
3	3	4	4	4	5	6
5	6	8	8	12	12	15
3	3	3	3	3	3	4
6	7	8	12	14	16	20
12	12	12	16	18	22	26
3	4	7	8	8	10	13
1809	1995	2411	3000	3512	3992	4987
231g/51%	261/52	318/53	378/50	468/53	5108/51	637/51%
138g/31%	141/28	152/25	192/26	212/24	254/25	306/25%
37g/18%	43/20	59/22	80/24	88/23	104/24	135/24%

2400 Calorie Menu Example

AM MEAL 1 –2 oz. protein 1 "milk" option 1-2 fruits 1-2 starch 1-2 fats	Sunday 1 egg omelette 100% whole grain English muffin with lowfat melted cheese kiwi slices lowfat milk option	Monday 1 cup of tart cherry juice 1 cup 100% whole grain cereal ¼ cup raisins 1 cup milk option	Tuesday 1 cup pome- granate juice 1 cup Greek yogurt 1 cup oatmeal with berries
AM SNACK Post workout shake or bar 1 oz. protein or milk option 1 fruit 1 fat	Apple slices with ¼ cup dried chickpeas	1 tbls nut butter of choice (or 2 tbls low fat nut butter) w/ sliced pear	Low fat chocolate milk option with 100% whole grain, organic breakfast bar
Afternoon Lunch 4-5 oz. protein 2-3 grains/high carb veggies 1 cups low cal veggies 1 milk option 1-2 fruits 1-2 fats	1 cup tart cherry juice 1 cup salad 4 oz tuna sand- wich on 100% whole grain wrap 12 whole grain pretzel nuggets 1 cup milk option	4 oz. sliced turkey or lean protein of choice on 100% whole grain sub roll with mixed veggies, 1 bag baked chips 1 cup milk option	1 cup water 1 orange 4 oz turkey or veggie burger 100% whole grain bun milk option
Snack—post workout shake or bar 1 protein, milk or fat options 1 fruit	16 oz. fruit smoothie with NSF approved whey protein serving	1 cup lowfat chocolate milk with 1/4 cup al- mond/walnut/ dried fruit mix	16 oz. fruit smoothie with milk option and fresh fruit
Evening Dinner 4-5 oz. protein 1 cup salad 1 milk option 2-3 grains/high carb veggies 1-2 fruits 1-2 fats	1 cup veggie soup 100% whole grain roll 5 oz. lean grass fed steak 8 baked fries w/ organic ketchup 1 cup steamed broccoli 1 cup milk option	1 cup green salad 5 oz. chicken and broccoli stir fry 1 cup soba noodles 1 cup milk option	1 cup veggies 5 oz. grilled fish taco w/ baked corn tortilla 1 cup brown rice with green peas 1 cup milk option

Wednesday	Thursday	Friday	Saturday
1 cup low fat high protein granola ½ banana sliced pineapple 1 cup lowfat milk option	100% whole grain cereal, 1 banana, egg white omelette with ham, 1 cup OJ	1 cup Legally Lean juice breakfast burrito w/ egg, lowfat cheese, veggies 1 cup low fat milk option	1 cup tart cherry juice 100% whole grain bagel 1 pear 1 cup low fat milk option
1 organic fruit/ nut bar and 16 oz. low sugar electrolyte/ sports drink	16 oz. fruit smoothie with 1 scoop NSF certified whey protein	1 plain lowfat Greek yogurt with sliced strawberries	¼ cup goji berries with ¼ cup dried edamame mix
1 cup green salad w/ ginger dressing Sushi roll with 4 oz. crab or fish of choice brown rice 1 cup milk option	1 cup citrus sections 4 oz grilled chicken sandwich on 100% whole grain pita 1 cup milk option	1 cup gazpacho soup 4 oz. grilled chicken on green salad chopped with veggies 1 cup milk option	4 oz. grilled fish sandwich on 100% whole grain pita 1 serving baked tortilla chips sliced watermelon 1 cup milk option
1-Greek yogurt with ¾ cup berries	Whole grain breakfast bar with nectarine	Coconut water with ¼ cup dried chickpeas	1 lowfat string cheese with 15 grapes
1 cup chili 4 oz. Jerk Turkey Burger on 100% whole grain roll(recipe, on page 200) 1 grilled corn cob 1 tsp Omega-rich spread 1 cup milk option	1 cup green salad 5 oz. grilled fish 1 sweet potato smashed with Omega-rich spread grilled asparagus 1 cup milk	1 cup salad w/ extra virgin olive oil-based dressing 1 cup Paella (brown rice with 4 oz. seafood/ chicken) 1 cup milk option	1 cup green salad 4 turkey meatballs on sub 1 cup 100% whole grain pasta 1 cup milk option

As you can see, the athlete's performance eating plans provide a more optimal training calorie range of 1,800 to 5,000 calories than the Legally Lean Core Program, weight cutting 1200 and 1500 calorie programs outlined on **page 65**. You CAN use the Core Food Lists and Food Choices in the Core Plan in Section III for mealtime options or follow the menus starting on **pages 112-113**.

Carbs, Protein, & Fat

The next step is to determine how many of your daily calories should come from carbohydrate, how many from protein, and how many from fat. To answer that question, first take into consideration your training intensity.

"Moderate training" means working out at between 50 and 70 percent of your maximum heart rate. (You can find out what 50 to 70 percent of your maximum heart rate is by taking 220 minus your age and multiplying that number by a number between .50 and .70.) Then take your heart rate manually or use a heart rate monitor while you exercise, and determine whether you fall into the 50 to 70 percent range. If you do, you can meet your daily fuel needs by using the following formula:

- 45-55% carbohydrates (3 to 5 grams/kilograms body weight/day)
- 10-15% protein (0.8 to 1.0 grams/kilograms body weight/day)
- 25-35% fat (0.5 to 1.5 grams/kilograms body weight/day)

To convert your weight in pounds to your weight in kilograms, take your weight in pounds and divide by 2.2. For example, if you weigh 120 pounds, divide 120 by 2.2. Your weight is 54 kilograms.

When you increase your training duration, or you add double or triple workouts, or your lifestyle added to your long training sessions adds up to several active hours each day (say you're going to classes or working on your feet as a coach, teacher, firefighter, or nurse), then you will probably need more carbohydrates and protein to prevent breaking down.

If you're an endurance "junkie" training consistently 3 to 4 hours daily for an Ironman, ultramarathon, or multiday adventure racing event, shoot for getting at least 50 percent, but 60 percent to 70 percent (especially in-season) of total calories from carbohydrates (5 to 8 grams/kg/day) to maintain adequate carbohydrate stores in muscles.

Set protein at 1.2 to 1.7 grams/kg body weight/day and fat at 20 percent to 30 percent of total calories. Don't be surprised if you're losing weight, because you may need even more to keep up with your training in season or for longer events like an Ironman. Experts suggest carbohydrate needs can reach 10 grams/kilogram/body weight a day and fat needs up to 35 percent of total calories in athletes who are training heavily.

These numbers are just a starting place for your performance eating plan. And as you know, when you get to a "starting line," anything can happen. Performance diets, like races, require trial and error. The more you try, the better you get. And, like selecting the right gear for your sport, keeping the following food tips in mind will help you to select the best food value for your calorie budget.

 Coach's Corner

Training Table Guidelines

Make your calories count. Eat a wide variety of foods, even within food groups and selection, to get the most vitamin and mineral bang for your buck. Some brands may also just work better for you.

Choose at least five colors a day (preferably each meal) for your plate, representing all the food groups on a daily basis. Include foods from the Legally Lean Food Guide Bar in the Core Performance Program for bonus vitamins, minerals, and phytonutrient compounds shown to accelerate speed, endurance, and recovery from training and promote optimal health.

Don't skip! Eat at least three meals and two to three snacks throughout the day to sustain energy levels, manage blood sugars, and assist with pre-workout and recovery fuel.

Choose wholesome and fresh foods. Whenever possible, limit additives, colorings, flavoring, and/or processing. If you have limited access to fresh and wholesome foods, go for frozen, organic, or without sauces/seasonings. The next best choice after frozen would then be canned, (BPA free), low sodium, and/or rinsed.

Here are sample 1,800- and 3,500-calorie menus to get you started. If you require more or less, adjust the portion sizes as needed. Always keep track of your actual diet with your Legally Lean Pocket Coach© to make sure you are actually eating enough. Often what an athlete thinks they're eating looks completely different when they put it down on paper!

1800 Calorie Sample Menu:

Pre-Workout AM (1 hour before): 1 cup green tea with half of a sport bar or 1 slice of 100 percent whole grain toast with 1 tsp. nut butter

During workout: Less than one hour: water, electrolytes as needed. More than one hour: coconut water or low sugar electrolyte-rich, naturally sweetened sports drink as needed. Organic energy chews, gels, or bar as needed for beyond 90 minutes (See more information later in this chapter.)

After workout: Recovery beverage to include a natural source of simple sugar with high-quality protein such as a NSF or Informed Choice approved protein powder (for example, a fruit smoothie with whey scoop)

Breakfast
Whole egg plus 4 egg white omelette with spinach, mushrooms, onions, and a side of sliced tomatoes, topped with low-fat shredded cheese and salsa
1 mini whole grain bagel with 1 teaspoon of almond butter
1 lowfat Greek yogurt
½ cup strawberries

Snack
1 ounce lowfat string cheese with a sliced apple

Lunch
1 cup gazpacho soup
4 ounces lean, antibiotic-free turkey breast
2 slices whole grain toast
Add deep greens, tomato slices and sprouts
1 teaspoon extra virgin olive oil or low-fat, olive-oil-based dressing
1 cup mixed tropical fruit salad with diced kiwi and citrus sections (for a potassium kick)

Snack
100% whole grain, high fiber, low-added-sugar breakfast bar and watermelon chunks

Pre-Afternoon-Workout Snack (if required)
(45 minutes to 1 hour before)
1 lite natural sport drink and banana
Or 12-ounce coconut water with 1 ounce of oat bran pretzel nuggets

Dinner
Spinach salad with shredded carrots, tomatoes, chickpeas, mushrooms and grilled corn topped with 1 ounce lite lowfat Feta cheese crumbles
5 ounce grilled turkey burger or veggie burger
1 whole grain bun
Handful of baked fried potatoes
1 cup stir-fried mixed veggies

Snack
Frozen natural fruit pop or ¾ cup berries with light whipped cream

3500 Calorie Sample Menu:

Morning
1 cup 100% orange juice
1 bowl vitamin fortified 100% whole grain cereal
1 cup lowfat "milk" group option
½ cup strawberries and sliced banana in cereal

Snack
1 lowfat string cheese snack
6 whole grain crackers
1 apple

Afternoon
1 green salad with carrots and tomatoes
1 ounce olive-oil-based salad dressing
12-inch turkey (6 oz.) sub on whole grain bread, loaded with veggies, lite cheese
1 bag baked potato chips
12 ounces low fat milk
1 orange

Snack

Pre workout: 1 whole grain breakfast bar or sports bar

During workout: water and sports drink, as needed

Post workout: recovery drink or fruit smoothie with fresh fruits and whey isolate protein powder

Evening

1 cup vegetable soup
1 whole grain roll, 1 tsp. butter
8 ounces grilled fish
1 cup of brown rice and beans or 1 large baked sweet potato
1 cup of peas and corn
1 cup steamed broccoli with parmesan cheese
1 cup of mixed berries with whipped cream

Snack—1-2 hours before bedtime

12 ounces low fat "milk" option

Nutritional Periodization

There is another nutrition topic which is vital for athletes to understand called *nutritional periodization.*

Nutritional periodization is a concept that involves altering one's diet to match the intensity, volume, and specificity of training as it changes throughout the year. Periodization involves taking into account different training cycles, including the exercise load, recovery, peak, and conditioning. These cycles are implemented according to the athlete's sport demands and competition schedules.

Essentially, *nutritional periodization* means devising a nutrition plan that correlates perfectly with the strength or training goals you have at any certain point in a cycle. This requires manipulating the percentage and amounts of carbohydrates, protein, and fat to work in tandem with training to maximize strength, muscle mass, and endurance.

For example, during the preseason, a time when an athlete is making the most significant changes in body composition, which is typically characterized by higher volume, higher intensity overload training and places additional strain on the muscular, immune and antioxidant systems, a periodization plan might call for additional calories, protein, and antioxidants. In season, since the goal is geared towards energy, endurance, and weight maintenance, adequate carbohydrate calories are critical, with enough protein and essential fats added to keep up with game-time needs and protect the system from unnecessary inflammation, injury, and illness.

A summary of the dietary changes throughout the *Nutritional Periodization* year can be found in the Coach's Corner.

Coach's Corner
Training Table Guidelines

	Pre-season	In-season	Post-season
Goals	Overload training High volume/ intensity 50-60%	Maintain energy Prevent injury 55-70%	Weight management Overall health 40-50%
Carbohydrates	Moderate	High	Moderate
Protein	20-30% (up to 35%)* High	15-20% Adequate-High quality Timing critical	15-25% Moderate
Fat	15*-35%** Moderate	20-30% Moderate-essential	20-35% (up to 50%)** Moderate as needed

* For athletes trying to lose/cut weight
**For athletes trying to gain weight/ keep up with calorie demands

Nutrition Periodization Science

Athletes involved in moderate- to high-volume training will need greater amounts of carbohydrates, protein, and fat to meet macronutrient needs. When an athlete is using *nutritional periodization*, the composition of his or her diet depends on training phase: pre-season, season, or off-season. It also depends on sport type, including intensity and duration of training. Lastly, it depends on weight and body composition goals.

In addition to varying macronutrient composition over the course of pre-season, in-season, and post-season, athletes need to take into account a smaller cycle: each 24-hour day. This concept is called *Nutrient Timing*. According to renowned exercise physiologist Dr. John Ivy, during a 24-hour period, there are three distinct phases of nutrient timing: energy, anabolic, and growth phase. Each phase has a unique set of metabolic characteristics that impact the percentage of carbohydrates, protein, and fat the athlete should consume during those phases.

Pre-season, out of competition time is an ideal time to understand the impact of the distribution of carbohydrates, fats, and protein on your 24-hour cycle, and to practice with manipulating them, so that you can maximize the opportunities for building endurance, recovering from training, and enhancing muscle growth and not interfere with performance.

Understanding the windows of opportunity for energy, anabolism and growth/rest is one thing. Taking them to the dinner table is another! If you're interested in reading more about Nutrient Timing, read Jon Ivy's *Nutrient Timing* and Heidi Skolnick and Andrea Chernus's *Nutrient Timing for Peak Performance* books. Sports Dietitian Bob Seebohar, RD also offers online education and resources on nutritional periodization.

If this topic seems complicated to you, don't feel overwhelmed. Because of the need and challenge to devise specific plans for each cycle, competitive, elite and Olympian athletes typically hire a sports dietitian/nutritionist to devise a nutrition periodization program. Sometimes university nutrition departments with sports nutrition programs will offer these services at a reduced fee or for free to give their graduate students experience in the field.

Protein Type, Timing, and Amount for Muscle Building

A hot topic amongst athletes and in the sports nutrition community, many known and yet to be understood factors appear to contribute to overall muscle hypertrophy. Nutritional factors that control protein anabolism (synthesis) during exercise are not well understood, leaving experts in discord about the type, amount, and timing of meals to enhance protein synthesis and muscle hypertrophy.

Both strength training and diet consistently appear to play a role in post-workout muscle protein synthesis. The metabolic basis for muscle growth appears to be a balance between muscle protein synthesis (MPS) and prevention of catabolism (breakdown), especially the balance of myofibrillar protein or contractile protein synthesis in which dietary protein and exercise play an important role.

Strength training enhances your body's ability to build by 40 to 100 percent over resting levels. Adding dietary protein immediately prior to and at least within 24 hours after helps the muscle building process to last for up to 24 hours.

Research suggests that the anabolic response to strength training and protein consumption works just as well with "whole food" proteins like a turkey sandwich as it does with sports fuel or supplemental proteins. Often athletes choose convenience over homemade meals, since taking a high protein shake or bar to training is more practical than carrying a chicken breast. Selecting Sport Certified, safe products with the NSF or Informed Choice logos ensure the quality and purity of the products (see Section V for more information on **pages 232**).

Puberty & Testosterone

Being a teen is one of the most challenging periods for keeping up with the nutritional needs that accompany growth. The physiological process of growing from a child into an adult is the only time other than right after birth when the velocity of growth actually increases.

Teens gain about 20 percent of their adult height and 50 percent of their adult weight during this period. At some point during the five to seven years of puberty, the majority of this growth happens very quickly, during an 18- to 24-month period called the "growth spurt." Everyone goes through growth spurts at different times and they can continue into the early 20s.

During the process, body composition changes, too. At prepuberty, body composition for boys and girls is about the same. But during puberty, boys gain about twice as much lean mass as girls. BMI and skin fold measurements are two ways to track the growth and changes.

The nutritional requirements for teenaged athletes can vary because of variations in growth rate and training. Calorie requirements are designed to maintain health, promote optimal growth and maturation, and support training needs. Athletes who compromise their diet during this time can impact their ultimate adult growth and health.

In other words, it's very important for the teen athlete to consume enough calories on a daily basis. The Coach's Corner provides a more general look at basic calorie needs for different age groups, based on the Food and Nutrition Board of the Institute of Medicine's Estimated Energy Requirements (EER).

Coach's Corner

Estimated Energy Requirements (EER) for Teen Athletes

Age	Ref weight (pounds)	Ref height (inches)	EER (calories/day)
10	70.3	54.7	2486
11	79.1	56.7	2640
12	89.2	58.7	2817
13	100.4	61.4	3038
14	112.3	64.6	3283
15	124	66.9	3499
16	134.1	68.5	3663
17	142.3	68.9	3754
18	148	69.3	3804

How Much Protein?

For athletes interested in building muscle, it appears that neither the type nor the amount of protein matters, as long as the day's total amount is within the recommended range for resistance-training athletes of 1.2 to 2 grams (2.4 grams maximum) of protein per kilogram of body weight per day, depending on many factors including age, size, gender, lean body mass, activity level and intensity and overall health. One study suggests that 2.3 grams per kilogram bodyweight (or about 35 percent) protein is more effective than 1.0 gram per kilogram bodyweight (or 15 percent) protein for maintaining lean body mass in athletes during short term, low calorie weight loss.

Protein experts suggest that 20 to 25 grams of a high-quality, complete protein containing 2.5 grams of the branched chain amino acid (BCAA) leucine per meal maximizes the response of protein synthesis following strength workouts. No differences have been shown between 20 and 40 grams, suggesting more is not better. Smaller protein portions consumed throughout the day, rather than large 20-ounce steaks, may be more beneficial for maintaining and building muscle.

If you are consuming a diet of primarily incomplete plant-based protein sources (for example, vegetables, beans, nuts, whole grains, soy or hemp), or if you are an older individual, more protein may be required to maximize the response of muscle synthesis.

Pre-workout essential amino acid fuel also appears to enhance the anabolic response. And while essential fat Omega-3 foods (such as fish, soy, and some nuts) and carbohydrates may not contribute to protein synthesis, they have been shown to play a role in the prevention of muscle breakdown (catabolism). The total fat content of post-workout snack may also have a positive impact on muscle protein synthesis. For example, in one study, whole milk enhanced synthesis more effectively than skim milk.

Training & Competition Fuel

When your training is picking up steam, staying energized is key for feeling great as you're building your longer workouts. Preventing energy depletion means replenishing sugars in your blood, muscles, and liver.

You don't have much sugar to spare—only about 60 to 90 minutes' worth of stored sugar (called "glycogen") in your liver and muscles. And even that store depends on your daily dietary intake of carbs and the intensity and duration of your daily training. If glycogen stores drop to critically low levels, training for any length of time and speed will be an effort, and as the veteran athletes say, you'll "bonk."

Glycogen depletion can be a gradual process—the result of repeated days of training without adequate carbohydrate replacement. You can also deplete with repetitive, high-intensity work, like pick ups—spurts of faster speeds on top of your longer steady state session. Long-term glycogen depletion can negatively impact the immune, endocrine, cardiovascular, muscuskeletal, and mental systems, and can lead to illness and injury which can take weeks, months, or sometimes years to recover from. Called Overtraining Syndrome, this phenomenon is summarized at the end of this chapter.

To avoid the bonk, both eating enough total daily carbs and carb-fueling before, during, and after running are imperative.

How much do you need before, during, and after your workouts?

Pre-Workout Meals

A pre-workout meal can improve performance compared with exercising in a fasted state. Athletes who train early in the morning before eating or drinking risk developing low liver glycogen stores that can impair performance, particularly if the exercise regimen involves endurance training.

The pre-workout snack helps to maintain optimal levels of blood sugar for muscles, and can help restore suboptimal liver glycogen stores. If you train first thing in the morning and cannot imagine eating anything first thing, then your last meal or snack the night before will serve as your pre-workout snack. If that's the case, your evening meal needs to be carb-loaded—a tennis ball size or two servings of 100 percent whole grain pasta, brown rice, potatoes, beans, peas, or corn with additional carbohydrate servings from fruit, vegetables, or low fat dairy. If the pre-workout snack is within one hour of training, keep it simple—leave the fibers, fat, and spices for other mealtimes, if you want to avoid training "trots" and indigestion. Exercising with a full stomach may cause indigestion, nausea, and vomiting. (More on gut distress later in this section.)

Get a snack that provides one to four grams of carbohydrates per kilogram body weight, one to four hours prior to your workout respectively. If you weigh 120 pounds, that means eating about 54 grams of carbs one hour before training. Foods recommended or crackers, a serving of fruit, and cup of coconut water.

You can calculate how much you need by multiplying your kilogram body weight by the number of hours before your workout you're eating, to get how many grams of carbohydrates you will need.

As a reference, a slice of toast, ½ cup of unsweetened cereal, or 6 saltines has about 15 grams of carbs; 14 grams for every 8 oz. of sports drink; 30 to 45 grams for a banana, and 21 to 40 grams for some of the more popular, high carbohydrate sport bars. Additional carbohydrate-rich foods can be found in the Coach's Corner.

Coach's Corner
Carbohydrates in Pre-Workout Food Options

Food	Serving Size	Calories	Carbohydrates
Sports drink	8 ounces	70	18
Endurance sports beverage	12 ounces	120	21
Sports bar	1 bar	240	45
Coconut water	12 ounces	60	15
Apple juice	1 cup	140	35
Cereal	1 cup	110	24
English muffin	1 medium	130	25
Pasta	1 cup	159	34
Pretzels	1 ounce	106	21
Tortilla	1 small	85	15
Sweet potato	1 medium	103	24
Apple	1 average	81	21
Applesauce	1 cup	232	60
Breakfast bar	1 bar	210	43
Toast	1 slice	75	13
Bagel	1 regular	165	31
Waffle	1 regular	200	27

Pre-Workout Fuel Summarized:

1. Get carbs and keep them simple.

It's important to get a good source of carbs before, during, and after training to keep energy levels high, to efficiently continue burning fat.

2. Being well fueled can accelerate the recovery process.

That way, you can work out again later in the day or within the next 24!

3. Before your workout:

You'll need about one gram of carbohydrate per kilogram (weight in pounds /2.2), one hour prior to exercise. That means if you weigh 130 pounds, you take your pounds and divide by 2.2 to get kilograms, which is 59 kilograms. You then take 59 kilograms and multiply that number by:

- One gram carbs/kg body weight for a 59 gram carbohydrate snack one hour before. Example: A banana (30 grams of carbs) and one serving of oatmeal (30g of carbs). Two grams carbs/ kg body weight, two hours before (about 118 grams of carbs). Example: One cup of whole grain cereal with almond milk and one banana.
- Three grams carbs/kg body weight, three hours before (about 177 grams of carbs). Example: One cup of black beans and one cup of brown rice with a green salad.

Examples of Competition Meals

For athletes who compete in events such as track, swimming meets, or soccer, or who play in basketball, volleyball, or wrestling tournaments, nutritious, easy-to-digest food and fluid choices require attention. Athletes need to consider the amount of time between eating and performance when choosing foods during these all-day events. Suggested pre-competition menus include the following:

One Hour or Less Before Competition—Approximately 100 kcal—One of these choices:

- Fresh fruit such as a banana or orange slices
- Half of most sports energy bars
- ½ plain whole grain bagel or English muffin
- 8 whole grain crackers

- Small box of dry low-fiber cereal
- 8-12 oz. of a natural sports or endurance sports drink
- ½ plain baked potato

Two to Three Hours Before Competition—Approximately 300-400 kcal—One of these choices:

- ½ of turkey sandwich with baked chips
- ½ whole grain bagel with fruit jam and 1 banana
- 2 whole grain waffles with natural maple syrup and berries
- 1 baked sweet potato with 0% Greek or Icelandic Yogurt dollop
- 32 fluid ounces of a natural sports drink or 32-ounce endurance drink with added protein
- 1 fruit smoothie with berries, banana, and scoop of added NSF/Informed Choice approved whey protein
- 1 sports energy bar, 1 cup sports drink, 1 cup water

Three to Four Hours Before Competition—Approximately 700 kcal—One of these selections:

- Scrambled egg + 4 egg whites with whole grain toast, fruit jam, and banana
- Whole grain bagel with nut butter, fruit jam, banana, and coconut water
- 6-inch turkey sub on Italian bread with lettuce, tomato, apple, and baked chips
- 3-ounce grilled chicken breast with baked potato, dill-spiked yogurt dollop, whole grain roll, and water
- 2 cups whole grain pasta, 2 meatballs, roll, glass of almond milk

Fuel During Exercise

One way to get fueled without interfering with your training or focus or upsetting the gut is with sports fuels, since these are especially designed for consumption while training or competing. Sports fuel comes in variety of forms, whether it is sports drinks, gels, blasts, or bars. They're typically high in carbs, low

Coach's Corner

Sports Fuel Options for Training and Competition

Sport Food	Characteristics
Sports drink	CHO: 5%-7% by volume (about 14 g/8 oz.) Sodium: (110-165 mg/8 oz.) 16-66mg/(cups) Potassium: Other electrolytes: Varier
Organic sport energy chews*	1 (45 gram) package provides both complex and simple carbohydrates, 36 grams total carbs, 17 grams sugars & 140 calories 110 mg sodium, 30 mg potassium
Energy gel blasts*	6 pieces = 130 calories, 30 grams carbohydrates, 2 grams protein Vitamin C = 10% daily values Electrolytes and antioxidants vary
Energy gel*	Carbs: 50% by volume (50g/100 ml or 15 g/oz.) Vitamins and minerals: trace or absent
Sports beans*	14 beans 100 calories Carbs: 25 g/1 oz. 10% DV of vitamins B1, B2, B3 20% DV of vitamins C and E

*Watch caffeine and additional herbs

Guidelines For Consumption In Exercise		
Before	**During**	**After**
Not necessary, can include 8-16 oz. along with water, tea, 1 hr. before exercise, as needed for energy	2-4 oz. every 15-20 minutes after 1 hour training to contribute to UP TO 60 grams/hour MAX	To replace losses along with water, recovery drink to meet 24 oz. for every lb. of body weight lost
As needed for carbohydrate energy calories in lieu of whole food pre-workout snack	As needed for carbohydrate and electrolyte fuel for endurance exercise over 1 hour duration	As needed for recovery for glycogen replenishment
6 pieces, as needed, about 30 to 45 minutes before training	6 -12 pieces every hour as needed for energy over 1 hour exercise	For glycogen replacement if whole food unavailable or desired
1 packet as needed before training; consume adequate fluid to promote absorption	If overall fluid intake is adequate, enough to supply 30 to 60 g carbs/hr.	For glycogen replacement when whole food is not available or desired.
NA	Up to 14 pieces/ hour for energy	NA

NA-Not applicable; *CHO*, Carbohydrate; *DV*, daily value; *RDA*, recommended dietary allowance.

in protein and fat, and designed for getting energy to the blood, brain, and muscles quickly.

Eating carbohydrates during longer workouts also improves performance, speeds recovery, and may help to prevent post-race respiratory illness. Although it can't prevent fatigue, it can definitely delay it. Eating during exercise can also spare muscle protein and carbohydrates so you'll recover faster and feel more energized for the next workout.

During the final minutes of exercise, when muscle glycogen is low and athletes rely heavily on blood glucose for energy, their muscles feel heavy, and they must concentrate to maintain exercise at intensities that are ordinarily not stressful when muscle glycogen stores are full. Studies show carbohydrates consumed during exercise can also spare endogenous protein help to maintain blood sugars, and improve performance.

Physiologically, the form of carbohydrate does not seem to matter in terms of staying fueled, although some athletes do better with some forms of sugars than others (see later in the chapter). Some athletes prefer a sports drink, while others like orange slices or a sports gel with water. Regardless, training is a great time to practice your workout fuel since not every choice works for every athlete, even if the fuel is designed for sports training. Trying different brands and flavors will help you to find the best one for you, so you can work out the GI kinks and compete without a snag on race day.

The recommended amount of carbs to consume during training is about 25 to 30 grams every 30 minutes. Sixteen ounces of most sports drinks have this amount unless they're diluted. Sip a few ounces every 15 to 20 minutes after you start your second hour of training.

Sport gummies, gels and beans also have approximately 25 to 30 grams of sugar per one ounce portion. However, be careful. Exceeding a total of 60 to 70 grams/hour from all sport fuels combined can cause major gut distress. Keeping mental tabs on your total consumption will help you to avoid unnecessary pit stops during your workout. The Coach's Corner highlights the nutrition composition of some sport fuel products.

Combining protein and carbohydrates in a sport fluid or snack may also improve performance, muscle protein synthesis and net balance, and recovery. A small amount of amino acids, ingested in small amounts, alone or in conjunction with carbohydrates, before or after exercise, appears to improve net protein balance and may stimulate protein synthesis and improve net protein balance at rest during exercise and post exercise recovery. Safe brands of amino acid fuel can be found at Informed Choice or NSF for Sports Certification websites (see Appendix).

It's important to make sure you try any of these products in training prior to competition. Sometimes the taste, amount, or sugar sources can upset your system. It is generally not recommended to consume more than 60 grams of the carbohydrates in these products combined per hour because they can cause gas and cramping. And while I do not like the idea of wasting any food or supplement, please don't feel compelled to consume the entire package. You may need less or more than the serving size to get you jump started and going, depending on your energy and stress levels, so go by your own feelings, not the portion size.

Summary of Fuel During Workouts

- Working out less than one hour doesn't require much beyond water. However, go over one hour of training, and it's a whole new ball game.
- You need to get something to keep you going, but not so much that your gut will ache. A sports drink, coconut water, few slices of fruit, or sports fuel gel will work.
- The rule of thumb is to consume no more than 60 grams of carbohydrates/hour to avoid gut distress. That's the equivalent of 12 ounces coconut water and one sliced orange or ½ banana.

Post-Workout Fuel

Recovery fuel strives to accomplish several goals—enhance recovery from the negative effects of exercise; promote more effective training adaptation; and enable you to return faster to training. The resulting improvement in training efficiency can lead to significant performance benefits and sport career longevity by supporting repetitive training and competition over time, helping to maintain immune status, and enhancing long term health.

On average, only a small percent (5 percent, to be exact) of the muscle glycogen used during exercise is resynthesized each hour following exercise. At least 20 hours will be required for complete restoration after all-out training sessions, and this will happen only when you replenish and consume carbohydrates throughout the remainder of the day. Waiting 'til you're showered and dressed and off to work to eat can slow down muscle replenishment two-fold and can impact your next workout.

 Coach's Corner

What to Look For in Sports Fuel

1. Include:
- Organic products which contain a blend of high and low glycemic carbohydrate sources.
- Bars, gels, and energy chews with sugars or sweeteners such as: honey, beet sugar, date sugar, brown rice syrup, black strap molasses, organic corn syrup, and calorie-free stevia and monk fruit.

2. Steer clear of all sport drinks with artificial flavors, obvious artificial colorings, and brominated vegetable oil (BVO). BVO is actually a flame retardant which was banned in Europe and Japan, but is still included in some of the most popular sports drinks here in the US! BVO is associated with:
- Reproductive and behavioral problems
- Skin lesions
- Memory loss
- Nerve disorders

3. Avoid sports drinks and products that contain:
- High fructose corn syrup
- Artificial colorings or flavorings, preservatives, and hydrogenated oils

4. Watch out for other potentially questionable ingredients:
- Unfamiliar herbs
- Caffeine in which no amount has been provided
- Added vitamins and minerals above 100 percent of the DVs

Delaying the consumption of carbohydrates for too long after training reduces overall muscle glycogen resynthesis. The highest capacity of muscle glycogen synthesis has been shown with the equivalent of 1 to 1.85 grams carbohydrates/kilogram/bodyweight/hour, consumed immediately after training and at 15- to 60-minute intervals thereafter, for up to five hours after a workout out. That means snacking on carbs throughout the remainder of the day and at main meals.

If you like sweets, this is the time to indulge, since sweeter carbs have been shown to result in higher muscle glycogen levels 24 hours after working out compared with the same amount of complex carbohydrates.

As for protein, adding approximately five to nine grams of protein with every 100 grams of carbohydrate has been shown to enhance muscle recovery, may further increase glycogen resynthesis rate, provides amino acids for muscle repair, and promotes a more anabolic hormonal response.

For example, if your weight is 220 pounds, you would need at least 100 grams carbohydrates and 22 grams of protein for recovery. A list of the post-workout carbohydrate and protein recommendations for other bodyweights can be found in Coach's Corner.

If you do intend to eat a full meal after a workout, you'll want to consume food and fluids that replenish your muscles as quickly as possible. Foods and drinks that are a cool temperature, contain simple carbohydrates, and are low in fiber and fat are the best for speeding up the delivery of carbohydrates to recovering muscles.

Whole-food meals and beverages that meet this criterion include organic "milk options" yogurt-based smoothies or shakes, frozen yogurt "sundaes" with fresh fruit topping, 100 percent whole grain bagel with nut butter, or a 100 percent whole grain raisin bran muffin with a low fat cheese stick. Chocolate milk has been shown to be an excellent post-workout recovery option for those with limited access or funds for smoothies and shakes. Research suggests that chocolate milk works as a recovery food, since it is a good source of carbohydrates, whey, casein, potassium, sodium, vitamins, and minerals.

Coach's Corner

Recovery Food Formula for Carbohydrates and Protein

Weight (pounds)	Carbohydrate (Gms)	Protein (Gms)
120	54	12
150	68	15
180	81	18
200	90	20
220	100	22
240	109	24
260	118	26
280	127	28
300	136	30
320	145	32
340	154	34

Recovery Supplements

Many athletes find it difficult to consume food immediately after exercise. Usually when body temperature or core temperature is elevated, appetite is depressed, and it is difficult to consume carbohydrate-rich foods. Many athletes find it easier and simpler to drink their carbohydrate or to consume easy-to-eat, carbohydrate-rich foods such as fruit pops, bananas, oranges, melon, or apple slices. That's when sports recovery shakes, bars, and fuel steps in.

Sports supplements may include easy-to-carry, easy-to-consume, and easy-to-digest meal-replacement powders, ready-to-drink supplements, energy bars, gummies and energy gels.

They provide a portable, easy-to-consume fuel that can be used before, during, or after training; while traveling; at work; in the car; or throughout the day at a multi-event meet such as in track and field, swimming, diving, or gymnastics.

As a competitive athlete myself, I appreciate all the great tasting, ready to drink and eat bars that I can blend up and toss into my training bag to consume right after my workout. I can honestly say that recovery fuel options have enabled me to continue to compete at a high level consistently and successfully over the past 30 years, enjoying complete muscle recovery and training, day after day. It's important to realize that when you choose the supplement route, there are risks associated with contamination and doping and selecting safety over promises is essential (see the Introduction and Section V). Several safe and recommended brands can be found at the website www.LegallyLean.com.

Many fitness-minded and athletic individuals also use these products as a convenient way to enhance their current diet. While these products are generally regarded as safe, if they are eaten in the place of whole foods on a regular basis, they can deprive you of a well-balanced diet.

Post-Workout Fuel Summarized

- Recovery fuel means getting all the carbs and nutrients you need to fuel and recover from your workouts.
- Replenish within the operative window of 30 minutes to two hours to completely restore glycogen energy in muscles.
- After workouts, get enough carbohydrates and high quality protein for complete muscle recovery and synthesis and prevention of catabolism.
- You'll need to experiment with different essential food combinations and amounts and then you will learn for yourself what is best and what is not and find the foods, snacks, and bars that work best for you.
- Keep in mind that these are all just recommendations. What works for one person does not necessarily work for the next.

Drink up!
Since the body is roughly 60 percent fluid, you'll need to replenish fluids through beverage and high-fluid food consumption (fruits and veggies) on a regular basis. If you don't replace what you lose, it could be extra stressful for your system just to get through the day, let alone a training session.

We need fluids and plenty of them—about 3.7 liters (13 cups) for men, 2.7 liters (9 cups) for women, says the DRIs, just to stay afloat—and up to 10 liters of fluid daily for longer than one-hour workouts in hotter weather, especially for "big losers."

You know you're a "loser" if you sweat excessively, indoors or out, even after training and showering, and if you sweat in air conditioned spaces. "Losers" are typically burdened with fatigue, late afternoon headaches, brain fog, cramping, nausea, and constipation. They also often have an "ashy" finish to their skin after racing, the "salts" of their labor. More serious symp-

Coach's Corner

Fluid's Responsibilities in the Body

- Regulating your body temperature, like in sweating, when heat is released, which leaves the body cooler

- Lubricating the digestive tract and keeping tissues moistened with mucus so your food flows freely down your digestive tract

- Assisting with cellular chemical reactions for creating energy

- Carrying away stressful waste products formed during reactions

- Acting as a shock absorber in joints and around the spinal cord, protecting you against the physical stress of training

- Transporting blood

- Surrounding and cushioning the unborn child in a pregnant woman

toms of heavy fluid loss include: excessive body temp, elevated heart rate, total body cramping, and even fainting. You see, just a one percent fluid loss can make you nauseous, lead to cramps, or even give you a migraine headache. If you lose more than one percent, you run the risk of dizziness, weakness, confusion, anxiety, lethargy, weakness, and even fainting.

Signs of Dehydration:

- Excessive thirst
- Fatigue
- Headache
- Dry mouth
- Little or no urination
- Muscle weakness
- Dizziness
- Lightheadedness, fainting
- Kidney failure

Suffice it to say, if fluid losses are not replaced, the consequences can be fatal.

Fluid Ins and Outs

Experts still debate the ins and outs of fluids—the best methods for assessing fluid needs. There is not general agreement on how much or what type of fluids athletes' need, under what conditions athletes need additional amounts, or even about whether or not dehydration makes any difference for sports performance.

A 2012 study on endurance athletes suggests mild dehydration during workouts of one hour or less does not affect performance. In fact, drinking too much water can work against you. Water alone actually *dilutes* the blood rapidly, increases its volume, and stimulates urination! Blood dilution also lowers the electrolyte, sodium and volume-dependent part of the thirst drive, removing much of your drive to drink and replace fluid losses.

However, pre-workout losses of three percent or more have been shown to negatively affect performance for longer than one-hour sessions. If you weigh 150 pounds, a fluid loss of three percent means at least a fluid loss of four to five pounds.

Coach's Corner

Are You Hydrated?

Methods for assessing hydration status include pre- and post-workout body weights, urine color, and urine specific gravity (typically performed by a professional sports medicine expert, dietitian, or physiologist in the office). Each method has its own strengths and drawbacks.

- **Pre-/Post-workout weights:** Take your weight before and after workouts, especially when the temps or your training changes. Replace each pound lost with 16 to 24 ounces of fluid.

- **Urine color:** Shoot for a lemonade urine color. Beyond that, and you may be dehydrated. However, be aware that if you take a B vitamin supplement, it may cause your urine to take on a yellow hue.

- **Thirst:** Thirst can be your best indicator of dehydration, although some of us are not great judges of thirst, ignore the sensations, or are too stressed during competition to deal with thirst until it's too late. Even if you can't swallow during competition due to feeling nauseous or dealing with reflux, a mouth "rinse" with sports drinks can help to keep you going.

How Much is Enough?

Health and sports organizations such as the ACSM, NATA, AND, USAT&F, and others offer the following guidelines. Remember, everyone is different, so use the recommendations like you would MapQuest, as a place to get started.

What About Electrolytes?

Electrolytes are minerals involved in the movement of water in and out of cells and in nerve and muscle transmission. In other words, electrolyte depletion can be even more serious and detrimental to performance than dehydration itself! Electrolyte depletion can cause nasty leg cramps or stitches in your gut. It can also cause the misfiring of information between your stomach and your brain and from the muscles to the kidneys—it's all connected!

Coach's Corner

Fluid Intake for Training

Before
- Drink approximately 14 to 22 ounces of water or sports
- Drink (approximately 17 ounces) two to three hours before the start of exercise.

During
- Drink six to 12 ounces of fluid every 15 to 20 minutes, depending on exercise intensity, environmental conditions, and tolerance.
- Drink no more than one cup (8 to 10 ounces) every 15 to 20 minutes, although individualized recommendations must be followed.

After
- Drink 25 percent to 50 percent more than existing weight loss to ensure hydration, four to six hours after exercise.
- Drink 16 to 24 oz of fluid for every pound of body weight lost during exercise.
- If you are participating in multiple workouts in one day, then 80 percent of fluid loss must be replaced before the next workout.

Sodium sweat losses differ from individual to individual, so one sport formula may not fit everyone. While leaner and also large athletes seem to sweat more, it's my experience that leaner, fitter athletes seem to cramp up faster. Typical losses are around 900 to 2,600mg sodium per liter of sweat lost.

Fluid overloading during prolonged workouts lasting more than four hours can cause hyponatremia (low blood sodium). Athletes who are less conditioned or prepared often produce a saltier sweat. If blood sodium levels fall below 130 mEq/L, you can become confused, have seizures, or lose consciousness. To avoid this, about 500 to 700 mg sodium is recommended for each liter of fluid consumed.

As for potassium, it's also an important major electrolyte inside the body's cells. Potassium works in tandem with sodium and chloride (salt) in maintaining body fluids, as well as in generating electrical impulses in the nerves, muscles, and heart. While you don't lose as much potassium as sodium in sweat (about 150mg/liter fluid) most athletes don't meet the four-gram-plus daily recommendation through food. (Five to 10 servings of fruits and veggies a day is where it's most often found.) Therefore, a good source of potassium is the 80 to 125 mg contained in most sports drinks.

Coconut water is even better than sports drinks for replacing potassium losses, with 500 to 600 mg of potassium typically found per serving. Foods also rich in potassium include bananas, kiwi, oranges, tomatoes, and potatoes—all also great carbohydrate boosters to fuel active muscles.

Will the Fluid Get Absorbed?

Healthy hydration is not simply reliant on drinking the right amount of fluid or the right amount of electrolytes. You also have to make sure they are absorbed!

I often hear athletes say they ordered the best blend of products from Company ABC, or their friend suggested blah, blah, blah for their Ironman Distance race and sadly, the fluid choice didn't get them to the finish. Instead, it caused GI distress, cramps, and nausea (see Gut Distress 101 on (pages 144-146). Not a simple issue, the speed at which fluid is absorbed depends on a number of different factors, including the amount, type, temperature, and osmolality (density of compounds) of the fluid consumed and the rate of gastric emptying.

Sugar is important, since it is actively absorbed in the intestines and can "escort" and increase both sodium and water absorption. A carbohydrate-electrolyte solution enhances exercise capacity, preventing brain drain and perceived exertion by elevating blood sugar and by maintaining a high rate of carbohydrate use by muscles.

To make sure you get enough, but not too much, carbs in your fluids, and to determine the ideal concentration of carbohydrate in your sports drink, you take the grams of carbohydrate or sugar in a serving, divided by the weight of a serving of the drink (usually 240 grams, the approximate weight of one cup of water).

Some experts suggest a 6 percent carbohydrate drink, which contains about 14 to 16 grams of carbohydrate per 8 ounces (1 cup) as the ideal amount. A 2013 study suggests a cold drink (about 60 degrees F) cools the body, inspires peripheral blood flow, decreases sweat rate, speeds up gastric emptying, and is absorbed more quickly when compared with warmer fluids. Iced slushy drinks and/or mouth rinses have also shown to prolong running time to exhaustion and reduce rectal temperature, supporting possible sensory and psychological effects of ice slushy beverages on performance, whether consumed or used as a mouthwash.
No doubt, we are all affected differently—knowing your threshold, and knowing the difference between how it feels to be energy-, water-, or electrolyte-depleted (which feel very different from one another), will ensure that hydration will never be your weak link again at any distance.

Fluid "Extras"

Four other players are important in the hydration game. These are magnesium, amino acids, beet juice, and caffeine.

Magnesium

Magnesium, the underestimated and overlooked mineral, supports more than 300 metabolic reactions in your body. For athletes, the energy, immune, hormonal, and muscle contraction/relaxation functions are the most pressing. Cause for concern, about 70 percent of my recreational to Olympic level athletes and the general population are deficient in magnesium. Magnesium deficiency causes muscle spasms, increasing heart rate and oxygen use even for the easiest of workouts.

Truth is, endurance training, excessive sweating while training, not eating enough whole grains, beans, nut and green veggies, and drinking too much alcohol are the top reasons athletes don't get enough magnesium. Fresh greens with black bean and whole grain brown rice salad, a hand full of nuts at snack time, or a training formula with added magnesium can help fill the gap and cover your needs of about 300 to 400mg/day.

Branched-Chain Amino Acids (BCAA)

Bless the BCAAs: leucine, isoleucine, and valine, which make up 35 to 40 percent of our essential amino acid (EAA) "pool", 14 percent of total muscle AAs. During training and competition stress, your body gets energy by breaking down muscle and BCAAs "fund" the cause more than any other EAA.

Research suggests BCAAs included in your pre/post workout formulas may decrease exercise-induced protein breakdown and muscle enzyme release (a sign of muscle damage) and increase protein synthesis and muscle gains beyond normal adaptation. Whey and egg protein are good sources, taken at mealtime or included in the hydration and recovery foods you whip up.

Beet Juice

"Beet" me to the finish—only with a nitrate boost, some experts say. Studies suggest natural sources of inorganic nitrate found in beetroot juice and powders, consumed immediately before, during, and after long-duration, endurance exercise for peak concentration may enhance performance by increasing vasodilation (blood flow) and muscular sugar uptake and reducing blood pressure and the oxygen cost of everyday workouts. In one cycling study, ½ liter beetroot juice daily for four to six days reduced the effort of steady training by five percent and extended the time to exhaustion during high intensity training by 16 percent. Nitrate levels peak within three hours and remain elevated for six to nine hours before returning to baseline which is ideal for athletes training or competing in multiday and/or endurance events like the Ironman triathlon, adventure races, or ultramarathon running. While there is a possibility that uncontrolled high doses of nitrate salts from processed meats such as hot dogs may be harmful to health, natural food sources also found in spinach, lettuce, and celery are most likely to promote health.

Caffeine

Not only can a cup of java give you an energy boost, but research suggests this fluid also improves strength and endurance, reduces rates of perceived effort, and improves hydration and recovery. Some of the ergogenic benefits include improving cognitive performance; mobilizing fat; sparing glycogen from muscles during exercise; increasing intestinal absorption and oxidation of ingested carbohydrates to speed the rate of glycogen resynthesis during recovery; and best of all, reducing perceived exertion and pain of training!

For most healthy adults who have a normal tolerance of caffeine, studies suggest a dose of 1.5 to 3 mg of caffeine per pound body weight (3.3 to 6.6 mg/kg) is enough to have an energy-enhancing effect. This is the equivalent of just a 10-oz cup of java for the 150-lb athlete. Know your threshold, because more is not better. At worst, too much caffeine can cause headaches, shakiness, GI irritation, reflux and bleeding, heart palpitations, increased urination, insomnia, and withdrawal, and may certainly limit performance in sport, health, and life.

To Check Your Hydration

In summary, follow these steps to make sure you are staying adequately hydrated for optimal health and performance.

1. **Step on the scale before your workout.**
   Then, weigh yourself again after your workout. Replace each pound with 16 to 24 ounces of fluid.

2. **Check your urine color.**
   Keep it light, but not clear.

3. **Drink Up!**
   Follow the minimum Dietary Recommended Intake (DRI) for Fluids.
   - For men: 19 to 50 years old, 3.7 liters/water/day (13 cups)
   - For women: 19 to 50 years old, 2.7 liters (9 cups)
   - (1 liter = 33 oz. (4 cups) = 1 quart)

4. **Water is ideal as a fluid replacer, particularly for activities lasting less than one hour.**
   Bottled water and safe tap water are your best options over sodas, sugar-free or otherwise, which are not great hydrators due to the carbonation.

143

5. **Don't drink so much fluid that you gain weight.**
   Drinking too much water can dilute the concentration of electrolytes and lead to hyponatremia, lightheadedness, nausea, and even fainting! More is not always better. While there is no specific amount that is excessive, we all have our own personal threshold. Too much can deplete your system of essential electrolytes.

6. **To maximize absorption, chill fluids to slightly below body temp.**

7. **Do not consume alcohol before, during, or after exercise.**
   Alcoholic drinks act as diuretics and prevent adequate fluid replenishment.

8. **Do not consume energy shots or drinks.**
   They can provide excessive amounts of caffeine, vitamins, herbs, and other substances. These don't improve performance, and they can be detrimental to your health and heart!

Gut Distress 101

Fueling for training and competition are critical for managing energy levels, staying hydrated and attaining full and complete recovery from exercise sessions. Your gut works very hard to make sure the rest of your body reaps the benefits of the food you eat.

As CEO of your diet, the gut is responsible for starting the digestion process and managing the temporary storage, assimilation, and delivery of nutrients to the blood, liver, muscles, and heart. As a result, your gut often works overtime and wears and tears over the years, whether it's from aging, poor and processed food choices, alcohol and over the counter pain medication use, stress, irregular eating behaviors, or hereditary factors.

If you have gut issues, you're not alone and there are probably dozens of other athletes playing their own "soundtrack" during training and competition!

Gut issues affect 45 to 85 percent of athletes and can include upper GI (as in the case of heartburn, chest pain, nausea, vomiting, gastritis, peptic ulcers, or stitches) or the lower GI (as in the case of gas, bloating, urge to defecate, diarrhea, hemorrhoids, and colitis/inflamed colon).

In addition to the pre-training/competition diet, stress, climate, dehydration, and non-steroidal anti-inflammatory drug (NSAIDs) use can affect gut health. Additional factors can include the obvious mechanical force of running, and less-obvious nuances like the stress of competition causing altered gut blood flow and changes to gut movement and neuro-endocrine (brain/hormone) balance in response to desiring a first place finish!

No worries. The solution is simple once the cause is determined. Sometimes you can find the culprit by asking yourself a few simple questions about your diet, drinking, and OTC drug habits, one month, week, day, or hour (or a few minutes) before you race.

Ruling out food-related issues may require a thorough dietary analysis; food sensitivity/allergy blood testing to determine if food intolerances to gluten, lactose, or other foods and spices exist; stool testing; or more invasive gut testing to see if there is a more serious issue like a bacterial infection like H. Pylori's, which causes chronic inflammation of the inner lining of the stomach. Supplementation advice such for probiotics, enzymes, and electrolytes/ multivitamins may also be necessary. If you can't narrow down the reason(s) off the top of your head, then hire a professional, like a sports dietitian (CSSD, RD) or medical doctor that specializes in guts called a gastroenterologist who can evaluate and order tests like an endoscopy or colonoscopy to help take a closer look at your gut.

If you're plagued by gut distress especially before competitions, then try the following:

- A low fiber/residue diet especially for three days prior to a competitive event. That means skipping all the grandé vegetable salads, fresh fruits with skin, and high fiber cereals!

- Eat small meals throughout the day rather than three big meals.

- Go lactose free, the milk sugar often responsible for gas and bloating for those who are sensitive or lactose intolerant.

- Get tested for celiac or gluten intolerance as you may be affected by the wheat protein component called gluten in your bread, cereals, pasta and snacks.

Overtraining Syndrome

As mentioned earlier in this section, when your dietary intake fails to keep up with the demands of training, competitive season, or the accumulating physical demands of school, work, and life, overtraining syndrome can result. When you become overtrained and get burned out, you're likely to hit the wall (or "bonk") before you ever really get started.

The "bonk" is a term to describe a physical breakdown in sports. It can be short term, due to poor training, nutrition, and fluid replenishment, or long term, due to overtraining. Short term bonking happens when your brain either shuts down from lack of carbohydrate fuel, not enough fluids, or from mental fatigue. Some say the short term bonk feels like you've just gotten hit on the head with a ton of bricks.

Difficult to diagnose and treat, the consequences of attempting to train for and recover from endurance activities without adequate nutrition can be devastating. Long-term effects of bonking may include same emotional features such as depression, anxiety, and fear. Research shows the symptoms are the same as those experienced by stressed, overworked men and women and by students taking exams.

The causes for long-term bonking are too much exercise, and an increase in training/overload too quickly, or even a combination of too much exercise with emotional stress. Research shows that overtrained athletes with stress are actually susceptible to more sports injuries than those without emotional stress.

Some of the signs of overtraining and poor recovery are summarized in the Coach's Corner.

A short term bonk is quickly reversible with the peri-training/ competition fuel and fluids and recommended eating plans discussed in this chapter. Long-term bonking requires rest and recovery. The extent of that rest and the treatment—whether

Coach's Corner

Signs of Overtraining and Poor Recovery:

- Premature fatigue
- Decline in performance
- Mood changes
- Emotional instability—anger, anxiety, and depression
- Decreased motivation
- Increased early morning heart rate
- Slow recovery of heart rate after exercise
- Postural hypotension
- Increased resting blood pressure
- Decreased performance
- Poor wound and injury recovery
- Disturbed sleep, depression, loss of drive and enthusiasm
- Increased fluid intake at night, muscle and joint pain, heaviness in legs
- Decreased appetite, weight loss
- Loss of libido, due to decreased testosterone levels
- Amenorrhea, due to decreased LH and FSH hormone levels in women

medical, nutritional, or psychological—are dependent on the severity of the overtraining syndrome.

The best way to treat overtraining syndrome is to prevent it by adhering to a well-nourished performance nutrition program, and by slowly and methodically increasing training volume and intensity, preferably guided by a certified athletic coach or expert, and by ensuring time built in to have fun! Life is too short to feel unhappy, dissatisfied with oneself, ill, or injured as a result of choosing to do what you love best: to exercise!

This section has taken you from start to finish, from the cellular level to performance eating plans, and provided you with strategies for staying hydrated, for tackling gut distress and for preventing overtraining syndrome.

If you're ready and fueled to digest Section V on Sports Supplements, go for it! This section will give you a taste of the supplement world, helping you to navigate the laws and labels, and will help you select safe supplements that MAY accelerate your efforts to reach optimal health and performance.

SECTION
V

SPORTS PERFORMANCE SUPPLEMENTS

Sometimes it is tempting to take the easy way out—drink, consume, or even inject your way to more energy, strength, muscle mass, or weight loss. But taking supplements is a risky business. This is especially true for collegiate, professional, and Olympic athletes, who are regularly tested for illegal and banned substances. But it is also true for young athletes participating in youth and high school sports who are still growing and maturing. Young athletes are potentially the most vulnerable to the health and emotional consequences of using illegal and dangerous substances, compounds, hormones, and drugs that are added to some sport supplements.

At best, supplements like caffeinated beverages, energy drinks, vitamins, or minerals, can give you a quick boost of energy, speed, or power. But at worst, they can cause a positive substance test, eliminate you from playing collegiately or professionally, or cause permanent damage to your body like heart, kidney, and liver problems—or even death.

While supplements may assist athletes in achieving optimal health and peak performance under specific circumstances (such as deficiency conditions or at certain times of high intensity or endurance training and competition), poor regulation of the supplement industry allows athletes to be bombarded with marketing hype that exaggerates or completely invents unproven benefits arising from the use of supplements.

Consequences of getting caught up in the supplement rat-race include:

- Distraction from the factors that can really enhance optimal health, recovery, and performance—FOOD!

- Money invested in supplements instead of equipment to prepare healthier foods such as homemade, process-free, organic and grass-fed, hormone-free lean protein

- Diversion from working on performance eating for training, competition, and recovery

- The possible risk of a positive doping outcome

This section will help you to make educated decisions about the efficacy, safety, and sound use of supplements as part of your optimal health and performance eating plan. It will also help you to understand the science and sort fact from fiction on several of the most popular supplements. Also included in this section is a list of comprehensive, evidenced-based, reliable scientific resources you can use to obtain additional information on sports supplements that are advertised at the store, in your favorite magazine, or in the news.

The supplements highlighted in this section and others are summarized in a Supplement Guide located in the Appendix on **pages 207-237.**

Food First Philosophy

"The best nutrition-based strategy for promoting optimal health and the risk of chronic disease is to choose a variety of nutrient-rich foods. Additional nutrients from supplements can help some people meet their nutritional needs as specified by science based standards such as the Dietary Reference Intakes (DRI).

Academy of Nutrition and Dietetics (AND)
Position Paper-Nutrient Supplementation, 2009

Before you jump onto the supplement bandwagon, consider that you might actually be getting enough vitamins and minerals through your daily diet. After all, as a nutritionally savvy athlete, you probably take advantage of the latest fortified foods on the market—wholesome foods which already have a high level of nutrients and which also have extra vitamins, minerals, and compounds added for health-minded people and athletes alike, such as antioxidants, electrolytes, Omega-3 essential fats, energy boosters etc.

The more foods you consume with these extras, the more likely you are to not only be meeting daily needs, but potentially exceeding them, increasing your risk for adverse reactions from excessive amounts. In addition, interactions between nutrients can interfere with the absorption and metabolism of each. For example, calcium binds iron, so combining a fortified calcium-rich beverage with a bowl of iron-rich whole grain cereal for breakfast may compromise your ability to get enough of the iron to meet your daily needs.

A similar example involves using tea as a healthy drink to maintain hydration. Tea contains trace minerals; including manganese, copper, and zinc, which are used by the endogenous antioxidants (see **pages 172-173**). A single bag of black tea provides nearly twice as much of the daily recommendations for manganese, which may compete with other minerals, such as magnesium and iron, in enzymes and other metabolic functions.

How much do you really need?

The United States Department of Agriculture (USDA) Food and Nutrition Information Center has a FREE interactive tool to calculate daily nutrient recommendations for dietary planning based on the Dietary Reference Intakes (DRIs). According to the website, the tool is based on the most current scientific knowledge on nutrient needs, developed by the National Academy of Science's Institute of Medicine, although depending on personal health, activity, and dietary factors, individual requirements may be higher or lower than the DRIs. The link to this interactive tool is: http://fnic.nal.usda.gov/fnic/interactiveDRI/.

After you visit the site to determine your daily needs, you can track your dietary intake and find out what you are actually getting through your diet before considering supplementation. Just keep a dietary log and have a sports nutrition expert analyze your diet to determine how much you are getting and missing through the food you eat, or analyze it for free online.

If you do come up short on one or more of the vitamins and minerals, check the Supplement Guide in the appendix to see if you are experiencing symptoms associated with deficiency in that vitamin, mineral, or nutrient. If you feel like you may be experiencing deficiency symptoms or performance deficits that may be impacting your overall health and performance, take a blood test to determine your levels of the nutrients of concern. Then you can make an informed decision about whether or not you are a candidate for dietary supplements and which ones you need to take.

For sports performance, you'll need to dig a little deeper to determine your need for a supplement and whether or not a specific dietary supplement may actually benefit your training.

Ask yourself the following questions:

1. Will this supplement help me to overcome dietary deficiencies?

If you *cannot* eat or drink and/or absolutely detest or desire to eliminate whole food groups from your diet (i.e. dairy, grains, fruits, or vegetables) and miss out meeting your daily recommended requirements of vitamins, minerals, and nutrients, it may make sense to consider supplements. This is probably one of the best reasons for using supplements and has been shown to improve performance—to correct a deficiency. There may be other medical and dietary reasons to supplement, as summarized in the Coach's Corner. A diet evaluation by a sports dietitian (RD or CSSD), including a thorough vitamin/ mineral blood test (see appendix), may reveal that you are coming up short on B vitamins; vitamin D; antioxidants like C, E, and glutathione; minerals such as iron, potassium, magnesium, or calcium; or essential fats such as Omega-3s.

2. Will this supplement help me achieve my personal goals and the physiological requirements for my sport?

As you know, different sports have different energy needs. If you're a bodybuilder or Cross Fitter, your energy sources and requirements are going to be significantly different than a marathoner or Ironman triathlete. Knowing the science behind the fuel that you've learned in Section IV, knowing how and when to fuel, and what compounds impact your ability to use the fuel, will help you enhance your performance.

3.Will this supplement offer a true ergogenic effect, which will *directly* enhance performance?

Sometimes a supplement helps you to reach, increase, or even saturate levels of substrate, nutrient, or compound levels. However does it enhance performance? The truth is, even though a compound may have a specific function in the body, taking more of that compound doesn't necessarily mean it will actually exert a performance enhancing-effect.

4. Will this supplement enhance my performance during this specific phase of training?

Think nutrition periodization—in other words, "go seasonal" when it comes to supplements. If you do choose the supplement route, make sure it's matched to your training and competitive season.

If you're a competitive year-round athlete in training, you'll probably need to reevaluate your supplement needs seasonally. For example, during pre-season your requirements will be significantly different than during the season, because you have different training regimens and goals. For pre-season, the aim might be to increase or to lose extra mass; supplements consumed for building muscle mass or losing weight are very different from those you would use during the season when continuous competitive energy is the priority and supplemental carbohydrate fuel, electrolyte replacement, or lactic acid buffers may be at the top of the supplement list.

After reading Section IV, you know that taking a high protein shake in the middle of a tennis match wouldn't be the best choice of supplement to help you maintain fluid balance, electrolytes, or energy, right? Similarly, supplements recommended for pre-training stamina in the gym are different from those used for recovery fuel after an Ironman triathlon.

You might also consider the fact that your need for a supplement may pass. Say you were found to have a vitamin deficiency, detected by a dietary analysis and blood test at your doctor or sport dietitian's office, and after a few weeks or months of supplementation, you reversed the deficiency. Why continue to take the supplement if the deficiency has passed?

Coach's Corner

Who May Need Dietary Supplements?

- Athletes/others with identified dietary deficiencies as determined by a blood or dietary analysis.

- Athletes/others with clinical issues such as anemia, vitamin D deficiency.

- Special needs athletes, i.e. those who are paralyzed; have autoimmune diseases such as rheumatoid arthritis (RA) or diabetes; have sickle cell anemia, concussions, or neurogenerative diseases such as Lou Gehrig's; or are pregnant.

- Older men and women, Master level athletes, postmenopausal women.

- Vegetarians, vegans, or athletes on restrictive diets which eliminate whole food groups such as dairy or grains.

- Individuals with allergies, food sensitivities, or personal aversions where whole food groups are eliminated or avoided (like dairy, whole grains, or meat).
- Imbalanced diets—fast- and processed-food dependent, alcohol drinkers, or snackers instead of whole meal eaters.
- Men and women with eating disorders or who are undernourished due to low-calorie dieting to make weight for sport (e.g., jockeys, wrestlers, rowers, boxers).
- Athletes taking prescription medications or recreational drugs which may interfere with vitamin or mineral absorption (see chart page 157).

In addition, the American Academy of Family Physicians (www.FamilyDoctor.org) adds the following groups who may also need a vitamin/mineral supplement:

- Women who are pregnant or trying to get pregnant
- Women who are breastfeeding
- Women who experience heavy menstrual periods
- Women who have gone through menopause
- People who have a medical condition that affects the way the body digests food, such as gastrointestinal disease, lactose intolerance, or food allergies
- People who have diseases of the stomach, liver, pancreas, or gall bladder

More questions you can ask yourself regarding the use of dietary supplements can be found at:

http://www.nutrition.gov/dietary-supplements/questions-ask-taking-vitamin-and-mineral-supplements .

Drug and Nutrient Interactions

In addition to special circumstances, medical conditions and medications used to manage those conditions can also interact with the absorption and metabolism of vitamins, minerals, and nutrients and determine whether or not you need to take a supplement. This is also true when taking over-the-counter (OTC) medications like Non-Steroidal Anti-Inflammatory Drugs (NSAIDS), birth control, or antibiotics for treating infections or acne. And if you are like many college-aged and beyond fitness-minded young men and women in the 21st century, taking social and recreational relaxation "remedies" such as alcohol or cannabis may also impact your daily dietary requirements.

Cheers, But Not So Fast, to Drinking Up

While maintaining adequate hydration is one of the foundations of performance nutrition, as you learned in Section IV, alcoholic beverages do not qualify as the healthiest beverage option.

The most popular recreational compound used on the planet, re-portedly used by 88 percent of intercollegiate athletes and dating back to the days of the Bible, alcoholic beverages such as wine, beer, and hard alcohol like vodka, gin, and whiskey are used for everything from relieving stress and inhibition to inducing sleep and celebrating performance successes. While a toast from time to time, on holidays and New Year's, is unlikely to impact your nutritional needs greatly, consuming alcohol on a regular basis can profoundly impact your performance, training, and recovery. It is also likely to increase your risk for illness and injury.

Never mind the fact that the average 12-ounce beer contains about 150 calories, and both 5 ounces of wine and 1.5 ounces of 80 proof distilled spirits have about 100 calories, adding mixers, juices, and sodas to cocktails or fancy frozen drinks can add an additional 400 to 500 calories of empty calories, devoid of and robbing you of essential vitamins and minerals.

Research has also shown the following negative impact on training, muscle hypertrophy, and body composition:

- Alcohol calories cannot be used by muscles for energy. The body converts alcohol calories to fat and this is typically stored as abdominal gut fat!
- Inhibits vitamin and mineral absorption impacting strength and endurance.
- Causes thermoregulatory issues making it challenging to stay cool!

- Impairs liver gluconeogenesis (new blood sugar formation) which impacts muscle protein synthesis during recovery.

- Impacts neural function—slows reaction time, hand-eye coordination, memory, sleep cycle, ability to learn new information. In fact, brain and body activities are compromised for up to 3 days after drinking 5 or more drinks! Two consecutive nights causes up to a 5-day impact!

- Increases heart rate, regardless of exercise intensity.

- Decreases blood testosterone levels, which impacts muscle hypertrophy and muscle recovery.

- Causes dehydration, headaches, and hangovers.

- Causes anemia by reducing absorption of folic acid.

- Impacts sleep which impacts hormones such as HGH and testosterone production, which aids recovery.

- Robs your body of HGH—decreases human growth hormone secretion needed for muscle building repair and recovery by as much as 70 percent.

- And that's just the short list of consequences! Add to the list permanent heart, liver, and brain damage, DNA and skin damage, and you have a disastrous prescription for failure in sport and in life!

Here is a summary of just some of the other common medications and recreational compounds and their vitamin/mineral interactions.

Drug and Food Interferences on Vitamin and Mineral Absorption and Performance

If you use this drug:	It may affect absorption, excretion, or metabolism of:
Alcohol	Potential deficiencies in B1, B3, B12, pantothenic acid, folic acid, vitamin C, magnesium, phosphorus, zinc.
Antacids (for indigestion, heartburn, Ulcers, GERD)	Decreases absorption of B12, iron; long term calcium

If you use this drug:	It may affect absorption, excretion, or metabolism of:
Amphetamines/cocaine	Weight loss; muscle and joint pain; arrhythmias, seizures, death
Analgesics (pain relievers) Non-steroidal, anti-inflammatory drugs (NSAIDS) i.e. Advil, Motrin	Iron deficiency; do not consume with alcohol – can cause gastrointestinal and liver damage
Antibiotics	Reduces fat, amino acid, folate, fat-soluble vitamins, B12 & minerals copper, iron, magnesium, potassium, phosphate and zinc; interferes with vitamin K and calcium synthesis; take mineral supplements 2-6 hours apart from drug
Aspirin	May increase urinary loss of vitamin C, potassium
Caffeine	May increase urine losses of sodium, potassium; decrease iron absorption, take iron separately by 2 hours; high cruciferous veggies like broccoli, cauliflower, Brussel sprouts, and cabbage may increase absorption
Cannabis/Marijuana	Alters taste and appetite; enhances preference and enjoyment of sweets; reduces nutrient density of diet due to high calorie, low quality foods; increases heart rate and blood pressure at rest; decreases physical work capacity by 25 percent
Cocaine	Reduces appetite; starvation causes loss of muscle mass, weight, water, nutrients; may lead to disordered eating

If you use this drug:	It may affect absorption, excretion, or metabolism of:
Nicotine	Lowers blood concentrations of Beta-carotene, vitamin C and selenium; and only in women, vitamin E
Oral Contraceptives (Birth control/estrogen replacement)	Decreases absorption of vitamin A and C; decreases blood levels of riboflavin, B6, B12, magnesium, and zinc

Sources: 17th Edition Food Medications Interactions™ (2012) Krause's Food and Nutrition Care Process, 13th Edition (2012), 2009 ADA Position Paper: Nutrient Supplementation (http:// www.eatright.org/About/Content.aspx?id=8409)nutrition).

Supplement Savvy

Once you've determined that taking a supplement is the right choice for you, how do you evaluate the many products available on the market? And how do you know for sure that the one you choose is safe, effective, and contains what it says it does?

If you aren't sure how to answer those questions, you are not alone. *"Consumers are confused,"* cites a report conducted by the U.S. Government Accountability Office (GAO). The report claims consumers have difficulty interpreting supplement labels, including structure and function claims and claims about whether or not the product can treat or prevent an illness. According to The US Anti-Doping Agency's Supplement 411 website, a portal for understanding and identifying tainted supplements, athletes are also confused believing that *"they need dietary supplements in order to compete at the best of their abilities, the most elite levels, and against the best competition."*

In addition to the confusion, consumers may not be well informed about the safety and efficacy of supplements and may have difficulty interpreting product labels.

Coach's Corner

Supplements 101 - Getting Started

The Office of Dietary Supplements (ODS) of the National Institutes of Health (NIH) FREE website and mobile app is an excellent place to start to clear up some of the confusion. The FDA instituted the office of Dietary Supplements (ODS) to fund supplement research and disseminate credible information to consumers like you. They have an awesome real-time website and mobile app, free subscription newsletter, and a hotline to report incidents. You can access the entire website at: http://ods.od.nih.gov/ and individual supplement fact sheets at: http://ods.od.nih.gov/factsheets/list-all/.

What is a Supplement?

The term "dietary supplement" is a legal definition set forth in the Dietary Supplement Health and Education Act 1994 (DSHEA).

The Food and Drug Administration (FDA) defines supplements as:

"... products other than tobacco which are used in conjunction with a healthy diet and contain one or more of the following dietary ingredients: a vitamin, mineral, herb orother botanical, an amino acid, a dietary substance for use of man to supplement the diet by increasing total daily intake, or a concentrate metabolite constituent, extract or combination of these ingredients."

According to DSHEA, the definition of a dietary supplement includes four key features:

- It is a product that contains a "dietary ingredient" (i.e. a vitamin, a mineral, an herb or other botanical, an amino acid, or a dietary substance) for use by people to supplement the diet by increasing the total dietary intake, or is a concentrate, metabolite, constituent, or extract of a dietary ingredient.

- It is something that is taken by mouth, though it may have many forms (tablet, capsule, powder, liquid, etc.).

- It is not intended to be consumed as a meal or as a meal replacement. (If it is intended to be a meal, a meal replacement, or a conventional beverage, then it is a food, no matter what the label says).

- The company represents the product as a dietary supplement.

Supplement Labels

- The Supplement Facts Panel defines how ingredients must be listed on the label. What does the FDA require on a Supplement Label? The label requires:

- Name of the product

- The word "supplement" or a statement that the product is a supplement

- Net quantity of contents

- Name and place of business of manufacturer, packer, or distributor

- Directions for use

Also included on Supplement Facts Panel:

- Serving size, list of dietary ingredients, amount per serving size (by weight), percent of Daily Value (%DV), if established.

- Whether or not the ingredient is a botanical, and if so, the scientific name of the plant or the common or usual name standardized in the reference Herbs of Commerce, 2nd Edition (2000 edition) and the name of the plant part used.

- If the ingredient is a proprietary blend (i.e., a blend exclusive to the manufacturer), the total weight of blend and components of blend in order of predominance by weight, like you see on the Nutrition Facts Panel for food and beverages.

- Other ingredients like non-dietary ingredients such as fillers, artificial colors, sweeteners, flavors, or binders; listed by common name or proprietary blend and by weight in descending order of predominance.

Supplement Claims

While manufacturers are allowed to publish limited information about the benefits of dietary supplements in the form of "statements of support", as well as so-called "structure" and "function claims," there are rules they need to follow (see box).

Supplement Label Claim Rules

Claim	Description
Health	Relationship between a food, food component, or dietary supplement ingredient, and reducing risk of a disease or health- related condition. Must be preapproved by the FDA.
Nutrient Content	Describes relative amount of nutrient or dietary substance in product. Must be preapproved by the FDA.
Structure/ Function	Describes how product may affect organs or systems of body but CANNOT mention any specific disease. Does not require FDA approval, but claim text must be submitted to FDA within 30 days of putting product on market. Most common claim used. i.e. calcium. In the case of structure claim, manufacturers CAN say, "Supports bone health." What they cannot say is "prevents osteoporosis."
	Labels containing structure claims must also include the disclaimer: "This statement has not been evaluated by the FDA. This product is not intended to diagnose, treat, cure, or prevent any disease."

Coach's Corner

Three Steps to Take Before Selecting a Dietary Supplement

1. Assess your need—meet with a sports nutrition expert/ medical doctor for dietary and blood testing.

2. Ask yourself questions on **pages 152-153.**

3. Learn how to read a Dietary Supplement label (see diagram).

Source: http://www.familydoctor.org

You can read more about the supplement label regulations at: http://www.fda.gov/Food/GuidanceRegulation/Guidance-DocumentsRegulatoryInformation/DietarySupplements/ucm070597.htm.

Who's Watching?

The Federal Trade Commission (FTC) has the primary responsibility of regulating claims made in advertising dietary supplements. In additional to false advertising and claims, product literature legally also cannot be displayed next to products, as it can mislead consumers.

When is the last time you reported a false claim or even an adverse side effect from a dietary supplement? For safety alerts, advisories, and recalls, visit: http://www.fda.gov/Safety/Recalls/default.htm. To report an adverse reaction from a dietary supplement, you can call the FDA directly at: 800-FDA-1088 or go online to: http://www.fda.gov/Food/DietarySupplements/ReportAdverseEvent/default.htm

Supplement Seals of Approval

Since dietary supplement certification is voluntary, not all companies pursue independent testing and certification. For some companies, financial reasons are sometimes the obstacle for certification, while for others, either the manufacturing facility has difficulty passing the Good Manufacturing Practices (GMP) audit or there is a processing, contamination, purity, and standardization problem with the actual product.

Some products cannot pass the certification process for other reasons, such as: the stated label nutrient content doesn't match what is actually in the product; they may fail because they have heavy metal or microbial contamination; or, in the case of sports supplements, the product does not pass the banned substance portion of the testing. Here are some of the organizing bodies that conduct certifications with their criteria and seals of approval:

 ### Good Manufacturing Practices (GMPs)

According to the FDA, "adherence to Good Manufacturing Practices (GMP) regulations assures the identity, purity, strength, and composition of dietary supplements." GMP requirements include: provisions related to the design and construction of physical plants that facilitate maintenance, cleaning, proper manufacturing operations, quality control procedures, testing of final product or incoming and in-process materials, handling of consumer complaints, and maintaining records. (Source: http://www.fda.gov/Food/GuidanceRegulation/ CGMP/ucm110858.htm.)

 ### US Pharmacopoeia
http://www.usp.org/

USP offers verification services for dietary supplement finished products, dietary ingredients, pharmaceutical ingredients, and excipients. Participation is voluntary and available to manufacturers worldwide. Products and ingredients that meet all USP verification requirements—including a GMP audit, product and ingredient testing, and manufacturing documentation review—are awarded use of the USP Verified Mark. USP's drug standards are enforceable in the United States by the FDA.

Consumer Lab
http://www.consumerlab.com

Certification dates back prior to USP and NSF tests products off store shelves for purity, quality and label identification.

NSF
http://www.nsf.org

The National Safety Foundation (NSF) certifies products against NSF/ANSI 173, and is the only American National Standard that establishes requirements for the ingredients in dietary and nutritional supplements.

NSF is an independent, third-party testing organization that conducts product testing to confirm that the actual contents of the supplement product match those printed on the label. NSF also checks to make sure no unlisted ingredients or potentially harmful levels of impurities are present in products that carry NSF certification.

The three main components of the NSF dietary supplements certification program are as follows:

- Label claim review to certify that what's on the label is in the bottle;
- Toxicology review to certify product formulation; and
- Contaminant review to ensure the product contains no undeclared ingredients or unacceptable levels of contaminants.

For a complete listing of NSF Certified Products, visit: http://info.nsf.org/Certified/dietary/.

Sport Specific Certifications

Informed Choice
www.informed-choice.org

 A quality assurance program for sports nutrition products, suppliers to the sports nutrition industry, and supplement manufacturing facilities is a world-renowned sports doping control and research laboratory. With over 50 years of expertise in anti-doping in sport, LGC has published over 300 scientific papers on methods for detection of trace levels of substances that are prohibited in sport.

Although there is no such thing as a "100 percent guarantee" that tested supplements are free of all banned substances, LGC's testing capability for supplements/ingredients includes the analysis of over 146 substances that are considered pro-hibited in sport and substances that pose a threat in respect of product contamination. These substances include drugs of abuse, anabolic agents, stimulants, beta-2-agonists, masking agents, etc. Testing methods used for a range of substances from these categories have been validated and accredited to the ISO 17025 standard in supplements/ingredients, in each of the relevant matrices: powders, bars, liquids, capsules, tablets, etc., with defined method capabilities/reporting limits. Reg-istered products and tested batches can be found at: http://www.informed-choice.org/registered-products.

National Science Foundation (NSF), Certified for Sport

http://www.nsfsport.com/

A program that focuses primarily on the sports sup-plement manufacturing and sourcing process pro-vides preventive measures to protect against adulter-ation of products, verify label claims against product contents, and identify athletic banned substances in the finished product or ingredients. Program designed for manufacturers and their products, includes product testing for more than 180 banned substances, label content confirmation, formulation and label review, production facility and supplier inspections, as well as ongoing monitoring in line with substance prohibitive lists. Program is recognized by NFL, NFLPA, MLB, MLBPA, PGA, LPGA, and CCES.

List of certified products: http://www.nsfsport.com/listings/certified products.asp.

Banned Substances Control Group

http://www.bscg.org/
Banned Substances Control Group (BSCG) offers the BSCG Certified Drug Free® independent third party supplement certification to responsible dietary supplement manufacturers to ensure finished products are free of more than 145 drugs on the WADA prohibited list and banned by sports organizations including the IOC, NFL, NHL, MLS, NCAA, MLB and others. BSCG includes additional testing for many drugs not banned in sports like pain killers, muscle relaxants, weight loss drugs and more. Label claim verification, contaminant testing and a toxicology review is conducted on each product. BSCG analyzes samples from each finished batch of a supplement using ISO 17025 validated methods with low detection limits (10 parts per billion for the majority of compounds). If no drugs are found in the sample above the detection limits BSCG issues a certification to the manufacturer for the batch from which the sample was taken. The BSCG Certified Drug Free® seal can be used on certified products and the product is listed on the BSCG Certified Products page.

Guide to Selected Sports Supplements

Supplements used to achieve optimal health and performance fall into several categories, depending on the intended purpose and objective. Some of the supplement categories overlap. For example, probiotics are used both for general health and for gut health.

A thorough physical exam, medical history, and biochemical testing (blood, urine, salivary) can help discover nutrition deficiencies which may warrant the use of a vitamin, mineral, or any other food or beverage supplement—but these should only be used under the supervision of a health expert. This is because serious side effects can occur if you combine certain supplements with each other or with medications, and also because some supplements can be dangerous if you have certain health conditions. Because of these issues, using supplements without proper guidance can put you at risk for injury, illness, and death.

Supplements Commonly Used to Achieve Optimal Health and Performance*

Objective	Examples
General health	vitamins, minerals, antioxidants, quercetin, glutathione, probiotics, Omega-3, fish oils
Gut health	probiotics, enzymes
Immune function	antioxidants, zinc, glutamine, phytonutrients, herbs (e.g., Echinacea)
Fuel replacement/ competition snacks	liquid meals, sports drinks, bars, gels, chews
Fluid and electrolytes	electrolyte supplements, sports drinks
Joint health	glucasomine, chondroitin, MSM
Muscle growth and repair	protein powders, amino acids (essential EAA), Branched Chain (BCAA), HMB
Fat reduction	caffeine, carnitine, pyruvate
Exercise metabolism	carbohydrates, nitrates, bi-carbonate, beta alanine, and betaine
Promoting recovery	protein powders, amino acids, carbohydrate bars/ drinks
Central Nervous System (CNS) stimulants	caffeine, taurine

Please note: This supplement list is NOT a recommendation guide. Everyone needs to meet with a medical doctor, sports dietitian, or healthcare professional that has knowledge of their medical history prior to taking any dietary supplement and prior to changing their diet, exercise, or lifestyle pattern.

Supplement Summary

This section provides a summary of some of the major categories and types of vitamin and mineral supplements. Pros, cons, safety, and efficacy of specific popular dietary supplements can be found in the guide located in Appendix A.

Vitamins and Minerals

Since multivitamins have been identified as the most popular supplement consumed by athletes and all consumers, let's start here.

There is no doubt that you need at least 13 vitamins and 16 minerals to maintain optimal health. Your daily requirements are based on your age, gender, health status, and activity level.

Vitamins fall into two groups:

- Water soluble vitamins: B vitamins (B1 thiamin, B2 riboflavin, B3 niacin, B12 (cyanocobalamin), B6 (pyridoxine), folic acid (folate), biotin, pantothenic acid, and vitamin C

- Fat soluble vitamins: A, D, E, and K, which are absorbed with and stored in fat and in the liver.

Minerals also fall into two groups, depending on how much your body needs. Both groups are equally important to health, nerve, and electrical conductivity which influences muscle contractions and heart function and water movement in and out of cells and helps to build bone strength.

The two groups of minerals are:

- Major minerals: sodium, potassium, magnesium, calcium, phosphorus, chloride, and sulfur

- Trace minerals: Iron, copper, iodine, manganese, molybdenum, zinc, selenium, fluoride, and chromium

The biggest misconception is that vitamins and minerals will *give* you energy— but they cannot. They do not have calories like protein, carbohydrates, and fats. Instead, they help you to use energy from food. They also influence a number of physiological reactions important to training and sport performance.

169

For example, the B vitamins are involved with processing carbo-hydrates and fats for energy, while the mineral iron is involved in hemoglobin production, which helps to deliver oxygen to cells. Antioxidants such as vitamins C and E help to prevent oxidative damage to cells, which in turn enhance recovery from training. vitamin D acts like a hormone that affects overall health in more ways than we ever imagined: It regulates more than 1,000 vitamin-D-responsive genes, acts directly on mus-cle to increase protein synthesis, works with calcium to impact bone strength, and can influence overall health and athletic performance.

Deficiencies in vitamins *have* been shown to impair sports performance. For example, a daily intake of less than one-third of the Recommended Dietary Allowances (RDAs) can lead to a decrease in VO2 max (the amount of oxygen you can move around the system at maximum intensity) and in aerobic threshold (your ability to sustain and maintain training) in as little as four weeks.

However, when vitamins are consumed in your diet in adequate amounts, research does not suggest that extra vitamins can en-hance performance. In some cases, extra vitamins can actually compromise performance and have adverse consequences.

Research has shown that most athletes can meet their daily dietary needs for vitamins and minerals through an optimally planned nutritious diet IF they consume enough calories and get enough variety from all the food groups and if they choose strategically and healthfully.

However, if unhealthy foods seem to dominate the nutritional playing field, the diet will be limited in numerous vitamins and minerals. And that risk is a reality for many athletes whose diets fall short of needs. One study showed that female athletes were deficient in calories, carbohydrates, folate, calcium, magnesium, and iron, while male athletes have a tendency towards deficien-cies in vitamins A, C, and D, folate, calcium, potassium, and magnesium. Athletes who also follow the latest dietary trends and eliminate whole food groups such as meat, dairy, grains, or fruits are at an even greater risk for deficiencies in calcium, zinc, iron, vitamin B12, and other nutrients.

No doubt, some athletes can benefit from a multivitamin supplement, especially if diets fall short of daily needs, and if training demands are high and/or they reside or train at high elevation or in polluted, hot climates. Injured athletes can also benefit from a multivitamin supplement during rehab and the recovery process when protein along with calcium, vitamin A, C, and D, magnesium, and zinc have been shown to promote healing.

Recently, there has been some debate over the safety and efficacy of taking a multivitamin (MVI) supplement after a large study called the Iowa Women's Health Study reported that women who took MVI supplements over a 19 year period had a 6 percent higher death rate than those who did not take the vitamin. The problem was, it was an observational study, which never looks at cause and effect. Just think: Maybe the women who took the multivitamin started taking it because they weren't feeling well, hence the real root of the cause of death. In fact, in another randomized control trial, the largest and longest for multivitamins called the Physicians Health Study II of more than 14,000 50 year old men over the course of 11 years, the risk for death between those taking verses not taking an MVI was not significantly different.

Coach's Corner

Tips for Selecting a Multivitamin

- Look for USP or NSF certification for purity.
- Don't count on a multivitamin to "cover all the bases," since some of the important ones to athletes, vitamin D, potassium, and probiotics are typically not present in amounts designed to reach optimal health.
- Chewable, liquid, and MVI gummies have fewer nutrients and more sugar, which tends to crowd out room for the essentials.
- Watch the added coloring, flavoring, and filling agents, as you might have sensitivities which will negate any positive benefits.
- Don't buy into the brands that promise more energy—since vitamins and minerals do not have calories, the company may have added caffeine to the formula.

Corner continued on pg.172

- Get enough folic acid (DV 400 mcg), especially if you are a woman in your childbearing years, but do not take more, since it may increase your risk for cancer. Also, check your fortified foods, since shakes and bars may also be fortified.

- Limit selenium to 100 mcg, since more may increase your risk for skin cancer and diabetes.

- Do not exceed 100 percent of the Daily Values for any of the nutrients.

- Go to www.consumerlab.com for an excellent review, cautionary notes, and recommendation list for multivitamins.

Source: Nutrition Action Health Letter November 2013, Nutrition Action Health Letter, June 2008,

For specific brand recommendations and information about their quality, purity, and safety, go to www.consumerlab.com or the NSF or Informed Choice.

Antioxidants

Antioxidants have been touted as being the key to preventing cancer, stopping arthritis, and slowing down aging. For performance, it's not clear whether supplementing protects the system and decreases muscular fatigue, or whether antioxidants are even safe to take in supplemental amounts.

Antioxidants are compounds produced within the body and also consumed through the diet that reduce the impact of free radicals. This is important, because free radicals are loose oxygen molecules produced with exercise. Antioxidants also help to repair cells already impacted by the blow of free radicals.

The body is armed with an endogenous first line of defense in the form of oxidative enzymes, superoxide dismutase, glutathione peroxidase, and catalase, which change the structure of damaging free radicals. These enzymes scavenge and squelch free radicals dead in their tracks. Dietary antioxidants, the body's exogenous line of defense in the form of vitamins A (carotenoids), C, E, selenium, and flavonoids, also help to prevent free radical damage. *Together*, these antioxidant systems work as a team to protect the body.

The amount of defense one has varies considerably and is dependent on age, genetic disposition to antioxidant armor, dietary intake, lifestyle habits (such as smoking and drinking alcohol), training, and exposure to environmental toxins. Trained athletes have more finely tuned endogenous antioxidant systems that are ready to tackle the free radical battle. Untrained individuals, athletes training early in season, athletes suddenly increasing training intensity or duration, or those training at high altitude and in extreme heat may be at a disadvantage and must build their antioxidant systems through exercise or by dietary fortification.

Although the answer is not yet clear, experts question whether or not exercise-induced radical production in skeletal muscle actually serves as an activator of beneficial adaptive responses. Maybe taking too much extra in the form of supplements can actually blunt the training adaptation. The jury is still out. And data supporting the use of antioxidant supplements to protect from free-radical-induced muscle damage is inconclusive.

What we do know is that an athlete's antioxidant status in some types of training can cause an imbalance between free radical production and availability of antioxidants to quench them. But the situation is not identical for all sports.

Susceptibility to oxidative stress appears to vary from person to person and the impact is not uniform for any population. Variables such as diet, lifestyle, environmental factors, and training make a difference. It is also unclear where the "cut-off" is regarding oxidative stress level before it starts to impact performance; which athletes encounter this effect; whether the benefit outweighs the risks; and whether additional dietary or supplemental antioxidants are warranted for athletes to defend against the damaging effects.

High doses of antioxidants (above the optimal dose) have been shown to actually shift the intracellular antioxidant balance and impair performance. If you do choose to take an antioxidant, stay under the Tolerable Upper Intake Level (UL), the highest level of daily intake of a nutrient that has been shown unlikely to pose a risk of adverse health effects for most people. The Tolerable Upper Limits for adult men and women are as follows: 2000 mg (2 grams)/day for vitamin C; 1,500 IU/day for vitamin E (any form of supplemental alpha-tocopherols); 10, 000 IU/day for vitamin A; and 400 mcg/day for selenium.

While there is no UL for beta carotene (the pro-vitamin form of vitamin A found in plant based foods such as carrots) high doses of beta-carotene supplements (30 mg/day or more), as well as the consumption of large amounts of carotene-rich foods, can result in a yellow discoloration of the skin (primarily palms and soles) known as carotenodermia.

Source: Institute of Medicine (IOC) http://iom.edu/Activities/ Nutrition/SummaryDRIs/~/media/Files/Activity%20Files/Nutrition/DRIs/ULs%20for%20Vitamins%20and%20Elements.pdf

A diet rich in fruits and vegetables can almost guarantee an adequate intake of antioxidants. Research also suggests that foods with phytonutrients (see Section III) are rich sources of antioxidants and may help with post-training inflammation.

Electrolytes

Muscle cramping has cost athletes great workouts, Olympic medals, and probably even our troops during battle. Although cramping can be caused by a number of reasons, when the cause is nutritional, it is often due to dietary deficiencies and the loss of electrolytes in sweat.

Electrolytes are minerals like sodium and potassium, which are added to most sport drinks. The electrolytes also include other minerals such as calcium, magnesium, chloride, bicarbonates, phosphate, and sulfate. Electrolytes send messages to nerves and muscles throughout the body. Electrolytes are involved with muscle contraction and relaxation while you're training, so an imbalance can impact the actual contraction of the muscle itself.

Sodium

Sodium losses through sweat are the most common cause of cramping. Excess water replacement in the absence of supplemental sodium during extended training can lead to *hyponatremia* or decreased plasma sodium concentrations. Research suggests that exercise-induced *hyponatremia* may also result from fluid overloading during prolonged training. Hyponatremia is also associated with calorie/sugar-conscious athletes who drink plain water in excess of their sweat losses or who are less physically conditioned and produce a more salty sweat.

When blood is diluted of sodium, your thirst drive is affected, too. So the key is to rehydrate with fluids that replace sodium. Healthy options for replacing sodium losses include commercial vegetable juices, juice bar juices, or your own juice spiked with a salt packet. You can also include in your diet salty whole foods such as pretzels, baked chips, salted almonds, pistachios, and organic canned foods.

Potassium

Potassium is an electrolyte involved with maintaining body fluids. As the major electrolyte inside the body's cells, potassium works in tandem with sodium and chloride to maintain body fluids and generate electric impulses in the nerves and muscles, including the heart. Loss of potassium from muscle has been linked with fatigue.

Although potassium supplements are not necessary, finding sports drinks and recovery beverages that include potassium is one way of meeting your needs. Sports drinks contain sodium and potassium in various amounts to prevent cramping. Snacking on organic baby food packets like bananas or sweet potatoes or adding them to a fruit smoothie are two easy, portable ways you can add a few hundred milligrams of potassium to your diet. The baby food will also help thicken your beverages naturally.

Potassium-rich foods go beyond bananas; in fact even though bananas are typically the first potassium food consumed by consumers for potassium, they're not even the best choice when it comes to trying to meet your daily needs. Try a serving of papaya, dried apricots, soy and lima beans, kiwi, tomatoes, avocados, artichokes, oat bran, cucumber, cantaloupe, mangoes, pears, baked potato, or peanuts and opt for a glass of milk or coconut water to stay hydrated.

Magnesium

Another electrolyte, magnesium is the fourth-most abundant mineral in the body, with about 50 percent found in bone. Magnesium is required for hundreds of functions in the body; the most important to athletes are energy production, oxygen uptake by muscles, and electrolyte balance. Magnesium helps the heart to beat steadily, supports the immune system, keeps bones strong, and is involved in protein synthesis required for building muscle. In addition, research suggests that deficiencies in magnesium can affect performance and amplify the stress to the cells from high intensity exercise.

Magnesium deficiency has been shown to impair athletic performance. Muscle spasms, increased heart rate, and increased oxygen consumption during submaximal exercise have been shown. Low magnesium levels have also been shown in athletes who sweat heavily; however, low levels appear to be transient, returning to normal values within 24 hours after exercise.

According to U.S. reports on the general population, 7 out of 10 individuals are deficient in magnesium. High intensity exercise can increase urinary and sweat magnesium losses by 10 to 20 percent. Female athletes are more likely to be deficient, in one study reportedly consuming less than 60 percent of the RDAs.

For deficient athletes, supplemental magnesium may improve performance by improving cellular function. In athletes with adequate intake and levels, performance outcomes are mixed. In one study with female volleyball players, magnesium supplementation improved alactic anaerobic metabolism, even though the players were not magnesium deficient. In another study, with young males participating in a strength training program for seven weeks, daily magnesium intake of 8 mg/kg of body weight demonstrated increases in muscle strength and power. In another study, marathon runners with adequate stores did not seem to benefit.

Getting enough whole grains, fresh organic greens, beans, and nuts can ensure meeting daily dietary requirements. Once grains are bleached, stripped of the brown fibrous whole grain, magnesium is lost. In addition to 100 percent whole grains, almonds, pistachios, peanut butter, soy and kidney beans, spinach, baked potatoes with the skin, black eyed peas, brown rice, and oatmeal are rich in magnesium. Supplementing with more than 300mg has a tendency to cause diarrhea in sensitive individuals.

B Vitamins

To break down and make energy from carbohydrates, protein, and fat for training, the body needs additional B vitamins. These include thiamin, riboflavin, niacin, pyridoxine, folate, biotin, pantothenic acid, and choline, which serve as part of coenzymes involved in regulating energy metabolism. While vitamin B deficiency can impair both anaerobic and aerobic performance, supplementation has not been shown to enhance performance when daily needs are met through food.

For some competitive athletes who consume low-calorie diets for long periods to make or maintain a low weight (e.g. wrestlers, jockeys, figure skaters, gymnasts, or rowers) and for athletes who have less-than-adequate intakes and may be prone to deficiencies, a B-vitamin complex supplement may be warranted. B12 deficiency could also potentially be an issue in strict vegans who do not consume fortified, plant-based foods. Athletes who indulge in alcohol on a regular basis are also at risk for B vitamin deficiencies.

Fat Soluble Vitamins

While vitamins A, D, E, and K have no direct role in energy metabolism, they do play supportive roles in using energy for sport. As discussed, vitamins A and E as antioxidants can reduce muscle damage from exercise, although supplementation is not advised. Vitamin K assists with coagulation and works with vitamin D in building strong bones.

Over the past few years, vitamin D has received the most attention, and has been acknowledged as playing an increasingly important role in sports performance beyond its role in working with calcium absorption and building bones.

Vitamin D

Vitamin D influences more than 1,000 genes involved with muscle protein synthesis, muscle strength, muscle size, reaction time, balance, coordination, endurance, inflammation, and immunity—all important to health and performance. Having an adequate blood level of vitamin D has been shown to:

- Increase muscle protein synthesis
- Increase ATP concentration
- Increase strength, jump height, jump velocity, jump power, and exercise performance
- Decrease muscle protein degradation and reverse myalgias
- Decrease bone fractures
- Impact the immune system, reducing cold and flu risk
- Reduce inflammation, especially after intense exercise periods
- Enhance recovery in peak isometric force, attenuate the immediate and delayed increase in circulating biomarkers representative of muscle damage.

Vitamin D deficiency is common in athletes, especially in specific groups:

- Lactose intolerant and those who avoid milk and dairy
- Those who do not eat fish
- Those who live in colder, less sunny climates
- Those with darker skin, even if they live and train in sunny climates
- Those who use sun block on exposed areas or wear extensive clothing

The prevalence of deficiency also varies by sport, training location and time, and skin color. Some studies suggest more than 75 percent of whites and 90 percent of African Americans and Latinos are deficient. In other studies, up to 77 percent of athletes who live in northern climates with little winter sunlight, and indoor athletes, including 94 percent of basketball players and 83 percent of gymnasts, have been shown to be deficient in vitamin D.

Although the specific amount of vitamin D needed to reverse deficiency has not been determined for several reasons, including the extent of the deficiency, get tested and guided to supplements by your sports medicine experts if you are diagnosed with a deficiency. Some reports suggest peak neuromuscular performance is associated with 25 (OH) D blood levels of 50ng/ml or more.

In addition to diet, fair-skinned individuals should get five minutes of exposure to sunlight on their arms, legs, and back several times a week without sunscreen. For dark-skinned individuals, 30 minutes several times a week without sunscreen has been recommended.

Minerals

Although many major and trace minerals have been shown to be essential for optimal health, the electrolytes sodium, potassium, and magnesium (discussed in the previous section) and iron and calcium have special roles which can impact overall health and performance.

Iron

Iron is critical for sport performance. As a component of hemo-globin, it is instrumental in transporting oxygen from the lungs to the tissues. It performs a similar role in myoglobin, which acts within the muscle as an oxygen acceptor to hold a supply of oxygen readily available for use by the mitochondria. Iron is also a vital component of the enzymes involved in the produc-tion of ATP.

Iron adequacy can be a limiting factor in performance, since deficiency limits aerobic endurance and the capacity for work. Even partial depletion of iron stores in the liver, spleen, and bone marrow, as evidenced by low serum ferritin levels, may have a detrimental effect on exercise performance, even when anemia is not present.

You may have heard of "sports anemia," a term which can be applied to three different situations: hemodilution, iron de-ficiency anemia, and foot-strike anemia. Athletes at risk for sports anemia include:

- rapidly growing adolescent males;
- female athletes with heavy menstrual losses;
- athletes adhering to energy-restricted diets;
- distance runners who may have increased GI iron loss, hematuria, hemolysis caused by foot impact, and myoglobin leakage;
- and those training heavily in hot climates with heavy sweating.

Recent research suggests that approximately 32 percent of female athletes may be anemic and that all athletes, especially adolescent and premenopausal females, long-distance runners, and vegetarians, should be screened periodically to assess their iron status.

Heavy endurance training, especially early in the season, can also cause a transient decrease in serum ferritin and hemoglobin. Known as "sports anemia" or "pseudoanemia," reduced hemo-globin levels due to expanding blood volumes are at the root of the problem; however, levels return towards pre-training normal, and performance is typically not affected. Some research suggests there actually may be improvements in aerobic capacity and performance.

Some athletes, especially long-distance runners, can experience GI bleeding, which causes low iron levels. GI bleeding is related to the intensity and duration of the exercise, the ability of the athlete to stay hydrated, how well the athlete is trained, and whether he or she has taken ibuprofen before the competition. Diagnosis can be determined by stool hemoglobin assays. Some athletes also experience iron deficiency without anemia, a condition with normal hemoglobin levels but reduced levels of serum ferritin (20 to 30 ng/mL). If you suspect that you fall into a risk group mentioned, my advice is to get a baseline measurement at the beginning of and during the training season using hemoglobin and serum ferritin blood test.

Those suspected to have sickle cell trait (SCT) should also be tested, since the rate of sudden death in SCT athletes is reported to be 10 to 30 times higher. Deaths have been reported more often than not early in season, during exhaustive drills in hot weather without adequate warm up time. In 2010, the NCAA instituted a universal screening program to test for SCT in all Division I athletes, although at the high school level, in the NBA, NFL, Navy, Marines, and Air Force, testing is not required.

Given the evidence suggesting iron's important role in optimal health and physical performance, there is no debate that athletes at risk or with suspected deficiencies should be identified and treated. Taking a supplement without deficiency remains controversial since there are health risks associated with having too much iron.

While male athletes typically get enough dietary iron, female athletes tend to consume less for a variety of reasons, including low energy intakes, reduction of animal products, or adherence to a vegetarian/vegan diet.

For those found to be deficient, increasing dietary intake of iron or supplementation under the guidance of a medical expert are the only ways to replace iron losses and improve status. Eating or drinking vitamin-C-rich foods like oranges, grapefruits, tomatoes, and potatoes at the same time as iron-rich meats and fortified cereals can improve iron absorption while eating or drinking calcium-rich dairy or cheese with iron-rich foods can compromise and interfere with absorption.

Iron supplementation is not free of side effects; nausea and constipation are just two of the most common complaints.

Calcium

Low dietary intake levels of calcium have been shown to contribute to stress fractures, decreased bone density, and osteoporosis, especially in young female athletes who have had interrupted menstrual function. Many athletes have been shown to have suboptimal levels of dietary calcium due to lactose intolerance or adherence to special diets that eliminate dairy, such as Paleo and vegan diets.

While low-fat and nonfat dairy products such as organic milk, yogurt, cheese and frozen desserts are one way to get enough calcium, fortified milk-free options such as almond, flax, rice and soy milks, and yogurt, cheese, and tofu made with calcium sulfate are also good sources. Sardines, plant-based fortified cereals, deep greens like kale and spinach, and vegetables like broccoli also contribute calcium to the diet.

Supplements Consumed by Athletes

There are dozens of supplements consumed by athletes to enhance sports performance. This section has summarized some of the major nutrients, vitamins, minerals, essential fats, and probiotics which all support the athlete's overall health, which in turn can optimize performance.

What about when just enough is not good enough? What about the athlete who wants to gain mass, go faster longer, and get stronger?

Rather than extending this section for hundreds of pages, I have compiled the pros and cons, functions and food sources, safety and precautions for some of the most popular supplements in a chart which you can find in Appendix A.

AND Position Paper on Nutrient Supplementation available FREE at: (http://www.eatright.org/About/Content.aspx?id=8409)nutrition.

SECTION
VI

READY RECIPES

Thanks to: Chef Mandy Twardowski, BS, DTR, graduate of the Johnson & Wales University Culinary Nutrition Program, for analyzing many of the recipes; Chef Goble, with whom I had the pleasure of creating the Sandals Spa Cuisine Program a decade ago; Culinary expert Michelle Austin; my colleagues and friends for their delicious, nutritious contributions. The nutrition analysis for the recipes was based on the food ingredients listed utilizing ESHA Food Processor SQL software program and BiPro® Super Fudge Recipe.

Beverages	Nutrients/Vitamins/Minerals
Legally Lean Power Juice	Protein, fiber, vit A, C, K, folate, calcium, potassium, magnesium, beta-carotene, nitrates
Ginger Papaya Cooler	Fiber, beta carotene, potassium, calcium, folate vit C

Appetizers/Dips/Salsas	Nutrients/Vitamins/Minerals
Avocado & Tomato Salsa	Fiber, beta-carotene, folate, potassium
Jicama Salsa	Fiber, vit A, C, folate, magnesium, calcium, potassium
Hot Mango Salsa	Beta carotene, vit C, potassium

Salads	Nutrients/Vitamins/Minerals
Mango Strawberry & Chayote Toss	Fiber, vit C, beta carotene, potassium
Korean Salad	

Soups	Nutrients/Vitamins/Minerals
Caribbean Style Island Soup	Protein, fiber, vit A, C, K, B3, folate, potassium, calcium, magnesium, choline
Ginger, Carrot & Pear Bisque	Fiber, vit A & C, folate, calcium, potassium, magnesium, choline
Phyto Veggie Soup	Fiber, vit A, C, K, B3, beta-carotene, calcium, potassium, choline, magnesium, lycopene

Entrees	Nutrients/Vitamins/Minerals
Legally Lean Chili	Protein, fiber, vit A, B3, C, K, iron, calcium, potassium

Cured Tuna Fillet with Coriander/Veg	Protein, vit A, B3, calcium, phosphorus, selenium
Turkey Meatballs	Protein, vit C, B3, beta-carotene
Jerk Turkey Burger	Protein, fiber, vit A, C, beta carotene, potassium, calcium
Grouper en Papillote	Protein, vit A, C, K, B3, folate, calcium, phosphorus, potassium
Zimbabwe Greens Stew with Chicken	Protein, fiber, vit A (190% DV), Vit C (270% DV), iron, calcium

Vegetarian Entrees	Nutrients/Vitamins/Minerals
Quinoa, Grilled Vegetables & Seitan	Protein, fiber, vit A, C, K, folate, beta carotene, potassium, magnesium, calcium, zinc
Pasta Tropical	Protein, fiber, vit A, C, Bs, potassium, magnesium, phosphorus, choline, beta carotene

Side Dishes	Nutrients/Vitamins/Minerals
Black Beans, Tomato & Bell Pepper	Protein, fiber, vit A, C, folate, iron, potassium, magnesium
Bahamian Peas & Grits	Protein, fiber, iron, Vit C, magnesium
Spiced Sweet Potato	Protein, fiber, vit C, B3, B6 & A (500%DV!), iron, potassium, calcium, magnesium, phosphorus, beta-carotene,
Mashed Potato & Parsnip	Protein, fiber, vit C, Bs, iron, calcium, potassium, magnesium, phosphorus, choline

Breakfast Dishes	Nutrients/Vitamins/Minerals
Confetti Egg Omelette	Protein, fiber, vit A, C, Bs, K, folate, potassium, beta carotene, choline
Oatmeal Banana Spiced Pancakes	Protein, fiber, B vitamins, folate, calcium, potassium, selenium, phosphorus, choline

Dessert/Bread	Nutrients/Vitamins/Minerals
Garbanzo Cake	Protein, B vitamins, fiber
Super Fudge	Protein, fiber

Nutrition Facts
Serving Size 1 (501g)
Servings Per Container 1

Amount Per Serving

Calories 250   Calories from Fat 10

	% Daily Value*
Total Fat 1g	2%
Saturated Fat 0g	0%
Trans Fat 0g	
Cholesterol 0mg	0%
Sodium 320mg	13%
Total Carbohydrate 49g	16%
Dietary Fiber 8g	32%
Sugars 25g	
Protein 16g	

Vitamin A 70%	•	Vitamin C 45%
Calcium 10%	•	Iron 10%

*Percent Daily Values are based on a 2,000 calorie diet. Your daily values may be higher or lower depending on your calorie needs:

	Calories:	2,000	2,500
Total Fat	Less than	65g	80g
Saturated Fat	Less than	20g	25g
Cholesterol	Less than	300mg	300mg
Sodium	Less than	2,400mg	2,400mg
Total Carbohydrate		300g	375g
Dietary Fiber		25g	30g

Calories per gram:
Fat 9 • Carbohydrate 4 • Protein 4

Legally Lean Power Juice - Serves 1

Ingredients:
1/2 cup beet juice
1/2 cup coconut water
1 cups organic frozen blueberries
1/2 frozen banana
2 cups fresh spinach
1/3 bottle ready-to-drink whey protein "juice" (15-20 grams protein)
Ice as needed

Directions: Blend, mix, and enjoy!

Nutrition Facts
Serving Size (179g)
Servings Per Container 2

Amount Per Serving

Calories 80   Calories from Fat 0

	% Daily Value*
Total Fat 0g	0%
Saturated Fat 0g	0%
Trans Fat 0g	
Cholesterol 0mg	0%
Sodium 10mg	0%
Total Carbohydrate 23g	8%
Dietary Fiber 2g	8%
Sugars 10g	
Protein 0g	

Vitamin A 8%	•	Vitamin C 170%
Calcium 4%	•	Iron 2%

*Percent Daily Values are based on a 2,000 calorie diet. Your daily values may be higher or lower depending on your calorie needs:

	Calories:	2,000	2,500
Total Fat	Less than	65g	80g
Saturated Fat	Less than	20g	25g
Cholesterol	Less than	300mg	300mg
Sodium	Less than	2,400mg	2,400mg
Total Carbohydrate		300g	375g
Dietary Fiber		25g	30g

Calories per gram:
Fat 9 • Carbohydrate 4 • Protein 4

Ginger Papaya Cooler - Serves 2

Ingredients:
1 large ripe papaya, deseeded and peeled
Juice of 2 key limes
3 tbsp. ginger, grated
Garnish Option - Mint leaf for garnish

Directions:
1.Place papaya in food processor or blender and puree.
2.Add lime juice and grated ginger.
3.Continue to blend.
4.Garnish with mint leaf.

Chef Tips:
Papaya can be substituted with passion fruit.

Nutrition Facts

Serving Size (105g)
Servings Per Container 8

Amount Per Serving

Calories 90   Calories from Fat 70

% Daily Value*

Total Fat 8g   12%
  Saturated Fat 1g   5%
  Trans Fat 0g
Cholesterol 0mg   0%
Sodium 5mg   0%
Total Carbohydrate 7g   2%
  Dietary Fiber 4g   16%
  Sugars 2g
Protein 1g

Vitamin A 2%   •   Vitamin C 26%
Calcium 2%   •   Iron 2%

*Percent Daily Values are based on a 2,000 calorie diet. Your daily values may be higher or lower depending on your calorie needs:

	Calories	2,000	2,500
Total Fat	Less than	65g	80g
Saturated Fat	Less than	20g	25g
Cholesterol	Less than	300mg	300mg
Sodium	Less than	2,400mg	2,400mg
Total Carbohydrate		300g	375g
Dietary Fiber		25g	30g

Calories per gram:
  Fat 9 • Carbohydrate 4 • Protein 4

Avocado And Tomato Salsa - Serves 8

Ingredients:

2 Florida avocados, peeled and chopped
2 fresh tomatoes, peeled, seeded, and chopped
2 tomatillo, chopped
¼ small red onion, finely chopped
1 tsp. minced garlic
½ Scotch Bonnet chili, seeded and chopped (use gloves when preparing to avoid capsaicin burn
1 tablespoon key lime juice
Salt, freshly ground black pepper
1/3 cup finely chopped cilantro
¼ cup fresh strawberries - chopped

Directions:

1.Mash ½ of avocados.
2.Combine first six ingredients (except the fresh herbs). Mix until well blended. Do not crush the avocado.
3.Add herbs just before serving. Taste and adjust seasonings as desired.
4.Delicately blend in fresh strawberries.
5.Serve with baked tortilla chips or raw veggies such as carrots, cucumbers, jicama and red pepper.

Chef Tips:

Like most fruits at the grocery store, avocados are primarily found unripe. To speed up the ripening process, like plantains, place in paper bag. When selecting an avocado, pick one that is blemish-free and heavy for size.

Nutrition Bite: Serve with fresh jicama, carrot, or cucumber sticks. Also delicious with baked tortilla chips.

Caribbean Style Chicken Soup - Serves 6

Ingredients:
32 oz. organic lite chicken stock
2 carrots chopped
2 celery stalks (no leaves)
1 small red pepper - chopped large pieces
½-1 whole yellow onion
2-3 garlic cloves
½ small calabasa (pumpkin)
1 plantain (semi-ripe)
½ sweet potato chopped into ½ moon qtr.
inch pieces (or sub malanga)
1 handfull of spinach (1/2-1 cup)
½ bunch of cilantro (cut off bottom stems)
3 chicken breasts
1 tsp. olive oil or chili/garlic oil
Kosher or sea salt, to taste
Black pepper, to taste
Garlic powder, to taste

Directions:
1. Cut all vegetables, chop garlic roughly, and put all in pot with chicken stock.
2. Bring to a boil for 15 minutes and reduce to low-medium heat.
3. Do not put in the spinach and cilantro.
4. Sprinkle salt, pepper and garlic on both sides of breasts.
5. In a separate sauté pan, heat oil, place chicken breasts in hot pan, sear on both sides until brown.
6. Remove from pan and cut into pieces and add to soup. Cook for 30 minutes.
7. In a food processor or blender, take spinach, cilantro and ladle a cup of soup and put in blender.
8. Blend together.
9. Incorporate puree into soup and cook 15 more minutes. Salt and pepper to taste.

Chef Tips:
Can add or substitute yucca and parsnip.

Can remove the Caribbean root vegetables and cilantro. Keep all other vegetables.

Add pre-cooked brown rice at the end of cooking to have a more traditional chicken and rice soup.

Nutrition Facts
Serving Size 4-6 (309g)
Servings Per Container 6

Amount Per Serving

Calories 140   Calories from Fat 5

% Daily Value*

Total Fat 0g — 0%
  Saturated Fat 0g — 0%
  Trans Fat 0g
Cholesterol 0mg — 0%
Sodium 410mg — 17%
Total Carbohydrate 28g — 9%
  Dietary Fiber 8g — 20%
  Sugars 14g
Protein 4g

Vitamin A 260% • Vitamin C 15%
Calcium 10% • Iron 2%

*Percent Daily Values are based on a 2,000 calorie diet. Your daily values may be higher or lower depending on your calorie needs:

	Calories:	2,000	2,500
Total Fat	Less than	65g	80g
Saturated Fat	Less than	20g	25g
Cholesterol	Less than	300mg	300mg
Sodium	Less than	2,400mg	2,400mg
Total Carbohydrate		300g	375g
Dietary Fiber		25g	30g

Calories per gram:
  Fat 9 • Carbohydrate 4 • Protein 4

Gingered Carrot and Pear Bisque - Serves 6
Prepare ahead of time. Serve hot or cold.

Ingredients:

1 c. diced onion
Organic cooking spray
2 large unpeeled pears, miniscule diced
1 tbsp. peeled ginger, minced
2 c. chicken broth, organic or unsalted canned
1 lb. carrots, peeled and cut into chunks
½ c. cooked rice
1 bay leaf
1 ½ c. fat-free half & half
Salt and pepper to taste
Garnish: Carrot shavings, fresh dill

Directions:

1.Sauté the onion in a large saucepan sprayed with Pam until the onion is translucent and tender.
2.Add ginger, and sauté another minute or two.
3.Add the chicken broth, carrots, pears, rice and bay leaf, and simmer, partly covered until the carrots are tender.
4.Remove the bay leaf. Puree the mixture in a blender or food processor, blending in the fat-free half & half to thin the soup to your taste.
5.Season with salt and pepper.
6.Reheat the soup gently, and serve it hot, or let it cool completely, and place in refrigerator for 2 hours.
7.Serve cold with a garnish of carrot shavings and fresh dill.

Phyto Veggie Soup - Serves: 8

Ingredients:

1 lb. cassava and yams, peeled, and cut into large chunks
Pam spray
1 small onion, chopped
1 red bell pepper, cut into strips
3 tomatillo, chopped
2 tbsp. fresh ginger chopped
1 small chayote, peeled and diced
½ c. chopped chives
2 garlic cloves, minced
1 can (14 oz.) tomatoes with juice
1 tbsp. chopped basil
1 tbsp. fresh thyme
2 tbsp. ginger
1 plantain - completely ripe
Organic or canned low sodium chicken broth

Nutrition Facts	
Serving Size 1 serving (197g)	
Servings Per Container 8	
Amount Per Serving	
Calories 130	Calories from Fat 5
	% Daily Value*
Total Fat 0.5g	1%
Saturated Fat 0g	0%
Trans Fat 0g	
Cholesterol 0mg	0%
Sodium 90mg	4%
Total Carbohydrate 32g	11%
Dietary Fiber 4g	16%
Sugars 9g	
Protein 3g	
Vitamin A 100% • Vitamin C 70%	
Calcium 4% • Iron 8%	

Directions:

1. Steam cassava and yam over high heat until tender. Remove and set aside.
2. Heat Pam in a sauté pan, add onion, and pepper. Sauté until fragrant, about 3 minutes.
3. Add chayote and cook.
4. Cover until tender, about 5 minutes.
5. Add chives, garlic, ginger and tomatoes, breaking the tomatoes with the back of spoon.
6. Then add the basil and thyme and cook covered for an additional 10 minutes over a low heat.
7. Season with salt and freshly ground black pepper.
8. Stir in steamed casava, tomatillo and combine.
9. Cook for about 1 to 2 minutes more.
10. Serve in clear bowls.

Chef Tips:

Plantains should be completely ripe for soup or they will get mushy and dissolve.

Nutrition Facts
Serving Size 1 (128g)
Servings Per Container 1

Amount Per Serving

Calories 120   Calories from Fat 5

% Daily Value*

Total Fat 0.5g   1%
  Saturated Fat 0g   0%
  Trans Fat 0g
Cholesterol 25mg   8%
Sodium 40mg   2%
Total Carbohydrate 18g   6%
  Dietary Fiber 1g   4%
  Sugars 16g
Protein 13g

Vitamin A 50%   •   Vitamin C 6%
Calcium 4%   •   Iron 6%

*Percent Daily Values are based on a 2,000 calorie diet. Your daily values may be higher or lower depending on your calorie needs.

	Calories:	2,000	2,500
Total Fat	Less than	65g	80g
Saturated Fat	Less than	20g	25g
Cholesterol	Less than	300mg	300mg
Sodium	Less than	2,400mg	2,400mg
Total Carbohydrate		300g	375g
Dietary Fiber		25g	30g

Calories per gram:
  Fat 9 • Carbohydrate 4 • Protein 4

Cured Tuna Fillet With Coriander & Vegetables - Serves 1

Ingredients:
2 oz. tuna fillet
1 oz. coriander
½ oz. salt
½ oz. sugar
½ oz. carrot
½ oz. onion
½ oz. zucchini
½ oz. fennel
Pam olive oil cooking spray

Directions:
1.Season tuna with salt, sugar, and coriander.
2.Set aside.
3.Sauté onion, carrot, zucchini, and fennel in Pam olive oil spray.
4.Add a dash of salt and pepper.
5.Remove from pan.
6.Turn heat up to high and sear tuna filet to level of doneness you desire.

Chef Tips:
Tuna is delicious cooked at medium rare.

"Cured" usually means there's brine or smoking process involved.

"Brunoise" means cut into small cubes.

Could serve with grilled fennel, which tastes like licorice.

Chili Recipe - Serves 8

Ingredients:
3 tbls.olive oil
2 tbls. chili powder
1 tbls. curry
½ tsp. cumin
½ tsp. paprika or cayenne
¼ tsp. black pepper and ¼ tsp. salt
¼ tsp. cinnamon and ¼ tsp. instant coffee
3 cloves of garlic mashed
1 large yellow onion
1 fresh tomato
1 red pepper- roasted (see below)*
1 green pepper
1 can pinto beans (15 oz.)
1 can large dark red kidney beans (15 oz.)
1 small red chili beans (15 oz.)
1 lb. ground turkey or ground meat substitute
(use ½ ground sirloin, ½ ground turkey for analysis)
1 can crushed tomatoes (seasoned with oregano and basil or
chile [can sub salsa]
Grated cheese to taste (lowfat cheddar or pepper jack)

Directions:
1. On oven range, put burner on high until range is red or use
grill, char outside of red pepper on all sides. Put in PAPER bag,
close, and let cool.
2. When completely cooled, peel black char off pepper and chop.
3. In a pan over medium heat, place olive oil, sauté onion, green
peppers til wilted, add garlic, red pepper, fresh tomatoes, add
meat, salt, pepper, ½ chili paste, and add beans with juice,
crushed tomatoes and rest of spices.
4. Simmer for 45-60 minutes.

Chef Tips:
Sometimes I do not use meat but use zucchini and squash and
bulgur (which I like very much). If using bulgur, add 2 cups of
water or as directed on label.

Can use all white beans to make a white bean chili and add kale,
and/or collard greens for a white bean chili.

Bison or beef tenderloin can be used.

Jicama Salsa - Serves: 4

Ingredients:
1 small red onion, chopped fine
Juice of 2 key limes
3 small mandarin oranges from can with
about 2 tbsp. juice
1-1 lb. jicama, diced small
½ cucumber, diced small

Optional:
1 Congo chili

Directions:
1.Cut the onion in half. Dice fine.
2.Place in a bowl with key lime juice. Let soak.
3.Slice mandarin oranges.
4.Peel the jicama and rinse in cold water.
5.Cut into quarters, and then slice finely. Add to a bowl of mandarin orange juice.
6.Cut the cucumber in half lengthwise, and then use a teaspoon to scoop out the seeds. Slice the cucumber and add to the bowl.
7.With gloves, remove the stem from the chile, slit it and scrape out the seeds with a small sharp knife. Chop the flesh finely and add to the bowl.
8.Add the sliced onion to the bowl with any remaining lime juice and mix well.
9.Cover and let stand at room temperature for at least 1-hour before serving.

Chefs Tips:
If not serving, refrigerate salsa. It will keep for 2 to 3 days.

Mango, Strawberry & Chayote Toss - Serves: 8

Ingredients:
2 c. fresh strawberries, sliced
1 med. chayote cut in ¼ inch cubes
1 large mango, peeled and cut into ¼ inch cubes
8 c. mixed torn salad greens

Dressing:
1/3 c. rice wine vinegar
1 tbsp. walnut oil
1 tbsp. granulated white sugar
1 ½ tbsp. fresh mint, chopped
¼ tsp. salt and pepper to taste

Nutrition Facts	
Serving Size (162g)	
Servings Per Container 8	
Amount Per Serving	
Calories 80	Calories from Fat 20
	% Daily Value*
Total Fat 2g	3%
Saturated Fat 0g	0%
Trans Fat 0g	
Cholesterol 0mg	0%
Sodium 20mg	1%
Total Carbohydrate 13g	4%
Dietary Fiber 3g	12%
Sugars 5g	
Protein 1g	
Vitamin A 50% • Vitamin C 50%	
Calcium 2% • Iron 4%	

Directions:
1.In a large bowl, whisk together vinegar, oil, sugar, mint, salt and pepper.
2.Add strawberries, chayote (Christophene) and mango.
3.Top greens with strawberry, mango and chayote mixture.
4.Divide greens among 8 clear plates.

Chefs Tips:
Can substitute cucumber (no guts) for chayote.

Black Beans With Tomato and Bell Pepper - Serves: 16 ½ c. servings

Nutrition Facts

Serving Size 1/2 cup (190g)
Servings Per Container 16

Amount Per Serving

Calories 80   Calories from Fat 5

% Daily Value*

Total Fat 0g	0%
Saturated Fat 0g	0%
Trans Fat 0g	
Cholesterol 0mg	0%
Sodium 250mg	10%
Total Carbohydrate 15g	5%
Dietary Fiber 4g	16%
Sugars 2g	
Protein 5g	

Vitamin A 10%   •   Vitamin C 25%
Calcium 4%   •   Iron 6%

*Percent Daily Values are based on a 2,000 calorie diet. Your daily values may be higher or lower depending on your calorie needs.

	Calories	2,000	2,500
Total Fat	Less than	65g	80g
Saturated Fat	Less than	20g	25g
Cholesterol	Less than	300mg	300mg
Sodium	Less than	2,400mg	2,400mg
Total Carbohydrate		300g	375g
Dietary Fiber		25g	30g

Calories per gram:
Fat 9 • Carbohydrate 4 • Protein 4

Ingredients:

5 c. dried or canned organic black beans
12 c. water
1 small red onion, chopped
1 red bell pepper, chopped
3 large bay leaves
4 c. chopped tomatoes
1 small onion, chopped
½ c. chopped garlic
1 fresh cilantro bunch, chopped
1 tbsp. ground cumin
Pam spray

Directions:

1. Boil 6 c. water.
2. Add beans and cook at medium heat for 30 minutes.
3. Drain in colander and remove foreign particles.
4. Return beans to pot.
5. Add 6 c. water to beans.
6. Add red onion, bell pepper and bay leaves and bring to boil.
7. Reduce heat to medium and cook until beans are tender, stirring occasionally.
8. Sauté tomatoes, onion, garlic and season in Pam sprayed frying pan.
9. Drain and add beans to mixture. Turn off heat and remove from stove.
10. Transfer to bowl, serving plate or dish.

Chef's Tips:

If you use canned beans, you can skip the method steps 1 to 7.

Just sauté the vegetables, add cilantro, and if you're not worried about fat and calories, in traditional Caribbean style, you can add a splash of extra virgin olive oil at the end of the cooking process.

Delicious with cooked rice, warm tostadas, mixed vegetable salad or with baked tortilla chips

Greens Stew - Serves: 4
From my Zimbabwe running "brother" Philemon Hanneck, Olympian

Ingredients:
4 cups collard greens, diced
16 oz. chicken stock
2 tomatoes, fresh, diced
1 onion, diced
2 bell peppers
chicken chunks
3 cups tomato sauce

Directions:
1)Place kale or collard greens in a pot with stock.
2)Dice tomatoes, onion, and bell pepper. Add to stew.
3)Add chicken chunks.
4)Boil, add tomato sauce, and let boil again.

Bahamian Peas and Grits - Serves: 6
From my Island sister, Marva Munroe, Bahamas

Ingredients:
2 tbsp. safflower oil
1 small onion, diced
¼ cups green pepper, diced
½ tsp. thyme leaves or ¼ teaspoon powdered thyme
1 tbsp. tomato paste
1 pinch black pepper
1 level teaspoon salt
1 cups pigeon peas, kidney beans, or black eye peas
2 cups vegetable stock or water
1½ cups grits

Directions:
1.Cook onion and green pepper in oil on low heat until soft.
2.Add thyme, tomato paste, black pepper, salt and cook tomato paste until well done.
3.Add peas and allow to simmer for 15 minutes, stirring occasionally.
4.Add stock or water and bring to a boil on medium heat.
5.Add and stir in rice.
6.Leave cooking with cover off until water disappears from the top of the grits.
7.Stir, put cover on pot and cook on low heat for 20 minutes.
8.Stir well and serve.

Quinoa with Grilled Vegetables and Seitan - Serves: 6
by Sharon Palmer, RDN, the Plant-Powered Dietitian™ and author of Plant-Powered for Life.

Nutrition Facts
Serving Size 1 (286g)
Servings Per Container 6
Amount Per Serving
Calories 330   Calories from Fat 80
% Daily Value*
Total Fat 8g 12%
Saturated Fat 0.5g 3%
Trans Fat 0g
Cholesterol 0mg 0%
Sodium 135mg 6%
Total Carbohydrate 45g 15%
Dietary Fiber 17g 68%
Sugars 7g
Protein 19g
Vitamin A 15% • Vitamin C 100%
Calcium 6% • Iron 25%
*Percent Daily Values are based on a 2,000 calorie diet. Your daily values may be higher or lower depending on your calorie needs.

Ingredients:
1 ½ cups quinoa, uncooked
Water
2 teaspoons vegetable broth base, reduced sodium
½ pound Brussels sprouts, trimmed, split in half
1 onion, sliced into rings (red or yellow)
1 red, orange or yellow bell pepper, sliced into wedges
4 small (i.e. Indian, Rosa Blanca) eggplants or 1 Japanese eggplant, sliced
1 medium zucchini
1 8 – ounce package seitan strips (unseasoned)
2 teaspoons extra virgin olive oil
2 teaspoons white balsamic vinegar
2 cloves minced garlic
1 teaspoon oregano
½ teaspoon smoked paprika
¼ teaspoon black pepper
Optional, pinch sea salt

¼ cup pistachio nuts (dry roasted)
3 tablespoons fresh basil, sliced

Directions:

1.Bring water (use the amount recommended on quinoa package) to a boil and add quinoa and vegetable broth base. Cover and simmer for about 45 to 55 minutes, until tender yet crunchy. Drain any remaining water. (May use a rice cooker to cook farro).

2.Meanwhile, place all vegetables (Brussels sprouts, onion, bell pepper, eggplant, and zucchini) and seitan in a shallow dish.

3.Mix olive oil, vinegar, garlic, oregano, paprika, black pepper, and sea salt (if desired) in a small dish. Drizzle over vegetables and toss together well; allow to marinate for at least 30 minutes while farro is cooking.

4.Heat a grill and grill the vegetables and seitan for about 5- 10 minutes on each side, until tender and browned (seitan will brown faster). (May also roast in top rack of the oven for about 30-40 minutes, stirring every 15 minutes, until golden brown.)

5.Spoon cooked farro onto a serving platter and arrange grilled vegetables and seitan over farro.

6.Sprinkle with pistachio nuts and chopped basil.

Chef's note:

Substitute quinoa with farro, brown rice or wheat berries. Just follow cooking instructions on package for water and cooking time.

Seitan is a wonderful, versatile alternative to meat. According to legend, this wheat-based, high-protein product was first discovered by Buddhist monks in seventh-century China when a batch of wheat dough went awry. The starch portion was washed away, revealing the gluten protein. Since then, it's been a traditional Asian element—simmered in broth, soy sauce, ginger and garlic. You can use it in a number of dishes to replace meat, such as this simple, rustic grilled vegetable dish.

Pasta Tropical - Serves: 8

Ingredients:
16 oz. tricolor or sport-shaped pasta like bicycle, tennis rackets, etc., cooked, drained and cooled, no salt used in cooking.
1 cup garbanzo beans, organic or regular rinsed
1 cup frozen peas, no salt added, thawed
1 cup corn, canned or frozen, no salt added
1 cup mandarin oranges, drained
¼ cup raisins

Dressing:
1 tbsp. flavorful oil like walnut oil
3 tbsp. fortified orange juice
1 tsp. cinnamon
¼ tsp. fresh ground ginger
¼ tsp. nutmeg
¼ tsp. orange peel

Directions:
1.Cook pasta according to directions. Remove from heat, rinse and drain.
2.Cool pasta in refrigerator for approximately 10 to 15 minutes. Remove.
3.Toss in peas, corn, garbanzo beans and raisins.
4.Prepare dressing by combining oil and spices thoroughly.
5.Toss pasta and dressing. Garnish with mandarin oranges.
6.Serve.

Nutrition Bite:
This is a colorful dish I've been preparing and serving for years, and featured in numerous magazines.

Nutrition Facts
Serving Size (176g)
Servings Per Container 8

Amount Per Serving
Calories 310   Calories from Fat 30

% Daily Value*
Total Fat 3.5g   5%
Saturated Fat 0.5g   3%
Trans Fat 0g
Cholesterol 0mg   0%
Sodium 190mg   8%
Total Carbohydrate 56g   19%
Dietary Fiber 4g   16%
Sugars 12g
Protein 11g

Vitamin A 15%   •   Vitamin C 20%
Calcium 2%   •   Iron 15%

*Percent Daily Values are based on a 2,000 calorie diet. Your daily values may be higher or lower depending on your calorie needs.

	Calories	2,000	2,500
Total Fat	Less than	65g	80g
Saturated Fat	Less than	20g	25g
Cholesterol	Less than	300mg	300mg
Sodium	Less than	2,400mg	2,400mg
Total Carbohydrate		300g	375g
Dietary Fiber		25g	30g

Calories per gram:
Fat 9 • Carbohydrate 4 • Protein 4

Turkey Meatballs - Serves: 4- medium size meatballs

Nutrition Facts
Serving Size 1 meatball (136g)
Servings Per Container 4

Amount Per Serving

Calories 110   Calories from Fat 10

% Daily Value*

Total Fat 1g   2%
Saturated Fat 0g   0%
Trans Fat 0g
Cholesterol 20mg   7%
Sodium 105mg   4%
Total Carbohydrate 6g   2%
Dietary Fiber 1g   4%
Sugars 2g
Protein 19g

Vitamin A 0%   •   Vitamin C 30%
Calcium 2%   •   Iron 6%

Ingredients:
1/2 lb. of ground white turkey meat
1/3 cup of yellow onion
1/3 cup of red and green pepper
1/4 cup of oatmeal
1 tsp. Worcestershire sauce
1 egg white
1/4 tsp. black pepper
1/2 tsp. oregano
1/2 tsp. thyme
1 tsp. of low sugar ketchup or tomato sauce
1/2 tsp. mustard

Directions
1) Mix all ingredients well.
2) Cook in oven until browned all the way through.

Jerk Turkey Burger - Serves: 1

Nutrition Facts
Serving Size (384g)
Servings Per Container

Amount Per Serving

Calories 350   Calories from Fat 40

% Daily Value*

Total Fat 4g   6%
Saturated Fat 0g   0%
Trans Fat 0g
Cholesterol 65mg   22%
Sodium 630mg   26%
Total Carbohydrate 39g   13%
Dietary Fiber 10g   40%
Sugars 12g
Protein 48g

Vitamin A 50%   •   Vitamin C 20%
Calcium 10%   •   Iron 20%

Ingredients:
6 oz. ground white turkey
¼ yellow onion chopped fine
1 tsp. barbeque sauce - low sugar
1 tsp. Jerk seasoning
1/2 tsp. Worcestershire sauce
Salt and pepper
Organic cooking spray
2 slices thick cut yellow onion- grilled
¼ cup mixed field greens with shredded carrot and jicama
Dash of apple cider vinegar
Dash of olive oil
Optional:
100% whole grain buns

Directions:
1. Combine all seasoning with ground turkey.
2. Spray pan with cooking spray.
3. Brown onion on each side - set aside to cool.
4. Cook on medium heat to desired temp.
5. In separate bowl, combine greens, carrot and jicama. Add little salt, pepper, vinegar, and oil, just enough to slightly wet and flavor
6. Lightly spray with organic cooking spray and dust with garlic powder.
7. Warm buns on cookie sheet in oven.
8. Assemble meat patty, onion and mixed green mixture.

Chefs Tips:
Variation: can use turkey 70%-30% white to dark meat, mix ½ turkey and ½ ground pork, grain fed bison or beef

Grouper en Papillote
(steamed in paper) - Serves 1

Fish Ingredients:
1- 8 oz. filet Grouper, Mahi Mahi, Tuna, Snapper, or Salmon

Marinade:
1.5 oz. low sodium soy sauce
1/4 jalapeno- seeded and chopped
1/2 tsp. ginger-peeled and grated
juice of 1 lime
6 sprigs cilantro
dash of curry

Vegetables (cooked in Paper) - Serves 1:

Ingredients:
1 cup of chopped spinach
1/4 red pepper sliced
1/4 red onion sliced thick
1/4 tsp. orange zest

1/2 tsp. ginger zest

1 tbls. of egg substitute

Parchment paper

Directions:
1. Blend all marinade ingredients together.
2. Coat fish.
3. Cover and refrigerate for a few hours.
4. Cut parchment paper into squares that measure 13 x 18.
5. Preheat oven 350 degrees
6 Toss together vegetables and put in paper.
7. Place fish on top of vegetables, pour extra marinade on top (up to 1 tbls) and top with dash of curry.
8 Brush the outer edges with egg white, fold and seal contents-twist at ends.
9 Put paper on baking sheet for approx. 15 minutes. The paper will pop up when cooked.

Chefs Tips:
Can change flavor combination by deleting spicy pepper and cilantro and adding basil and roasted garlic.

Any dark green vegetable can be added, kale, bok choy.

Can add thin sliced sweet potato or Yukon gold potato to veggie mix.

Spiced Sweet Potato - Serves 1

Ingredients:
1 medium sweet potato
1 tsp. of butter
1 tsp. of 0% plain Greek or Icelandic yogurt
1 ounce of chopped walnuts
½ tsp. cinnamon
½ tsp. ginger
½ tsp. nutmeg
Kosher salt

Directions:
1. Cook sweet potato until tender in oven or for approx. 10 min if microwave.
2. Slice open and scoop out the meat inside.
3. Put in a bowl, add butter, spices, and yogurt and stir together.
4. Put back in potato skin, and top with chopped nuts.

Mashed Potato and Parsnip - Serves 1

Ingredients:
1 medium mashed potato-Yukon gold
½ parsnip
¼ cup low fat milk
1 tsp. butter
1 tsp. of 0% plain Greek or Icelandic yogurt
½ tsp. parsley
Dash of cayenne pepper
Salt and fresh ground black pepper

Directions:
1. Boil potato and parsnip.
2. Mix all ingredients.

Nutrition Facts	
Serving Size (264g)	
Servings Per Container	
Amount Per Serving	
Calories 230	Calories from Fat 40
	% Daily Value*
Total Fat 4.5g	7%
Saturated Fat 3g	15%
Trans Fat 0g	
Cholesterol 15mg	5%
Sodium 65mg	3%
Total Carbohydrate 40g	13%
Dietary Fiber 3g	12%
Sugars 5g	
Protein 7g	
Vitamin A 4% • Vitamin C 70%	
Calcium 15% • Iron 10%	

Confetti Egg White Omelette - Serves: 1

Ingredients:
3 oz. egg whites fresh or commercial
1 tsp. fresh black pepper

Fillings:
1 oz. pepper, chopped
1 oz. mushroom, chopped
1 oz. onion, diced
1 oz. tomato, diced
(Additional veggies are welcome!)

Organic cooking spray

Nutrition Facts	
Serving Size 1 (205g)	
Servings Per Container 1	
Amount Per Serving	
Calories 80	Calories from Fat 0
	% Daily Value*
Total Fat 0g	0%
Saturated Fat 0g	0%
Trans Fat 0g	
Cholesterol 0mg	0%
Sodium 200mg	8%
Total Carbohydrate 9g	3%
Dietary Fiber 2g	8%
Sugars 4g	
Protein 11g	
Vitamin A 20% • Vitamin C 70%	
Calcium 2% • Iron 2%	

Garnish:
Fresh Florida orange slice

Directions:
1.Mix eggs with veggies.
2.Pour into hot frying pan which has been sprayed with organic cooking spray.
3.Cook until firm and slightly browned.

Banana Spiced Pancakes - Serves 1

Ingredients:
½ cup steel cut oats
¼ cup Greek or Icelandic yogurt
2 egg whites
2 tablespoons milk (soy, almond alternative if desired)
1 ripe banana
¼ teaspoon cinnamon
¼ teaspoon nutmeg

Directions:
1. Process the oatmeal, 0% plain Greek or Icelandic yogurt, egg whites, milk, cinnamon, nutmeg and 1/2 banana in a blender until smooth.
2. Heat a nonstick skillet over low to medium-low heat.
3. Pour 1/3 cup of batter onto hot skillet. Wait until the batter bubbles and the edges look slightly dry (about 1-2 min) and then flip the pancake and cook for 1 minute longer.
4. Serve with a layer of thinly sliced the other half of the banana on top with a little bit of honey drizzled over it.

Chef's Notes:
Try adding blueberries to mixture after it's blended.

Chocolate chips or chocolate whey protein can be added. If using a scoop of whey protein, add a few tablespoons of water to loosen thickness.

Garbanzo Cake - Serves: 10

Ingredients:
2- 10 oz. cans garbanzo beans, organic or regular, rinsed and drained
1 cup Egg Beaters
zest and juice of 1 orange
1 cup unsweetened applesauce
1 tsp. baking powder
2 tsp. ground cinnamon

Nutrition Facts	
Serving Size (108g)	
Servings Per Container 10	
Amount Per Serving	
Calories 100	Calories from Fat 15
	% Daily Value*
Total Fat 1.5g	2%
Saturated Fat 0g	0%
Trans Fat 0g	
Cholesterol 0mg	0%
Sodium 170mg	7%
Total Carbohydrate 15g	5%
Dietary Fiber 0g	0%
Sugars 3g	
Protein 6g	
Vitamin A 6% • Vitamin C 8%	
Calcium 4% • Iron 6%	

*Percent Daily Values are based on a 2,000 calorie diet. Your daily values may be higher or lower depending on your calorie needs.

	Calories:	2,000	2,500
Total Fat	Less than	65g	80g
Saturated Fat	Less than	20g	25g
Cholesterol	Less than	300mg	300mg
Sodium	Less than	2,400mg	2,400mg
Total Carbohydrate		300g	375g
Dietary Fiber		25g	30g

Calories per gram:
Fat 9 • Carbohydrate 4 • Protein 4

Directions:
1.Preheat the oven to 350° F.
2.Tip the chickpeas in a colander, drain them thoroughly, then rub them between palms of your hand to loosen and remove the skins.
3.Put the skinned chickpeas in a food processor and process until smooth.
4.Spoon the puree into a bowl and stir in the egg substitute, sugar, baking powder, cinnamon, orange rind and juice. Use Baker's Spray to spray a loaf pan.
5.Pour the cake mixture into the pan, level the surface and bake for about 1 ½ hours or until a skewer inserted into the center comes out clean.
6.Remove the cake from the oven and let stand in the pan, for about 10 minutes.
7.Remove cake from the pan. Place on a wire rack.
8.Let cool completely before serving.

Super Fudge - Serves: 10 pieces

Ingredients:
¼ cup raw honey
¼ cup peanut butter (can substitute almond butter)
¼ cup raw almonds, finely chopped
¼ cup cocoa powder
¼ cup BiPro® natural unflavored
3 tbls. ground flax meal
1 tsp. vanilla

Directions:

1 Combine all ingredients in a bowl and mix until smooth and cohesive dough forms.
2. Divide into mini-muffin pan cups and chill for 1 hour.

APPENDIX A

Guide to Selected Supplements

This guide covers a list of some of the popular supplements which have been marketed to or consumed by athletes and consumers to enhance health or performance. However, it would be nearly impossible to cover them all!

Some of the selected supplements, such as caffeine, creatine, omega-3, nitrates (beet powder/juice) probiotics and Vitamin D have very strong evidence to suggest a health, healing, performance and/or recovery benefit. Others have the potential to have some positive benefits such as BCAAs, conditionally essential amino acids (glutamine, arginine), beta alanine, beta glucan, betaine, choline, glutathione, HMB, magnesium, quercetin, taurine tumeric (curcumin); while supplements like antioxidants and glucosamine/chondroitin have mixed research findings.

Because the topic is so broad, I wanted a second opinion and enlisted the help of some of the top sports nutritionists/dietitians and performance experts* in the country to inquire about their supplement experience. Here's what I asked:
• What top 5 supplements were their athletes consuming?
• Which top 5 supplements they were consuming?
• What top 5 supplements were they most likely to recommend?

The results were not remarkable, but were consistent with the research presented in previous sections of this book. The results were as follows:

**Supplements/Supplemental foods
your athletes most likely to consume:**
1. Protein Shakes/Powders/Protein Bars
2. Multi vitamins
3. Creatine
4. Energy Drinks/Caffeine
5. NO/Beet Juice

Supplements the experts consume:
1. Multivitamins
2. Protein Bars/Shakes
3. Omega-3 essential fats
4. Probiotics
5. Turmeric (Curcumin)

**Supplements/Supplemental food experts
most likely to recommend:**
1. Protein Shakes/Powders
2. Multi vitamins
3. NO/Beet Juice
4. Protein Bars
5. Pre-Workout Formulas

Multivitamins seem to pop up on nearly every list. Being the most popular supplement consumed by athletes and every-day consumers, I provided a summary and how-to guide for selecting multivitamins in Section V along with other selected important vitamins, minerals, and antioxidants. Several are also included individually on this chart. Another popular, albeit food supplement like sport bars, recovery shakes, electrolyte drinks, competition fuel such as energy chews, gels, and beans were also discussed previously in Section IV in the Performance Nutrition for Athletes section.

Heads up: You may or may not find your favorite supplement on the chart because there are too many to include within the scope of this book. There are plenty of excellent supplement resources located in Appendix B. One reference hot off the press and used as a resource for some of the information in this chart is Sports Dietitians Kimberly Mueller and Josh Hingst's book, *The Athlete's Guide to Sports Supplements* (Human Kinetics, 2013.)

Important Note Before You Proceed

This supplement list is NOT a recommendation guide. Every athlete, man and woman, should discuss all diet, lifestyle, and supplement choices with their personal medical doctor prior to making any changes. A thorough physical exam, medical history, and biochemical testing (blood, urine, salivary) may be used to diagnose nutrition deficiencies which may then warrant the recommendation from your medical doctor to use of vita-min, mineral, or any other food or beverage supplement.

As with any dietary compound or supplement, there could be potentially serious side effects, from combining or consuming one with another or with any medications you are taking for a health condition. If you have, or suspect you have, a serious health issue, or you are pregnant, lactating, or under 18 years old, you are not advised to take any supplement without a physician's guidance, since it may cause serious injury, illness, or death. If you take a supplement and experience any negative reaction or ill side effect, you can file a report to the FDA at: *http://www.safetyreporting.hhs.gov/*

Water Soluble Vitamins and Antioxidants	Function	Deficiency Signs/ symptoms	Evidence for Enhancing Sports Performance
Antioxidant Vitamins (A,C,E)	Protect cells against oxidative damage	Depletions dependent on athlete level, training, intensity, training environment, and training cycle; See vitamin A,C,E for deficiency signs	Mixed results—Vitamin A, C and beta carotene may improve VO2 Max, peak cycle power & output & peak lactate and threshold; supplementation also may actually be detrimental to performance
B$_1$ (Thiamin)	Supports energy metabolism and nerve and mental function	Weakness, decreased endurance, muscle wasting, weight loss, increased lactic acid, fatigue, reduced performance; alcoholics at increased deficiency risk	To correct deficiency; otherwise, no benefits shown
B$_2$ (Riboflavin)	Supports energy metabolism; normal vison, skin, cell function and growth; also recycles glutathione antioxidant	Cracks and sores around the mouth and nose; nervous function limited	In athletes whose food availability is limited; also, needs increase at initiation of heavy training or increased physical activity; supplements may improve pain associated with migraine headaches
B$_3$ (Niacin)	Supports energy metabolism, skin health, nervous system, and digestive system	Mouth sores, skin rashes, diarrhea	Shown to be adequate in most athletes; no impact on performance shown
B$_6$	Amino acid and fatty acid metabolism, gluconeogenesis, red blood cell production	Anemia, irritability, patches of itchy skin	Not shown to be effective for improving performance
Folic acid	Supports DNA synthesis, new cell and hemoglobin formation	Impaired cell division; anemia; diarrhea; gastrointestinal upsets, fatigue	In deficiency only

Safety & Toxicity Issues/Concerns	Food Sources	Other FYI
See individual vitamin A,C,E and selenium	Fresh fruits and vegetables; see A, C, E	Phytocompounds in selected foods fruits, veggies, and spices; also antioxidants (see Section III)
Excess usually excreted through kidneys	Chicken, pork loin, peas, brown rice, lentils, pistachios, pinto beans, baked potato, peanuts broccoli, flaxseed, sunflower seeds	Highest concentrations found in muscle; destroyed in food by heat, baking, pasteurization, refining, canning; enzymes in raw fish, rice bran and antagonists in tea, coffee interfere with B1 absorption
Sensitivity to light, itching, numbness, and burning/prickling sensations	Lean meat, milk, salmon, chicken egg, green leafy veggies; spinach, broccoli	Taking riboflavin supplements may cause a bright yellow hue in urine due to an iridescent compound in vitamin; destroyed in food by light and baking soda
Skin irritation, gut discomfort, nausea, vomiting, flushing, abnormal liver function tests	Chicken, fish, beef, dairy, peanuts, avocado, bagels, baked potato, beans, mango	Supplements contraindicated for those with ulcers, reflux, liver disease, or alcohol abuse
Peripheral neuropathy (nerve damage) leading to weakness, numbness, tingling in hands and feet, difficulty walking, loss of reflexes	Garbanzo beans, sunflower seeds, banana, avocado, baked potato, soybeans, brown rice, beef, carrots, peas, milk	Medications like antibiotics, hypertensive, anti-inflammatories alcohol, and caffeine can compromise absorption. May help symptoms of carpel tunnel syndrome and PMS, although results mixed.
Excess linked to increased risk of colon cancer for those with genetic mutation	Spinach, orange, romaine lettuce, peanut butter, milk, beef, fortified cereals, bread, pasta	While brown rice has greater amounts of most nutrients, white rice is higher in folic acid; many foods fortified with folic acid, so watch amounts, add up.

Water Soluble Vitamins and Antioxidants	Function	Deficiency Signs/ symptoms	Evidence for Enhancing Sports Performance
B$_{12}$	New blood cell synthesis; helps break down fat and amino acids; supports nerve cell maintenance	Rare except in strict vegetarians; tiredness, irritability, depression, anemia	In deficiency only
Choline	Considered essential nutrient; required for fat metabolism, structural integrity of cells, precursor to acetylcholine a neurotransmitter	Fatigue, weight loss; may be low following endurance exercise and/or heavy drinking	No performance benefits in those with adequate stores. Increased time to fatigue; improved work performance
C (antioxidant)	Neutralizes free radicals; cofactor in collagen formation; supports bone and immune health; amino acid metabolism; helps iron absorption	Smokers, alcoholics, drug users at risk for deficiency; muscle weakness, fatigue, loss of appetite bleeding gums; easy bruising; infections	In depleted states, including environmental stress (altitude), high temperatures, infection, cigarette smokers may enhance immune function and facilitates recovery from intense training.

Fat Soluble Vitamins	Function	Deficiency Signs and Symptoms	Evidence for Enhancing Sports Performance
A	(Beta Carotene form in plants-antioxidant) Supports vision, skin, bone and tooth growth, immunity and reproduction; contributes to cell integrity	Loss of appetite; dry, rough skin; lowered resistance to infection; dry eyes; decreased collagen synthesis, increased infection risk	No evidence to suggest taking extra improves performance
D	Considered a hormone and vitamin; regulates calcium and phosphorus; supports immune and bone health	May impact muscle protein synthesis, strength, size, reaction time, balance, coordination, endurance, inflammation, immunity	Increase ATP concentration; increase strength, jump height, jump velocity, jump power, exercise performance; decrease muscle protein degradation; decrease bone fractures; reduce cold/ flu risk; reduce inflammation, especially after intense exercise periods; Enhanced recovery in peak isometric force, attenuate the immediate and delayed increase in circulating biomarkers representative of muscle damage

Safety & Toxicity Issues/Concerns	Food Sources	Other FYI
No adverse effects shown	Oysters, crab beef, salmon, egg, chicken, milk, fortified foods	Medications, including antibiotics and antacids, which reduce stomach acidity interfere with absorption; blood levels may also be low in older athletes due to lower stomach acid associated with aging
Supplementation may cause fishy odor due to breakdown and excretion of a compound "trimethylamine"	Eggs, egg yolk , wheat germ, soybeans, soy lecithin, brewer's yeast, broccoli, cauliflower, chicken, turkey, salmon, codfish	About 50% of population has a genetic variation that may increase dietary needs; Avoid supplements if you have health condition called "gout"
Diarrhea, double vision, hair loss, bone and joint pain, vomiting, liver damage, birth defects	Spinach, broccoli, bell peppers, Brussels sprouts, snow peas, tomato juice, kiwi, mango, papaya, orange, grapefruit, raspberries, strawberries, potatoes	Aspirin and NSAIDS increase urine losses Excessive intake may interfere with copper absorption Maximum absorption achieved by several doses of less than 1000 mg, not by taking 1 large dose

Safety/Toxicity Issues and Concerns	Food Sources/ Recipes	Other FYI
No more than 4000 IU recommended in MVI Supplements may increase lung cancer risk/heart disease in middle aged male smokers Supplementing while pregnant can cause birth defects	Liver; apricots, beet greens, broccoli, carrots, collard greens, corn, mango spinach, sweet potatoes	Excess beta carotene may cause orange palms and soles of feet Some forms of vitamin A (retin A) used successfully to treat acne
Increased blood calcium levels, headaches, irritability, weakness, appetite loss, nausea, kidney stones	Egg yolks, liver, fish oil, fortified milk and breakfast cereals	Darker athletes, and those who use sunscreen at risk for deficiency (see Section V for a more detailed discussion)

Water Soluble Vitamins and Antioxidants	Function	Deficiency Signs/ symptoms	Evidence for Enhancing Sports Performance
E (Antioxidant)	Neutralizes free radicals; supports immune and heart health	Rare, anemia; nerve and muscle damage	In regards to reducing exercised induced "oxidative" damage, may reduce inflammation and oxidation, muscle soreness
K	Essential role in bone health by regulating blood calcium; also helps to prevent bone demineralization; may have a role in energy production	Defective blood coagulation; greater risk for stress fractures; medications may block absorption	Bone health, may reduce arterial (blood vessel) stiffness; in female athletes, increased vitamin K associated with increased calcium-binding capacity of osteocalcin; low-estrogen group vitamin K supplementation induced 15-20% increase of bone formation markers and parallel 20-25% decrease of bone resorption markers

Minerals	Function	Deficiency Signs and Symptoms	Evidence for Enhancing Sports Performance
Calcium	Formation of bones and teeth, supports blood clotting; 99% of the body's calcium stored in bones and teeth	Osteoporosis, stress fractures	Improved bone density, reduced fractures
Copper	Cofactor in numerous enzymes; oxygen transport and utilization, immune function, connective tissue synthesis, antioxidant defense	Fatigue, frequent infections, stress fractures	Athletes who restrict calories for long periods at risk for deficiency, poor immune status, low bone density
Iron	Part of the protein hemoglobin (carries oxygen throughout body's cells)	Skin pallor; weakness; fatigue; headaches	In iron deficient athletes, in non-anemic, some evidence of enhanced muscle function
Magnesium	Supports bone mineralization, protein building, muscular contraction, nerve impulse transmission, immune function	Nausea, irritability, muscle weakness; twitching; cramps, cardiac arrhythmias	May increase muscle strength, improve cellular function; lowers lactic acid and oxygen uptake in exhaustive rowing

Safety & Toxicity Issues/Concerns	Food Sources	Other FYI
Increased tendency to hemorrhage	Wheat germ, sunflower & pumpkin seeds, hazelnuts, wheat germ, avocado, mango, papaya, mustard greens, broccoli	Supplementation in some men associated with prostate cancer and stroke in smokers. Need fat for absorption, i.e. use salad dressing/ olive oil on greens!
No reported risks	Found in plants or produced from intestinal bacteria; Brussels sprouts, leafy green vegetables, spinach, broccoli, cabbage, liver. Fermented soy foods, i.e. natto in tempeh and miso contain significant amounts of K2 (formed by bacteria)	Microwaving may increase rate of absorption of vitamin K from plant sources; Light reduces K content in food; Both vitamin A & E can compete for absorption with vitamin K if taking supplement mega doses

Safety/Toxicity Issues and Concerns	Food Sources/ Recipes	Other FYI
Constipation, kidney stones	Milk, yogurt, cheddar cheese, Swiss cheese, tofu, sardines, green beans, spinach, broccoli, chia seeds	Binds iron, should not be consumed at same meal, especially in iron deficient athletes on supplements to correct deficiency; also aluminum- and magnesium- containing antacids increase urinary calcium excretion
Supplements should never be consumed without a doctor's recommendation	Sesame seeds, garbanzo beans, nuts, soybean, lentils; shellfish, avocado, flax, pumpkin, sunflower seeds; beef, fortified shakes and bars	Excess amounts associated with increased dementia development
Heart disease; prooxidant	Artichoke, parsley, spinach, broccoli, green beans, tomato juice, tofu, clams, shrimp, pumpkin, sunflower & hemp seeds, beef liver	See Section V for comprehensive summary
Nausea, vomiting, diarrhea, low blood pressure, muscle weakness	Spinach, broccoli, artichokes, tomato juice, green, navy &, pinto beans, black-eyed peas, hemp, flax & sunflower seeds, tofu, nuts, whole grains, halibut	Avoid taking over 350 mg in supplement to avoid possible diarrhea

Minerals	Function	Deficiency Signs/ symptoms	Evidence for Enhancing Sports Performance
Potassium	Major electrolyte found IN cells; maintains fluid and electrolyte balance, cell integrity, muscle contractions and nerve impulse transmission	Nausea, anorexia, muscle weakness, irritability; Loss of potassium from muscle may cause fatigue during athletic events; more serious, cardiac arrest	Potassium losses in sweat very small, 160-320mg/liter sweat, unlikely to cause deficiency; supplements may reduce blood pressure in those with hypertension, however achievable with potassium rich diet
Selenium (antioxidant)	Trace element, reproduction, thyroid function, DNA synthesis, antioxidant	Selenium deficiency could exacerbate iodine deficiency, possible connection to hypothyroidism; cardiomyopathy	No benefits reported
Sodium	Maintains fluid and electrolyte balance, supports muscle contraction and nerve impulse transmissions	Hyponatremia, muscle weakness, cramping, nausea, lightheadedness, headache	Prevent muscle cramping in heavy sodium "sweaters," athletes who have white ashy skin after exercise
Zinc	Part of 200+ enzymes, involved in production of genetic material and proteins; glycolysis; transports vitamin A, taste perception, wound healing, sperm production and normal fetus development	Eye/skin lesions, weight loss Slow healing of wounds; slow grow, immune abnormalities; loss of taste	May benefit with suboptimal intake; may increase dynamic isokinetic strength and endurance

Safety & Toxicity Issues/Concerns	Food Sources/ Recipes	Other FYI
Supplements NOT advised-large doses can cause gastrointestinal lesions, hemorrhage, arrhythmias & death; hyperkalemia (high blood potassium) in those with kidney disease	Potatoes, acorn squash, artichoke, spinach, broccoli, carrots, green beans, tomato juice, avocado, grapefruit juice, watermelon, banana, strawberries, cod, dairy	See Section V for more detailed summary; Less than 2% US achieve recommended minimum adequate intake; diets high sodium offset intake; long term fasting and diarrhea may cause deficiencies
Hair loss, tissue damage; skin lesions; nausea, diarrhea, skin rashes, mottled teeth, fatigue, irritability, nervous system abnormalities	Fish, red meat, eggs, whole grains, wheat germ, orange juice, nuts, flaxseed (Food amount dependent on soil content)	Excess associated with garlic odor in the breath and metallic taste in mouth Brazil nuts contain very high amounts of selenium (68–91 mcg per nut) may cause selenium toxicity if consumed in high amounts regularly DO NOT take more than 400 mcg in MVI
Hypertension in some men & women; high risk groups, i.e. over 51 years old, African Americans, those with kidney disorders rec'd to consume about ≤1500 mg daily	Salt, soy sauce, bread, milk, meats	Most individuals meet daily recommended goals by consuming a normal diet; greater losses seen with vomiting/diarrhea, eating disorders
High intake may compromise immune function, interfere with copper & iron absorption	Grass fed beef, wheat germ, garbanzo beans, sunflower seeds, chicken, brown rice, nonfat milk, egg, codfish	Supplements may reduce the absorption of antibiotics; strict vegetarians may be at greater risk of deficiencies

Non-Vitamin/ Mineral Supplements in Alphabetical Order	Function	Deficiency Signs/ symptoms	Evidence for Enhancing Sports Performance
Alpha Lipoic Acid (ALA)	"Vitamin-like" antioxidant; water and fat soluble; involved in energy metabolism	None reported	Antioxidant potential; short-term supplementation may selectively protect DNA & fats against exercise-induced oxidative stress (not in muscle mitochondria); May improve endurance and strength;Used with diabetics to treat insulin resistance, symptoms of diabetes (peripheral neuropathy)
Arginine (conditionally essential amino acid)	Conditionally essential amino acid; important for regulation of blood flow & nitric oxide production; protein synthesis; precursor to creatine & potential to increase growth hormone (GH); precursor to nitrous Oxide (NO)-endogenous gas release by vascular endothelium	Body may not be able to produce enough during growth, metabolic stress, heavy exercise for lymphocyte production, RNA synthesis, collagen deposition	Mixed results: may improve aerobic endurance performance, reduce O2 consumption during sub max exercise; may reduce lactic acid levels after high intensity training
Betaine	Derivative of the amino acid glycine, one of the main functions of betaine is to maintain body cells' water retention Liver function, cellular reproduction, and helping make carnitine. It also helps the body metabolize homocysteine	None reported.	2 weeks' supplement mixed with 8 oz sports drink improved muscle endurance in lower-body workout—increasing number (#) reps performed in squat exercise; improving workout quality improving # reps performed at 90% mean & max power outputs;May reduce inflammation; may also contribute compounds necessary to synthesize creatine in muscles; improvements in bench press, throw power, vertical jump power, and isometric squat force
Beta Alanine	Non-essential AA, building block of carnosine, a molecule that helps to buffer acid in muscles (and	None; Carnosine primary muscle buffering substance synthesized from two amino acids, beta alanine and histidine, synthesis may be limited by beta alanine availability	Can assist with buffering in muscle—associated with improved strength, anaerobic endurance, body composition, muscle mass & performance on various measures of anaerobic power output during exercises between 60 to 240 second exercise bouts; may be an antioxidant; may delay fatigue onset

Safety & Toxicity Issues/Concerns	Food Sources	Other FYI
Nausea, vomiting, & vertigo, reported doses ≥ 600mg May cause allergic skin reactions & hypoglycemia; may exert pro-oxidant-especially in presence of iron	Organ meats (liver), spinach and yeast (brewer's yeast).	May benefit cardiovascular disease risk factors, i.e. blood lipids, protection against LDL oxidation, hypertension—evidence mixed
Doses of 10 g have been noted to cause diarrhea	Dairy, beef, pork, chicken, seafood wheat germ, granola, oatmeal, nuts, chick peas, cooked soybeans, and seeds.	Despite increasing nitric oxide formation, does not appear to impact performance as nitrates do from other food and supplement sources (see nitrates-Beet powder)
Stomach upset, nausea, diarrhea Supplements may raise cholesterol levels & interact with medications; those with kidney disease should not take supplements	Synthesized from choline (see foods) Daily intake of estimated 1 gram to 2.5 grams/day whole grains, spinach, beets, shellfish	With B6 , B12, folic acid my help reduce higher levels of homocysteine and may reduce heart disease risk
Short term supplementation range of 3.2-6.6 grams a day appears to be safe; Large doses taken at once may cause face tingling aka paresthesia— harmless, temporary side effect, can be avoided by taking time release formulation or lower doses multiple times daily	Meat, fish, poultry	Supplementation not dependent on timing in relation to exercise; can be taken at multiple points throughout the day

Non-Vitamin/ Mineral Supplements in Alphabetical Order	Function	Deficiency Signs/ symptoms	Evidence for Enhancing Sports Performance
Beta Glucan	Soluble fiber derived from cell walls of algae, bacteria, fungi, yeast, mushrooms	None reported	Research double-blind pilot study, elite athletes randomized showed may decrease risk of upper respiratory tract infections (URTI) associated with exercise stress
B-Hydroxy-β-Methylbutyrate (HMB)	Metabolite of the essential amino acid leucine	None reported	May reduce muscle damage; shorten recovery time; inhibit muscle proteolysis; enhance protein synthesis, increase body mass across the young, elderly, untrained, trained, and clinically cachexic; and less stress-induced muscle protein breakdown. Acute and chronic HMB supplementation associated with less exercise-induced muscle damage and soreness.
Branched Chain Amino Acids (leucine, isoleucine, and valine)	May decrease exercise-induced protein degradation and muscle enzyme release	Protein deficiency symptoms in sources of BCAA, uncommon	Leucine: most readily oxidized BCAA; most effective at causing insulin secretion from pancreas, lowering blood sugar levels, aiding in growth hormone (GH) production; works in conjunction with other BCAAs to protect muscle and act as fuel; promotes bone, skin, muscle tissue healing, often recommended for recovering from surgery. Isoleucine stabilizes regulates blood sugar and energy levels. Also needed for the formation of hemoglobin; Valine aids in muscle metabolism, tissue repair, and maintenance of proper nitrogen balance
Caffeine	Stimulant found in numerous beverages and foods	None reported	Stimulate reaction time, increase mental alertness & visual information processing; reduce perceptions of fatigue, stimulate fat burning, causing a glycogen sparing effect; May improve carbohydrate absorption when consumed together in a beverage.
Carnitine	Involved in energy metabolism, concentrated in tissues like skeletal and cardiac muscle that utilize fatty acids as fuel; made in the body and consumed via food.	Deficiency seen in genetic disorder-(cardiomyopathy, skeletal-muscle weakness, and hypoglycemia). may also occur in chronic renal failure/ use of certain antibiotics that reduce carnitine absorption/ increases excretion	May decrease muscle damage, oxidation, fatigue & improve power output

Safety & Toxicity Issues/Concerns	Food Sources/ Recipes	Other FYI
Safe but avoid with known allergy or hypersensitivity to beta-glucan or algae, bacteria, fungi, yeast, and plants that contain beta-glucan	OOats, oat bran, barley, rye, mushrooms	May also reduce LDL bad cholesterol and increase good HDL cholesterol; Beta-glucan from baker's yeast or brewer's yeast on FDA's Generally Recognized as Safe (GRAS) list
Safe with dose of 3 grams or less daily for 8 weeks; may interact with some medications	Catfish, grapefruit, and alfalfa	May lower LDL cholesterol and blood pressure. Several certified safe for sport products include in recovery mixtures. Check NSF or Informed Choice websites
Mild gut distress for some Excessively high level of valine can lead to a crawling sensation in the skin, so taking valine as a supplement is not advised.	Leucine: Meat, dairy, nuts, beans, brown rice, soy flour, and whole grains	35 to 40 % of body's protein; 14 % of total AAs in muscle; During stress, BCAAs required more than any other EAA; See Section IV for additional information
Insomnia, GI irritation, bleeding; increased urine flow, muscle tremor, coordination impairment, mental over arousal; adverse metabolic & heart disturbances; diarrhea, anxiety, shakes & nausea	Isoleucine: Chicken, eggs, fish, meat, rye, almonds, cashews, chickpeas, lentils, soy protein, and most seeds Valine: meat, mushrooms, peanuts, dairy products, grains, soy	May also help to kick up metabolism, decrease appetite in athletes who need to lose weight Athletes who drink caffeinated beverages on regular basis less likely to experience an ergogenic effect
May interfere with hypertension medications	Coffee, tea, chocolate, foods and beverages supplemented with caffeine Meat, fish, poultry, milk	Does not appear to burn fat unless otherwise deficient

Other Performance Supplements	Function	Deficiency	Evidence for Enhancing Sports Performance
Creatine	Normal component of muscle; Important energy source for high intensity	Deficiencies seen as a result of genetic disorder Breaks down in body to creatinine; body needs 2 grams/day to replace urine losses; vegetarians have little stores while meat eaters get about 1 gm/day;	Safe method to enhance muscle strength & size during resistance training; Supplements can increase creatine & creatine phosphate in muscles; improve performance in muscle strength & power events; In glycogen depleting endurance exercise, taken after in series of carbohydrate meals shown to stimulate synthesis
Essential Amino Acids	EAA include: methionine, isoleucine, leucine, phenylalanine, tyrosine, histidine, valine, and tryptophan	Deficiency unlikely in healthy individuals; signs—illness, hair loss, skin changes, muscle tone loss	3 to 6 grams of essential amino acids prior to and following training may stimulate protein synthesis & muscle building
Glucosamine/Chondroitin/ MSM (Methyl-sulfonyl-methane)	Glucosamine, Chondroitin and (MSM) occur naturally in the body; MSM -sulfur containing molecule	No deficiencies reported	Glucosamine/Chondroitin may help to enhance structural integrity & resilience of bone cartledge; may reduce associated pain & slow osteoarthritis progression; MSM used for its antioxidative & anti-inflammatory properties, joint health
Glutamine	Provides energy source; involved in muscle building	In catabolic states, becomes conditionally essential; athletes who overtrain may experience decreased plasma glutamine levels which may impair immune system/ predispose athlete to illness	Shown to improve glycogen synthesis / muscle protein levels; Improve glucose utilization post-workout, strength, increase growth hormone levels; marathon and ultra-marathon runners supplementing with glutamine shown to have decrease upper respiratory infections (URI) one week after competition Shown to be effective in recovery from illness, injury, trauma, burns, surgical healing

Safety & Toxicity Issues/Concerns	Food Sources/ Recipes	Other FYI
May cause a rapid weight gain of 1-4 kg, which may be an advantage in some sports, detriment in others Some athletes report GI distress in doses over the standard 3-5 gm daily dose Research shows no adverse effects on kidney or liver for healthy individuals with 5 grams-20 grams, 0.25 to 5.6 years or impairs heat tolerance or hydration during exercise	Meat and fish, milk	Creatine monohydrate most widely studied by researchers; Uptake stimulated by insulin combined with carbohydrate/amino acid fluids/foods; Exercise stimulates uptake into muscles Benefits may go beyond sports- shown to positively impact Type 2 diabetes; reducing damage to heart muscle following a heart attack, protecting cells against stress (like antioxidant), for neurodegenerative diseases like muscular dystrophy and building, maintaining muscle for healthy aging
None reported	Animal meats, dairy, eggs and supplemental certified protein powders	Well-controlled studies show glucosamine may slow down progression of osteoarthritis/control chronic knee pain, in older individuals;; premature to assume all athletes can benefit —research mixed results
Bloating and diarrhea Those with shellfish allergies: buyer beware, since many glucosamine supplements are from fish sources	Trace amounts in shrimp, lobster, crab and crawfish shell but difficult to digest, ground for supplements MSM found in many foods —meat, fish, certain fruit, vegetables, grains, however destroyed when foods are processed	National Institutes of Health (NIH) GAIT study (Glucosamine/Chondroitin Arthritis Intervention Trial) showed did not prevent narrowing of joint space in knee; only reduced pain in those with moderate to severe complaints
No side effects reported with 0.1mg to 0.6mg per kilogram bodyweight	Beef, chicken, fish, eggs, milk, dairy products, wheat, cabbage, beets, beans, spinach, and parsley	Muscle mass responsible for about 90 % of body's synthesis; supplements not recommended for those with liver or kidney disorders

Other Performance Supplements	Function	Deficiency	Evidence for Enhancing Sports Performance
Glutathione	Endogenous antioxidant synthesized from amino acids cysteine, glutamic acid & glycine; supports immune function; DNA synthesis & repair; prostaglandin synthesis; detoxifies toxins & carcinogens	Challenging to maintain blood levels through food alone, depleted by poor diets, stress, medications, infections; associated with diabetes, lung cancer and Parkinson's Disease	Supports immune system, as an antioxidant maintains C & E in active forms; prostaglandin synthesis which is responsible for muscle contraction/relaxation
Nitrates	Inorganic nitrate (NO3-) endogenously produced food product that appears to have a critical role in blood pressure & cardiovascular health Mitochondrial efficiency and contractile function	None reported	Enhanced performance by increasing vasodilation, glucose uptake, reduced blood pressure, O2 cost of submaximal exercise; supplementing diet with 0.5 liters of beetroot juice/powder day for four to six days reduced steady state cost of submaximal exercise by 5% & extended time to exhaustion during high intensity cycling by 16 %
Omega-3	Essential polyunsaturated fats not made by body 3 sources: alpha-linolenic acid (ALA), plants; eicosapentaenoic acid (EPA) and docosahexaenoic acid (DHA) in fatty fish Body partially converts ALA to EPA and DHA Required for digestion, fertility, cell division, growth. brain development; also anti-inflammatory, antioxidant; cell membrane structure, fluidity, signaling to cell; regulates blood pressure, blood clotting; cognitive function	Dry skin, eczema, small bumps like chicken skin on back of upper arms/legs; mood swings, fatigue, poor sleep; inflammation/joint pain	Upregulates enzymes (GLUT4) which may help make cells more permeable to glucose & amino acids; attenuates oxidative stress & inflammatory markers; decreases heart rate, peak heart rate & O2 production during incremental workloads to exhaustion; lowered steady state submax exercise heart rate O2 consumption & BP; decreases muscle damage; stimulates protein synthesis, increases fat metabolism, decreases body weight, prevent weight gain; Higher omega 3 index associated with decreased delayed onset muscle soreness (DOMS)

Safety & Toxicity Issues/Concerns	Food Sources/ Recipes	Other FYI
Supplementation of 250 mg & 1000 mg both shown to be effective for maintaining adequate blood & cellular levels; support immune system	Whey protein best source; low fat dairy, chicken, turkey, eggs, red peppers, garlic, onions, broccoli, Brussel sprouts, lentils wheat germ	Cooking can reduce levels by 30-60% Canning completely eliminates
None reported	Beetroot, spinach, lettuce, celery	Take 30 minutes prior to exercise; ½ liter beetroot juice shown to increase blood nitrite, level peaks within 3 hours; remains elevated 6-9 hours; beet juice may turn susceptible individuals' urine pink
GI upset, fishy odor with supplementation Increased risk of bruising in some individuals & bleeding, Increased low-density cholesterol (LDL) cholesterol levels, Altered blood sugar control, Need to discontinue before any surgery; supplement safety critical since some may be contaminated with heavy metals, mercury (see Consumer Lab)	Fish, salmon, tuna, halibut, krill; algae, flaxseed, almonds, pistachios and canola oil	May also help lower risk of heart disease, cancer, arthritis & depression; Supplement: 1 to 2 grams/day for healthy individuals; for high blood pressure, heart disease-higher doses recommended under medical supervision

Other Performance Supplements	Function	Deficiency	Evidence for Enhancing Sports Performance
Probiotics	Live microorganisms (bacteria) that favorably alter intestinal microflora balance, inhibit harmful bacteria growth, promote good digestion, boost immune function, increase resistance to infection	None reported	Ergogenic effect lacking; however, may provide secondary health benefit to positively affect athletic performance through enhanced recovery from fatigue, improved immune function, & maintenance of healthy gastrointestinal tract; double-blind trial, supplementation reduced frequency of upper respiratory tract infections training athletes during winter
Quercetin	Natural flavonoid has many beneficial biological benefits as anti-inflammatory, anticarcinogenic, cardioprotective, & neuroprotective compound		May enhance performance through anti-inflammatory properties; increases number & function of mitochondria May have a performance benefit via "caffeine-like boost" to central nervous system ; May increase exercise endurance, VO2 Max, and time before fatigue
Sodium Bicarbonate	Molecule that acts as a buffering agent against acidity in the human body	No deficiencies	200 to 300 mg/kg range taken 60 to 90 minutes before anaerobic activities May decrease lactic acid/acidosis, improve power endurance, VO2 max, rate of perceived exertion, neuromuscular function, training volume
Taurine	Nonessential sulfur-containing amino acid; component of bile acids, used to help absorb fats and fat-soluble vitamins Plays role in several metabolic processes, i.e. heart contraction; modulation of calcium signaling, antioxidant Also helps maintain cell membrane stability	None reported; low or negligible on strict vegan diet	May favorably influence cardiac parameters, i.e. increased stroke volume; 2014 study- during training recovery showed supplementation may decrease muscle damage/oxidative stress after eccentric exercise; 2007 study reported 7 days of taurine supplementation induced significant increases in VO2max & cycle ergometer exercise time to exhaustion; ergogenic effects attributed to taurine's antioxidant activity & cell protection
Tumeric (Curcumin)	Related to ginger, spice from India antioxidant/ anti-inflammatory properties	None reported	May help with knee osteoarthritis pain; free radical scavenger & antioxidant; may reduce oxidative DNA damage associated with training

Safety & Toxicity Issues/ Concerns	Food Sources/ Recipes	Other FYI
No known safety issues; some may experience ga ; Dose measured in viable living organisms "units" or "colonizing units" Recommended intake varies depending on strains, typically between 1 & 10 billion cells/day;	Yogurt, kefir, sauerkraut, cabbage kimchee, and soybean-based miso and natto	Strand specific to condition management (see Consumer Lab) keep supplements refrigerated & out of light
Supplementation since high doses can actually have pro-oxidant effects and may produce pain in small joints	Blueberries, tomatoes, apples, black tea, purple grapes, and red onions	Recent double-blind clinical trial comprising 60 athletic males showed increases in lean body mass, total body water, basal metabolic rate, total energy expenditure in quercetin group
Rapidly ingesting the drink, or taking too much, is likely to induce stomach pain & nausea followed by diarrhea/ flatulence ; While 500 mg/kg slightly more effective, tends to be associated with higher degree of intestinal side effects if taken all at once.	Baking soda	Limit use by individuals with salt-sensitive hypertension
Possible diarrhea; some drug interactions	Cheese, milk, yogurt, game meats, ingredient in some energy drinks	May be effective in reducing fatigue & improving mood & endurance, although typically researched with other compounds (e.g. caffeine) which have that same effect.
Minimal or no adverse effects; May cause nausea, diarrhea, skin reactions May be toxic to liver long term; not recommended for those with gallbladder disease or taking blood thinners; May bind iron-not suggested for those with anemia	Primarily used in curry blends and mustards and food coloring (yellow)	In traditional Chinese & Ayurveda medicine, used to aid digestion & liver function, relieve arthritis pain, regulate menstruation May relieve symptoms/pain associated with rheumatoid arthritis (RA), ulcerative colitis and atypical depression

Resources (also see Appendix B):

ODS SUPPLEMENT FACT SHEETS
http://ods.od.nih.gov/factsheets/list-all/

http://scan-dpg.s3.amazonaws.com/resources/DOCS/transfat/SCAN%20Supplement%20Guide%20by%20Ellen%20Coleman%202010.pdf

http://www.foodinsight.org/Content/3842/Final%20Functional%20Foods%20Backgrounder.pdf

www.ConsumerLab.com

AUSTRALIAN SPORTS COMMISSION
http://www.ausport.gov.au/ais/nutrition/supplements/classification

UNIVERSITY OF MARYLAND MEDICAL CENTER
http://umm.edu/health/medical/altmed/supplement/betaine#ixzz3AlSroitX

http://www.betaglucan.org/

http://www.naturalproductsinfo.org/index.php?src=gendocs&ref=Aisle7_Vitamins&category=Main&resource=%2fassets%2fa-z-index%2fa-to-z-index-of-vitamins-minerals-and-herbs%2f%7edefault

SUPPLEMENT GOALS REFERENCE GUIDE
http://examine.com/store/reference/

MUELLER K AND HINGST J. THE ATHLETE'S GUIDE TO SPORTS SUPPLEMENTS
(Human Kinetics, 2013.) http://www.humankinetics.com/products/all-products/Athletes-Guide-to-Sports-Supplements-The

Nutrition and performance experts who contributed to the professional's survey:

Leslie Bonci, MPH, RD, CSSD, RDN, sports dietitian, author: *Sports Nutrition for Coaches, Better Digestion, and Bike Your Butt Off*
http://www.amazon.com/Leslie-Bonci/e/B001ITTU5S

Tavis Piattoly, MS, RD, LDN, Co-owner of My Sports Dietitian
www.mysportsdconnect.com

Roberta Anding, MS, RD/LD, CDE, CSSD, Director,
Sports Nutrition, Texas Children's
Texas Children's Blog: http://www.texaschildrensblog.org/author/randing/

Ruth Carey, RD, CSSD, Sports RD, Portland Timbers MLS
http://www.ruthcarey.com/rc/Welcome.html

Nancy Clark, MS, RD, CSSD, sports dietitian
http://www.nancyclarkrd.com/

Amy Goodson, MS, RD, CSSD, LD, Sports dietitian,
Texas Health Ben Hogan Sports Medicine
http://www.texashealth.org/SportsNutrition#amygoodson

Tricia Griffin, RD, CSSD, Sports Dietitian, Director of Nutrition Marketing at
NEOGENIS Sport

Chris Herrera, DPT, CSCS, USAW, Founder & CEO, Jaguar Therapeutics, Miami
http://www.jaguartherapy.com/

Douglas Kalman, PhD, RD, FACN, CCEC, FISSN, Director, Nutrition Miami Research Associates/Director,
https://www.google.com/#q=doug+kalman+phd+books&tbm=shop; Melissa
Kaplan, RD, LD/N http://kaplannutrition.blogspot.com/

Ludmilla Marzano, BS Zumba Education Specialist / Zumba Master Trainer;
http://ludmillamarzano.zumba.com/

James Meder & Irik Johnson, Fast Twitch Performance Training;
http://www.areyoufasttwitch.com/

Sharon Palmer, RDN, author: *Plant Powered Diet and Plant Powered for Life*;
http://www.sharonpalmer.com/

Ryan Reist, MS, RD, LD, Sports Dietitian/Exercise Physiologist with Personal
EDGE; Owner: R3sportsnutrition
http://www.r3sportsnutrition.com/#!

Francesco Zampogna, RSP Nutrition,
http://www.rspnutrition.com/

APPENDIX B

Sports Specific Agencies,
Organizations, & Resources

Sports Dietitians Who
Contributed to This Book

Selected Book References

Resources for Supplement Information

Office of Dietary Supplements (ODS)
http://ods.od.nih.gov/

The FDA instituted the office of Dietary Supplements (ODS) to fund supplement research and disseminate credible information to consumers like you. They have an awesome real-time website and mobile app, free subscription newsletter, and hotline to report incidents.

http://nccam.nih.gov/

The National Center for Complementary and Alternative Medicine (NCCAM) of the US Department of Health & Human Service (HHS) and National Institutes of Health (NIH) defines the usefulness and safety of complementary and alternative medicine interventions and their roles in improving health and healthcare through research. They offer A-Z information, and news on dietary supplements, herbs, and alternative therapies such as acupuncture and massage and other health topics.

Natural Products Association (NPA),
http://www.npainfo.org/

Founded in 1936, this nonprofit group advocates for the rights of consumers to have access to retailers. NPA provides comprehensive GMP certification program for the dietary supplement industry. An A-Z index of supplements can be found at: http://www.naturalproductsinfo.org/index.php?src=gendocs&ref=Aisle7_Vitamins&category=Main&resource=%2fassets%2fa-z-index%2fa-to-z-index-of-vitamins-minerals-and-herbs%2f%7edefault.

https://www.cspinet.org/

A non-profit organization that surveys health claims made about supplements and reports false and misleading claims to the Federal Trade Commission (FTC). They offer lots of free information online at their website and through a print newsletter on health issues, food products, and hot health topics called the Nutrition Action Health Letter. Subscriptions are low-cost and are well worth the investment. http://www.cspinet.org/nah/index.htm.

Consumer Lab
www.Consumerlab.com

A privately held company founded in 1999 by Dr. Tod Cooperman, medical doctor, Consumer Lab purchases supplement products on the open market. Its research group, under the direction of Dr. Mark Anderson, a pharmacologist/toxicologist, analyzes the quantity, identity, and purity of key ingredients, and evaluates other issues of product quality, such as proper pill disintegration, through expert testing in-house and at other independent laboratories. They publish reports on nearly every popular supplement category and hundreds of name brand products at their website www.consumerlab.com. You can subscribe to the service to obtain detailed reports on everything from multivitamins to protein powders to popular herbs, including related clinical information, the latest recalls, and warnings. This is one of my favorite go-to websites for gathering the latest information on supplement-specific purity, safety, efficacy, and quality. www.consumerlab.com. Join at https://www.consumerlab.com/ NewSubscriber.asp , and sign up for their FREE Newsletter at https://www.consumerlab.com/ list.asp .

Natural Standard
https://naturalmedicines.therapeuticresearch.com/

A subscription service well worth the investment if you're considering taking or researching supplements. "Founded by healthcare providers and researchers to provide high-quality, evidence-based information about complementary and alternative medicine including dietary supplements and integrative therapies. Graded for strength of available scientific data for or against the use of each therapy attributed to a specific medical condition."

Natural Medicines Comprehensive Database
http://naturaldatabase.therapeuticresearch.com/home.aspx?cs=&s=ND

Database provides a comprehensive listing of brand name product ingredients for evidence-based information on this topic. A great go-to resource for complete and practical information on medical conditions, conventional treatment, and natural, holistic integrative/functional approaches. New information is continually added, hundreds of monographs are updated, and thousands of new references are added each year.

University of Maryland School of Medicine Center for Integrative Medicine (CIM)
http://www.umm.edu/altmed/

"Founded in 1991 by Brian Berman, M.D., the Center for Integrative Medicine (CIM) is an interdepartmental center within the University Of Maryland School Of Medicine. A leading international center for research, patient care, education, and training in integrative medicine, the CIM is a National Institutes of Health (NIH) Center of Excellence for research in complementary Medicine. Great FREE resource.

Memorial Sloane- Kettering Cancer Center—Integrative Medicine
http://www.mskcc.org/cancer-care/integrative-medicine

"Site provides objective information for oncologists and healthcare professionals, including a clinical summary and details about constituents, adverse effects, interactions, and potential benefits or problems. Evaluations of alternative or unproved cancer therapies, as well as products for sexual dysfunction are included. Consumer version of each monograph also is available to help you deal with the often confusing claims made for over-the-counter products and regimens." Great FREE Resource.

Sports Specific Agencies, Organizations, & Resources

World Anti-Doping Agency
www.USADA.Org

Source: http://www.wada-ama.org/
Athlete Handbook: http://www.usada.org/uploads/athletehandbook.pdf
International independent agency composed and funded equally by the sport movement and governments of the world established in 1999. WADA works towards a vision of a world where all athletes compete in a doping-free sporting environment. WADA's key activities include scientific research, education, development of anti-doping capacities, and monitoring of the World Anti-Doping Code – the document harmonizing anti-doping policies in all sports and all countries. Its seat is in Lausanne, Switzerland, and its headquarters are in Montreal, Canada. Site also contains the Supplement 411 High Risk List of products that have been found to contain substances that are banned in high-level athletic competition. List is accessible FREE of charge but requires viewers to register.

TrueSport

TrueSport of the United States Anti-Doping Agency (USADA)
http://www.truesport.org/resources/substances/dietary-supplements
https://www.usada.org/truesport

Powered by the U.S. Anti-Doping Agency (USADA), "brings action to the idea that sport can and should teach valuable life lessons. TrueSport is grounded in a solid platform of guiding principles centered on competing strong, playing fair, and achieving more."

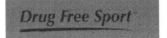

Supplement Safety Now
http://www.supplementsafetynow.com/

A public protection initiative founded by the U.S. Anti-Doping Agency, a nationwide effort to protect Americans whose health is threatened by the consumption of dangerous over-the-counter products disguised as "healthy" supplements. Mission is to urge Congress to establish a regulatory framework that ensures that all supplements sold over-the-counter in retail stores and online are safe and effective. Supported by Major League Baseball, the National Football League, the U.S. Olympic Committee, the National Basketball Association and the National Hockey League.

Drug Free Sport
http://www.drugfreesport.com

Drug-testing authority "dedicated to upholding the integrity of the game. Committed to policy development, drug testing, program management and customized education."

Support Clean Sport
http://www.supportcleansport.com

Proactive vision for the future of Clean Sport inspired by the 501(c)(3) public charity Anti-Doping Research (ADR), headed by renowned sports testing pioneer Don Catlin, M.D. and son Oliver Catlin. For too long we have fought for clean sport through drug testing and research alone, relying on a punitive enforcement based system to solve the problems. Support Clean Sport changes the paradigm giving all people the ability to take part in a grassroots event and e-community based effort for fostering Clean Sport.

LEGALLY LEAN

Resource Exchange Center
http://www.drugfreesport.com/rec/

With support from the NCAA, subscription-based service dedicated to ensuring athletes and others involved in athletics are provided with up-to-date, confidential, and accurate information on dietary supplements and dangerous or banned substances. Subscribing organizations include the NCAA, MLB, NFL, PGA TOUR, LPGA, USATF, state high school associations and many others.

Taylor Hooton Foundation
http://taylorhooton.org/

Founded in memory of Taylor Hooton, the high school baseball player who committed suicide as a consequence of taking steroids. His legacy lives on through this foundation started by his father. Education programs, resources for athletes, coaches and parents created to help raise awareness about the dangers of appearance and performance enhancing drugs (APEDs). 10% of the proceeds from this book will be donated to this organization.

I Play Clean
http://www.iplayclean.org/

Website/organization, according to website, mission: "devoted to educating and encouraging high school students to make the right choice of playing clean – that is, training hard, eating well and playing with attitude, instead of resorting to illegal and dangerous steroids and performance enhancing products." You can pledge to be and be featured as a Play Clean athlete at the website and on the Facebook page.

Global Drug Reference Online
http://www.globaldro.com/default.aspx

Provides athletes and support personnel with information about the prohibited status of specific substances based on the current World Anti-Doping Agency (WADA) Prohibited List.

Industry Watchdogs

Digital Citizens Alliance
http://www.digitalcitizensalliance.org/cac/alliance/default.aspx

Consumer-oriented coalition focused on educating the public and policy makers on the threats that consumers face on the Internet and the importance for Internet stakeholders individuals, government and industry "to make the web a safer place."

Great appreciation to the following nutrition experts who contributed to this book:

Leslie Bonci, MPH, RD, CSSD, RDN, sports dietitian, author
Director of Sports Nutrition, UPMC Center for Sports Medicine
Author: Sports Nutrition for Coaches, Better Digestion, and Bike Your Butt Off
http://www.amazon.com/Leslie-Bonci/e/B001ITTU5S

Tavis Piattoly, MS, RD, LDN, Co-owner of My Sports Dietitian,
www.mysportsdconnect.com

Sharon Palmer, RDN, author: Plant Powered Diet and Plant Powered for Life
http://www.sharonpalmer.com/

Selected References

1. Academy of Nutrition and Dietetics. Sports Nutrition Care Manual. 2014
2. Achten J, Jeukendrup AE: Optimizing fat oxidation through exercise and diet, Nutrition 20:716, 2004.
3. Aerenhouts D1, Deriemaeker P, Hebbelinck M, Clarys P. Dietary acid-base balance in adolescent sprint athletes: a follow-up study. Nutrients. 2011 Feb;3(2):200-11..
4. Ambrose PJ, Tsourounis C, Uryasz FD, Patterson E.Characteristics and trends of drug and dietary supplement inquiries by college athletes. J Am Pharm Assoc (2003). 2013 May-Jun;53(3):297-303.
5. American College of Sports Medicine, Exercise and Fluid Replacement Position Stand, Med Sci Sports Exer. 2007:39;377-390.
6. American Dietetic Association; Dietitians of Canada; American College of Sports Medicine, Rodriguez NR, Di Marco NM, Langley S. American College of Sports Medicine position stand. Nutrition and athletic performance. Med Sci Sports Exerc. 2009 Mar;41(3):709-31.
7. Anderson LL, et al: Effect of resistance training and combined with timed ingestion of protein muscle fiber size and muscle strength, Metabolism 54:151, 2005.
8. Anton, L Disordered Eating in Adolescent Athletes: Prevelence and Risk Factors. SCANS Pulse, Winter 2010 Vol 29, No.1. pp 9-12.
9. Artioli GG, Gualano B, Smith A, Stout J, Lancha AH Jr.Role of beta-alanine supplementation on muscle carnosine and exercise performance. Med Sci Sports Exerc. 2010 Jun;42(6):1162-73.
10. Askari G, Hajishafiee M, Ghiasvand R, Hariri M, Darvishi L, Ghassemi S, Iraj B, Hovsepian V.Quercetin and vitamin C supplementation: effects on lipid profile and muscle damage in male athletes. Int J Prev Med. 2013 Apr;4(Suppl 1):S58-62.

11. Askari G, Ghiasvand R, Karimian J, Feizi A, Paknahad Z, Sharifirad G, Hajishafiei M. Does quercetin and vitamin C improve exercise performance, muscle damage, and body composition in male athletes? J Res Med Sci. 2012 Apr;17(4):328-31.

12. Astorino TA, Matera AJ, Basinger J, Evans M, Schurman T, Marquez R. Effects of red bull energy drink on repeated sprint performance in women athletes. Amino Acids. 2012 May;42(5):1803-8.

13. Astorino T, et al: Is running performance enhanced with creatine serum ingestion? J Strength Cond Res 19:730, 2005.

14. Australian Institute of Sport. http://www.ausport.gov.au/ais/nutrition

15. Badshah H1, Ullah I, Kim SE, Kim TH, Lee HY, Kim MO.Anthocyanins attenuate body weight gain via modulating neuropeptide Y and GABAB1 receptor in rats hypothalamus.Neuropeptides. 2013 Oct;47(5):347-53.

16. Bahrke MS, Morgan WP, Stegner A.Is ginseng an ergogenic aid? Int J Sport Nutr Exerc Metab. 2009 Jun;19(3):298-322.

17. Bailey RL1, Gahche JJ, Miller PE, Thomas PR, Dwyer JT. Why US adults use dietary supplements. JAMA Intern Med. 2013 Mar 11;173(5):355-61.

18. Baker LB, et al: Sex differences in voluntary fluid intake by older adults during exercise, Med Sci Sports Exerc 37:789, 2005.

19. Barker T et al. Supplemental vitamin D enhances the recovery inpeak isometric force shortly after intense exercise. Nutrition & Metabolism 2013, 10:69

20. Bennett L1, Abeywardena M, Burnard S, Forsyth S, Head R, King K, Patten G, Watkins P, Williams R, Zabaras D, Lockett T.Molecular size fractions of bay leaf (Laurus nobilis) exhibit differentiated regulation of colorectal cancer cell growth in vitro. Nutr Cancer. 2013;65(5):746-64.

21. Bishop D: Dietary supplements and team-sport performance, Sports Med 40:995, 2010.

22. Boden BP, Breit I, Beachler JA, Williams A, Mueller FO.Fatalities in high school and college football players. Am J Sports Med. 2013 May;41(5):1108-16.

23. Bonci, L. Sports Nutrition for Coaches. Human Kinetics 2009

24. Bemben MG and Lamont HS. Creatine Supplementation and Exercise Performance. Sports Med. 2005;35(2):107-125.

25. Betts JA, Stevenson E.Should protein be included in CHO-based sports supplements? Med Sci Sports Exerc. 2011 Jul;43(7):1244-50.

26. Bloomer RJ. Nitric oxide stimulating dietary supplements: where is the evidence? Nitric oxide supplements. Sports Nutrition. 2009;20(1):40-42.

27. Bobovčák M1, Kuniaková R, Gabriž J, Majtán J.Effect of Pleuran (β-glucan from Pleurotus ostreatus) supplementation on cellular immune response after intensive exercise in elite athletes. Appl Physiol Nutr Metab. 2010 Dec;35(6):755-62..

28. Braam LA1, Knapen MH, Geusens P, Brouns F, Vermeer C.

29. Factors affecting bone loss in female endurance athletes: a two-year follow-up study. Am J Sports Med. 2003 Nov-Dec;31(6):889-95.

30. Brisswalter, J, Louis J.Vitamin Supplementation Benefits in Master Athletes. Sports Med. 2013 Dec 10.

31. Buell , Jackie L et al. National Athletic Trainers' Association Position Statement: Evaluation of Dietary Supplements for Performance Nutrition Journal of Athletic Training 2013;48(1):124–136

32. Buford TW, et al: International Society of Sports Nutrition position stand: creatine supplementation and exercise. Int Soc Sports Nutr 30:4, 2007

33. Burdon CA, Hoon MW, Johnson NA, Chapman PG, O'Connor HT. The effect of ice slushy ingestion and mouthwash on thermoregulation and endurance performance in the heat. Int J Sport Nutr Exerc Metab. 2013 Oct;23(5):458-69.

34. Burke LM, Deakin V, eds. Clinical Sports Nutrition. 4th ed. Sidney, Australia: McGraw-Hill Australia Pty Ltd; 2010.

35. Burke LM. Fueling strategies to optimize performance: training high or training low? Scand Med Sci

Sports. 2010 Oct;20 Suppl 2:48-58.

36. Byars A, et al: The influence of a pre-exercise sports drink (PRX) on factors related to maximal aerobic performance, J Int Soc Sports Nutr 7:12, 2010.

37. Byrne C, et al: Water versus carbohydrate electrolyte replacement during loaded marching under heat stress, Mil Med 170:715, 2005.

38. Campos-Ferraz PL, Bozza T, Nicastro H, Lancha AH Jr.Distinct effects of leucine or a mixture of the branched-chain amino acids (leucine, isoleucine, and valine) supplementation on resistance to fatigue, and muscle and liver-glycogen degradation, in trained rats. Nutrition. 2013 Nov-Dec;29(11-12):1388-94.

39. Candow DG, Kleisinger AK, Grenier S, Dorsch KD. Effect of sugar-free Red Bull energy drink on high-intensity run time-to-exhaustion in young adults. J Strength Cond Res. 2009 Jul;23(4):1271-5.

40. Cannell JJ, Hollis BW, Sorenson MB, Taft TT, and Anderson JJB. Athletic Performance and Vitamin D. Med. Sci. Sports Exerc., 2008;41(5):1102-1110.

41. Cannell JJ, Hollis BW. Use of Vitamin D in Clinical Practice. Alternative Medicine Review. 2008;13(1):6-20.

42. Cermak, N et al Nitrate Supplementation's Improvement of 10-km Time-Trial Performance in Trained Cyclists. International Journal of Sport Nutrition and Exercise Metabolism, 2012, 22, 64 -71

43. Chen YJ, Wong SH, Chan CO, Wong CK, Lam CW, Siu PM. Effects of glycemic index meal and CHO-electrolyte drink on cytokine response and run performance in endurance athletes. J Sci Med Sport. 2009 Nov;12(6):697-703.

44. Cherniack EP. Ergogenic dietary aids for the elderly. Nutrition. 2012 Mar;28(3):225-9.

45. Dabidi Roshan V, Babaei H, Hosseinzadeh M, Arendt-Nielsen L. The effect of creatine supplementation on muscle fatigue and physiological indices following intermittent swimming bouts. J Sports Med Phys Fitness. 2013 Jun;53(3):232-9.

46. Cohen PA1, Travis JC, Venhuis BJ.A methamphetamine analog (N,α-diethyl-phenylethylamine) identified in a mainstream dietary supplement. Drug Test Anal. 2013 Oct 14.

47. Craciun AM1, Wolf J, Knapen MH, Brouns F, Vermeer C. Improved bone metabolism in female elite athletes after vitamin K supplementation Int J Sports Med. 1998 Oct;19(7):479-84.

48. Daneshvar P, Hariri M, Ghiasvand R, Askari G, Darvishi L, Mashhadi NS, Khosravi-Boroujeni H.Effect of eight weeks of quercetin supplementation on exercise performance, muscle damage and body muscle in male badminton players. Int J Prev Med. 2013 Apr;4(Suppl 1):S53-7.

49. Darvishi L, Ghiasvand R, Hariri M, Askari G, Rezai P, Aghaie M, Iraj B, Khosravi-Boroujeni H, Mashhadi NS.Quercetin supplementation does not attenuate exercise performance and body composition in young female swimmers. Int J Prev Med. 2013 Apr;4(Suppl 1):S43-7.

50. da Silva LA1, Tromm CB, Bom KF, Mariano I, Pozzi B, da Rosa GL, Tuon T, da Luz G, Vuolo F, Petronilho F, Cassiano W, De Souza CT, Pinho RA. Effects of taurine supplementation following eccentric exercise in young adults. Appl Physiol Nutr Metab. 2014 Jan;39(1):101-4.

51. DellaValle DM.Iron supplementation for female athletes: effects on iron status and performance outcomes. Curr Sports Med Rep. 2013 Jul-Aug;12(4):234-9.

52. De Lorenzo A, Bertini I, Candeloro N, Piccinelli R, Innocente I, Brancati A. A new predictive equation to calculate resting metabolic rate in athletes. J Sports Med Phys Fitness. 1999 Sep;39(3):213-9.

53. Denham BE. Dietary supplements--regulatory issues and implications for public health. JAMA. 2011 Jul 27;306(4):428-9.

54. Deuster PA, Singh A, Coll R, Hyde DE, Becker WJ.Choline ingestion does not modify physical or cognitive performance. Mil Med. 2002 Dec;167(12):1020-5.

55. DiLuigi L, et al: Androgenic-anabolic steroids abuse in males, J Endocrinol Invest 28:81S, 2005.

56. Doyle Lucas, A et al. Energy Availability and the Female Athletic Triad in a Unique Population: Elite Ballet Dancers. SCAN Pulse, Fall 2008 Vol 27, No 4.

57. Drinkwater B et al Compromising the Competitive Edge, American bone Health, Foundation for Osteoporosis research and Education, 2007.

58. Driskell Judy and Wolinsky, Ira. Nutrition Assessment of Athletes, 2nd Edition. CRC Press, Boca Raton

Florida, 2011.

59. Drummond M and Rasmussen B Leucine-enriched nutrients and the regulation of mammalian target of rapamycin signaling and human skeletal muscle protein synthesis. Current Opinion in Clinical Nutrition and Metabolic Care 2008, 11:222–226

60. Dugas JIce slurry ingestion increases running time in the heat. Clin J Sport Med. 2011 Nov;21(6):541-2.

61. Dunford M, Doyle JA. Nutrition for Sport and Exercise, 2e. Belmont, CA: Thomson/Wadsworth: 2012.

62. Eijsvogels TM, Scholten RR, van Duijnhoven NT, Thijssen DH, Hopman MT. Sex difference in fluid balance responses during prolonged exercise. Scand J Med Sci Sports. 2013 Mar;23(2):198-206.

63. Engeln R, Sladek MR, Waldron H.Body talk among college men: content, correlates, and effects. Body Image. 2013 Jun;10(3):300-8.

64. Eckerson JM, Bull AJ, Baechle TR, Fischer CA, O'Brien DC, Moore GA, Yee JC, Pulverenti TS. Acute ingestion of sugar-free red bull energy drink has no effect on upper body strength and muscular endurance in resistance trained men. J Strength Cond Res. 2013 Aug;27(8):2248-54.

65. Ferguson-Stegall L, McCleave EL, Ding Z, Doerner PG 3rd, Wang B, Liao YH, Kammer L, Liu Y, Hwang J, Dessard BM, Ivy JL. Postexercise carbohydrate-protein supplementation improves subsequent exercise performance and intracellular signaling for protein synthesis. J Strength Cond Res. 2011 May;25(5):1210-24.

66. Field AE, Sonneville KR, Crosby RD, Swanson SA, Eddy KT, Camargo CA Jr, Horton NJ, Micali N. Prospective Associations of Concerns About Physique and the Development of Obesity, Binge Drinking, and Drug Use Among Adolescent Boys and Young Adult Men. JAMA Pediatr. 2013 Nov 4.

67. Fitzsimmons S, Tucker A, Martins D. Seventy-five percent of National Football League teams use pregame hyperhydration with intravenous fluid. Clin J Sport Med. 2011 May;21(3):192-9

68. Fogarty MC1, Devito G, Hughes CM, Burke G, Brown JC, McEneny J, Brown D, McClean C, Davison GW.Effects of α-lipoic acid on mtDNA damage after isolated muscle contractions. Med Sci Sports Exerc. 2013 Aug;45(8):1469-77.

69. Fogarty MC1, Hughes CM, Burke G, Brown JC, Davison GW.Acute and chronic watercress supplementation attenuates exercise-induced peripheral mononuclear cell DNA damage and lipid peroxidation. Br J Nutr. 2013 Jan 28;109(2):293-301.

70. Foster GD, et al: A policy-based school intervention to prevent overweight and obesity, Pediatrics 121:e794, 2008.

71. Franz KB, Ruddel H, Todd GL, et al. Physiologic changes during a marathon, with special reference to magnesium. J Am Coll Nutr1985;4:187-94.

72. Gammone MA1, Gemello E2, Riccioni G3, D'Orazio N4.Marine bioactives and potential application in sports. Mar Drugs. 2014 Apr 30;12(5):2357-82.

73. Garth AK, Burke LM. What do athletes drink during competitive sporting activities? Sports Med. 2013 Jul;43(7):539-64.

74. Gatterer H, Greilberger J, Philippe M, Faulhaber M, Djukic R, Burtscher M. Short-term supplementation with alpha-ketoglutaric acid and 5-hydroxymethylfurfural does not prevent the hypoxia induced decrease of exercise performance despite attenuation of oxidative stress. Int J Sports Med. 2013 Jan;34(1):1-7.

75. Giannopoulou I1, Noutsos K, Apostolidis N, Bayios I, Nassis GP. Performance level affects the dietary supplement intake of both individual and team sports athletes. J Sports Sci Med. 2013 Mar 1;12(1):190-6. eCollection 2013

76. Gibbs JC, Williams NI, De Souza MJ Prevalence of individual and combined components of the female athlete triad. Med Sci Sports Exerc. 2013 May;45(5):985-96

77. Gibson JC, Stuart-Hill L, Martin S, Gaul C. Nutrition status of junior elite Canadian female soccer athletes. Int J Sport Nutr Exerc Metab. 2011 Dec;21(6):507-14.

78. Gleeson M1, Siegler JC, Burke LM, Stear SJ, Castell LM.A to Z of nutritional supplements: dietary supplements, sports nutrition foods and ergogenic aids for health and performance--part 31. Br J Sports

Med. 2012 Apr;46(5):377-8.

79. Goldstein ER, Ziegenfuss T, Kalman D, Kreider R, Campbell B, Wilborn C, Taylor L, Willoughby D, Stout J, Graves BS, Wildman R, Ivy JL, Spano M, Smith AE, Antonio J. International society of sports nutrition position stand: caffeine and performance. J Int Soc Sports Nutr. 2010 Jan 27;7(1):5.

80. Goodman C1, Peeling P, Ranchordas MK, Burke LM, Stear SJ, Castell LM. A to Z of nutritional supplements: dietary supplements, sports nutrition foods and ergogenic aids for health and performance--Part 21. Br J Sports Med. 2011 Jun;45(8):677-9.

81. Goston JL, Correia MI. Intake of nutritional supplements among people exercising in gyms and influencing factors. Nutrition. 2010 Jun;26(6):604-11.

82. Goulet ED, Rousseau SF, Lamboley CR, Plante GE, Dionne IJ. Pre-exercise hyperhydration delays dehydration and improves endurance capacity during 2 h of cycling in a temperate climate. J Physiol Anthropol. 2008 Sep;27(5):263-71.

83. Graef JL, et al: The effects of four weeks of creatine supplementation and high-intensity interval training on cardiorespiratory fitness: a randomized controlled trial, J Int Soc Sports Nutr 6:18, 2009.

84. Hall M, Trojian TH. Creatine supplementation. Curr Sports Med Rep. 2013 Jul-Aug;12(4):240-4. Harris KM, Haas TS, Eichner ER, Maron BJ.Sickle cell trait associated with sudden death in competitive athletes. Am J Cardiol. 2012 Oct 15;110(8):1185-8.

85. Hawley JA.Fat adaptation science: low-carbohydrate, high- fat diets to alter fuel utilization and promote training adaptation. Nestle Nutr Inst Workshop Ser. 2011;69:59-71; discussion 71-7.

86. Hawley JA, Burke LM, Phillips SM, Spriet LL. Nutritional modulation of training-induced skeletal muscle adaptations. J Appl Physiol (1985). 2011 Mar;110(3):834-45.

87. Havemann L, et al: Fat adaptation followed by carbohydrate loading compromises high intensity sprint performance, J Appl Physiol 100:194, 2005.

88. Heaney S, O'Connor H, Michael S, Gifford J, Naughton G.Nutrition knowledge in athletes: a systematic review. Int J Sport Nutr Exerc Metab. 2011 Jun;21(3):248-61.

89. Heaney S, et al: Comparison of strategies for assessing nutritional adequacy in elite female athletes' dietary intake, Int J Sport Nutr Exerc Metab 20:245, 2010.

90. Heikkinen A1, Alaranta A, Helenius I, Vasankari T. Use of dietary supplements in Olympic athletes is decreasing: a follow-up study between 2002 and 2009. J Int Soc Sports Nutr. 2011 Feb 4;8(1):1.

91. Hillman AR, Turner MC, Peart DJ, Bray JW, Taylor L, McNaughton LR, Siegler JC.A comparison of hyperhydration versus ad libitum fluid intake strategies on measures of oxidative stress, thermoregulation, and performance. Res Sports Med. 2013;21(4):305-17.

92. Hoffman JR, Kraemer WJ, Bhasin S, Storer T, Ratamess NA, Haff GG, Willoughby DS, Rogol AD. Position stand on androgen and human growth hormone use. J Strength Cond Res. 2009 Aug;23(5 Suppl):S1-S59

93. Hoffman JR, Ratamess NA, Faigenbaum AD, Ross R, Kang J, Stout JR, Wise JA.Short-duration beta-alanine supplementation increases training volume and reduces subjective feelings of fatigue in college football players. Nutr Res. 2008 Jan;28(1):31-5.

94. Hoon MW, Johnson NA, Chapman PG, Burke LM.The effect of nitrate supplementation on exercise performance in healthy individuals: a systematic review and meta-analysis. Int J Sport Nutr Exerc Metab. 2013 Oct;23(5):522-32.

95. Horswill CA, Stofan JR, Lacambra M, Toriscelli TA, Eichner ER, Murray R. Sodium balance during U. S. football training in the heat: cramp-prone vs. reference players. Int J Sports Med. 2009 Nov;30(11):789-94.

96. Hosseinlou A, Khamnei S, Zamanlu M. The effect of water temperature and voluntary drinking on the post rehydration sweating. Int J Clin Exp Med. 2013 Sep 1;6(8):683-7.

97. Howatson G, et al: Influence of tart cherry juice on indices of recovery following marathon running, Scand J Med Sci Sports 37:843, 2010

98. Hulmi JJ, et al: Protein ingestion prior to strength exercise affects blood hormones and metabolism, Med Sci Sports Exerc 37:1990, 2005.

99. IOC consensus statement on sports nutrition 2010.J Sports Sci. 2011;29 Suppl 1:S3-4.

100. Institute of Medicine (IOM), Food and Nutrition Board: Dietary reference intakes (DRIs) for water, potassium, sodium and chloride and sulfate, Washington, DC, 2004, National Academies Press.

101. Institute of Medicine (IOM), Food and Nutrition Board: Dietary Reference Intakes for Calcium and Vitamin D, Washington, DC, 2011, National Academies Press.

102. International Food Information Council Foundation. Functional Foods. http://foodinsight.org

103. Irving LM, Wall M, Neumark-Sztainer D, Story M.Steroid use among adolescents: findings from Project EAT. J Adolesc Health. 2002 Apr;30(4):243-52.

104. Jäger R, Purpura M, Kingsley M.Phospholipids and sports performance. J Int Soc Sports Nutr. 2007 Jul 25;4:5.

105. Jamurtas AZ, Tofas T, Fatouros I, Nikolaidis MG, Paschalis V, Yfanti C, Raptis S, Jiang DQ1, Guo Y, Xu DH, Huang YS, Yuan K, Lv ZQ. Antioxidant and anti-fatigue effects of anthocyanins of mulberry juice purification (MJP) and mulberry marc purification (MMP) from different varieties mulberry fruit in China. Food Chem Toxicol. 2013 Sep;59:1-7

106. Kanayama G, Boynes M, Hudson JI, Field AE, Pope HG Jr.Anabolic steroid abuse among teenage girls: an illusory problem? Drug Alcohol Depend. 2007 May 11;88(2-3):156-62. Epub 2006 Nov 28.

107. Koutedakis Y. The effects of low and high glycemic index foods on exercise performance and beta-endorphin responses. J Int Soc Sports Nutr. 2011 Oct 20;8:15.

108. Kaminasky P and Woodruff, E. Male Body Dissatisfaction and the Growing Concerns about Muscle Dysmorphia. SCANS Pulse, Winter 2010, Volume 29, No 1 pp 6-8

109. Kass LS, Skinner P, Poeira F.A pilot study on the effects of magnesium supplementation with high and low habitual dietary magnesium intake on resting and recovery from aerobic and resistance exercise and systolic blood pressure. J Sports Sci Med. 2013 Mar 1;12(1):144-50.

110. Kenefick RW, Cheuvront SN. Hydration for recreational sport and physical activity. Nutr Rev. 2012 Nov;70 Suppl 2:S137-42.

111. Kerksick C, Leutholz B: Nutrient administration and resistance training, J Int Soc Sports Nutr 2:50, 2005.

112. Kern BD, Robinson TL.Effects of β-alanine supplementation on performance and body composition in collegiate wrestlers and football players. J Strength Cond Res. 2011 Jul;25(7):1804-15.

113. Kim BY1, Cui ZG, Lee SR, Kim SJ, Kang HK, Lee YK, Park DB. Effects of Asparagus officinalis extracts on liver cell toxicity and ethanol metabolism. J Food Sci. 2009 Sep;74(7):H204-8.

114. Kondric M, Sekulic D, Uljevic O, Gabrilo G, Zvan M. Dietary Sport nutrition and doping in tennis: an analysis of athletes' attitudes and knowledge. J Sports Sci Med. 2013 Jun 1;12(2):290-7.

115. Koncic MZ, Tomczyk M. New insights into dietary supplements used in sport: active substances, pharmacological and side effects. Curr Drug Targets. 2013 Aug;14(9):1079-92.

116. Kondric M, Sekulic D, Petroczi A, Ostojic L, Rodek J, Ostojic Z.Is there a danger for myopia in anti-doping education? Comparative analysis of substance use and misuse in Olympic racket sports calls for a broader approach. Subst Abuse Treat Prev Policy. 2011 Oct 11;6:27.

117. Kreider RB1, Wilborn CD, Taylor L, Campbell B, Almada AL, Collins R, Cooke M, Earnest CP, Greenwood M, Kalman DS, Kerksick CM, Kleiner SM, Leutholtz B, Lopez H, Lowery LM, Mendel R, Smith A, Spano M, Wildman R, Willoughby DS, Ziegenfuss TN, Antonio J. ISSN exercise & sport nutrition review: research & recommendations. J Int Soc Sports Nutr. 2010 Feb 2;7:7.

118. Kressler J, Millard-Stafford M, Warren GL.Quercetin and endurance exercise capacity: a systematic review and meta-analysis. Med Sci Sports Exerc. 2011 Dec;43(12):2396-404.

119. Kuehl KS, Perrier ET, Elliot DL, Chesnutt JC: Efficacy of tart cherry juice in reducing muscle pain during running a randomized controlled trial, J Int Soc Sports Nutr 7:17, 2010.

120. Larsen FJ, Weitzberg E, Lundberg JO, Ekblom B. Effects of dietary nitrate on oxygen cost during exercise. Acta Physiol (Oxf). 2007 Sep;191(1):59-66. Epub 2007 Jul 17.

121. Larson-Meyer DE, Willis KS: Vitamin D and athletes, Curr Sports Med Rep, 9:220, 2010

122. Lembke P1, Capodice J2, Hebert K2, Swenson T3.Influence of omega-3 (n3) index on performance

and wellbeing in young adults after heavy eccentric exercise. J Sports Sci Med. 2014 Jan 20;13(1):151-6. eCollection 2014.

123. Loucks AB. Energy availability, not body fatness, regulates reproductive function in women. Exerc Sport Sci Rev. 2003 Jul;31(3):144-8.

124. Loucks AB. Introduction to menstrual disturbances in athletes. Med Sci Sports Exerc. 2003 Sep;35(9):1551-2.

125. Lukaski, H. Vitamin and Mineral Status: Effects on Physical Performance. Nutrition Volume 20, Numbers 7/8, 2004

126. Lunn WR, Pasiakos SM, Colletto MR, Karfonta KE, Carbone JW, Anderson JM, Rodriguez NR.Chocolate milk and endurance exercise recovery: protein balance, glycogen, and performance.Med Sci Sports Exerc. 2012 Apr;44(4):682-91.

127. Malaguarnera M, Gargante MP, Cristaldi E, Colonna V, Messano M,Koverech A, et al. Acetyl L-carnitine (ALC) treatment in elderly patients with fatigue. Arch Gerontol Geriatr 2008;46:181–90.

128. Majtan J.Pleuran (β-glucan from Pleurotus ostreatus): an effective nutritional supplement against upper respiratory tract infections? Med Sport Sci. 2012;59:57-61.

129. Manore, M, Meyer, N and Thompson Sport Nutrition for Health and Performance, 2nd edition page 16, Human Kinestics, 2009.

130. Mason MA, Giza M, Clayton L, Lonning J, Wilkerson RD. Use of nutritional supplements by high school football and volleyball players. Iowa Orthop J. 2001;21:43-8.

131. Mason BC, Lavallee ME. Emerging supplements in sports. Sports Health. 2012 Mar;4(2):142-6.

132. Maughan RJ, Shirreffs SM.IOC Consensus Conference on Nutrition in Sport, 25-27 October 2010, International Olympic Committee, Lausanne, Switzerland. J Sports Sci. 2011;29 Suppl 1:S1.

133. Maughan, R et al. The use of dietary supplements by athletes. Journal of Sports Sciences, 25:S1, S103-S113

134. Maughan RJ, Shirreffs SM. Development of hydration strategies to optimize performance for athletes in high-intensity sports and in sports with repeated intense efforts. Scand J Med Sci Sports. 2010 Oct;20 Suppl 2:59-69.

135. Maughan, RJ Fasting and Sport: an Introduction. Br J Sports Med, Vol 44, No 7, June 2010.

136. Maravelias, C eta al Adverse effects of anabolic steroids in athletes A constant threat. Toxicology Letters 158 (2005) 167–175

137. Maughan RJ: Contamination of dietary supplements and positive drug tests in sport, J Sports Sci 23:883, 2005.

138. McArdle, William, Katch, Frank & Katch, Victor. Sports & Exercise Nutrition, 4th Edition, Six Core Areas of Research and Study in the Field of Exercise Nutrition Chart, Lipincott Williams and Wilkins, Philadelphia, 2013

139. McClung JP1, Gaffney-Stomberg E2, Lee JJ Female athletes: A population at risk of vitamin and mineral deficiencies affecting health and performance. J Trace Elem Med Biol. 2014 Jul 5. pii: S0946-672X(14)00127-8.

140. Megna M, Amico AP, Cristella G, Saggini R, Jirillo E, Ranieri M. Effects of herbal supplements on the immune system in relation to exercise. Int J Immunopathol Pharmacol. 2012 Jan-Mar;25(1 Suppl):43S-49S. Mettler S, Mannhart C, Colombani PC Development and validation of a food pyramid for Swiss athletes. Int J Sport Nutr Exerc Metab. 2009 Oct;19(5):504-18.

141. Michael-Titus AT1, Priestley JV2.Omega-3 fatty acids and traumatic neurological injury: from neuroprotection to neuroplasticity? Trends Neurosci. 2014 Jan;37(1):30-8.

142. Millard-Stafford M, et al: Recovery from run training: efficacy of a carbohydrate-protein beverage? Int J Sport Nutr Exerc Metab 15:610, 2005.

143. Moore LJ, Midgley AW, Thurlow S, Thomas G, Mc Naughton LR. Effect of the glycaemic index of a pre-exercise meal on metabolism and cycling time trial performance. J Sci Med Sport. 2010 Jan;13(1):182-8.

144. Morente-Sánchez J, Zabala M. Doping in sport: a review of elite athletes' attitudes, beliefs, and

knowledge. Sports Med. 2013 Jun;43(6):395-411

145. Mountjoy M1, Sundgot-Borgen J, Burke L, Carter S, Constantini N, Lebrun C, Meyer N, Sherman R, Steffen K, Budgett R, Ljungqvist A.The IOC consensus statement: beyond the Female Athlete Triad-- Relative Energy Deficiency in Sport (RED-S). Br J Sports Med. 2014 Apr;48(7):491-7.

146. Mullen G Nutrition Supplements for Athletes: Potential Application to Malnutrition Nutr Clin Pract. 2013 Dec 13.

147. Murray S1, Lake BG, Gray S, Edwards AJ, Springall C, Bowey EA, Williamson G, Boobis AR, Gooderham NJ. Effect of cruciferous vegetable consumption on heterocyclic aromatic amine metabolism in man. Carcinogenesis. 2001 Sep;22(9):1413-20.

148. Murray R: Fluids, electrolytes, and exercise. In Danford M, editor: Sports nutrition: a practice manual for professionals, ed 4, Washington, DC, 2006, American Dietetic Association.

149. Murray SB, Rieger E, Touyz SW, De la Garza García Lic Y. Muscle dysmorphia and the DSM-V conundrum: where does it belong? A review paper. Int J Eat Disord. 2010 Sep;43(6):483-91.

150. Myburgh KH.Polyphenol supplementation: benefits for exercise performance or oxidative stress? Sports Med. 2014 May;44 Suppl 1:S57-70.

151. Nazem TG, Ackerman KE. The female athlete triad. Sports Health. 2012 Jul;4(4):302-11.

152. Nieman DC. Immunonutrition support for athletes. Nutr Rev. 2008 Jun;66(6):310-20. Nichols AW. Probiotics and athletic performance: a systematic review. Curr Sports Med Rep. 2007 Jul;6(4):269-73.

153. Novak, Jeff. Healthy Living Eat Healthy, Live Better A Guide to Plant Based Nutrition. Kaiser Permanente, 2014. http://www.jeffnovick.com/RD/Articles/Entries/2014/8/22_Healthy_Living__Eat_ Healthy,_Live_Better_A_Guide_To_Plant_Based_Nutrition_files/HEALTHYLIVINGPROGRAMBOOK_2.pdf

154. Ogan D, Pritchett K.Vitamin D and the athlete: risks, recommendations, and benefits. Nutrients. 2013 May 28;5(6):1856-68.

155. Oosthuyse T, Bosch AN. The effect of the menstrual cycle on exercise metabolism: implications for exercise performance in eumenorrhoeic women. Sports Med. 2010 Mar 1;40(3):207-2

156. Oppliger RA, Utter AC, Scott JR, Dick RW, Klossner D.NCAA rule change improves weight loss among national championship wrestlers. Med Sci Sports Exerc. 2006 May;38(5):963-70.

157. Palisin T, Stacy JJ: Beta-hydroxy-methylbutyrate and its use in athletics, Curr Sports Med Rep 4:220, 2005.

158. Peake J: Heat, athletes and immunity, Am J Lifestyle Med 4:320, 2010.

159. Pedlar CR, Whyte GP, Burden R, Moore B, Horgan G, Pollock N. A case study of an iron-deficient female Olympic 1500-m runner. Int J Sports Physiol Perform. 2013 Nov;8(6):695-8. Epub 2013 Feb 20.

160. Pennings B, et al: Exercising before protein intake allows for greater use of dietary protein—derived amino acids for de novo muscle protein synthesis in both young and elderly men, Am J Clin Nutr 93(2)322, 2010.

161. Peschek K, Pritchett R, Bergman E, Pritchett K. The effects of acute post exercise consumption of two cocoa-based beverages with varying flavanol content on indices of muscle recovery following downhill treadmill running. Nutrients. 2013 Dec 20;6(1):50-62.

162. Pesta et al. The effects of caffeine, nicotine, ethanol, and tetrahydrocannabinol on exercise performance Nutrition & Metabolism 2013, 10:71

163. Pialoux V, et al: Effects of acute hypoxic exposure on prooxidant/antioxidant balance in elite endurance athletes, Int J Sports Med 30:87, 2009.

164. Pialoux V, et al: Antioxidant status of elite athletes remains impaired 2 weeks after a simulated altitude training camp, Eur J Nutr 49:285, 2010.

165. Pigeon WR, et al: Effects of a tart cherry juice beverage on the sleep of older adults with insomnia: a pilot study, J Med Food 13:579, 2010.

166. Pope HG Jr, Kanayama G, Athey A, Ryan E, Hudson JI, Baggish A. The lifetime prevalence of anabolic-androgenic steroid use and dependence in Americans: Current best estimates. Am J Addict. 2013 Sep 20.

167. Pope HG, Jr, Phillips, Olivardia. The Adonis complex: the secret crisis of male body obsession. Free

Press, New York (2000)

168. Prelack K, Dwyer J, Ziegler P, Kehayias JJ.Bone mineral density in elite adolescent female figure skaters. J Int Soc Sports Nutr. 2012 Dec 27;9(1):57.

169. Pritchett K, Pritchett R.Chocolate milk: a post-exercise recovery beverage for endurance sports. Med Sport Sci. 2012;59:127-34.

170. Pritchett K, Bishop P, Pritchett R, Green M, Katica C. Acute effects of chocolate milk and a commercial recovery beverage on postexercise recovery indices and endurance cycling performance. Appl Physiol Nutr Metab. 2009 Dec;34(6):1017-22

171. Reid, K Performance Food: Promoting Foods with a functional benefit in sports performance. British Nutrition Foundation Nutrition Bulletin, 38: 429-437, 2013.

172. Reidy PT, Walker DK, Dickinson JM, Gundermann DM, Drummond MJ, Timmerman KL, Fry CS, Borack MS, Cope MB, Mukherjea R, Jennings K, Volpi E, Rasmussen BB. Protein blend ingestion following resistance exercise promotes human muscle protein synthesis. J Nutr. 2013 Apr;143(4):410-6.

173. Rodriguez NR, et al: Position of the American Dietetic Association, Dietitians of Canada, and the American College of Sports Medicine: nutrition and athletic performance, J Am Diet Assoc 109:509, 2009.

174. Rogol AD. Drugs of abuse and the adolescent athlete. Ital J Pediatr. 2010 Feb 18;36:19.

175. Rosenbloom CA, Coleman E, ed. SCAN Dietetic Practice Group. Sports Nutrition: A Practice Manual for Professionals. 5th ed. Chicago, IL: American Dietetic Association; 2012

176. Rosenkilde M, Reichkendler MH, Auerbach P, Bonne TC, Sjödin A, Ploug T, Stallknecht BM.

177. Changes in peak fat oxidation in response to different doses of endurance training. Nat Prod Res. 2012;26(18):1741-5.

178. Saab AM1, Tundis R, Loizzo MR, Lampronti I, Borgatti M, Gambari R, Menichini F, Esseily F, Menichini F.Antioxidant and antiproliferative activity of Laurus nobilis L. (Lauraceae) leaves and seeds essential oils against K562 human chronic myelogenous leukaemia cells. Scand J Med Sci Sports. 2013 Dec 18.

179. Rowlands DS, Clarke J, Green JG, Shi X.L-Arginine but not L-glutamine likely increases exogenous carbohydrate oxidation during endurance exercise. Eur J Appl Physiol. 2012 Jul;112(7):2443-53

180. Sacirović S, Asotic J, Maksimovic R, Radevic B, Muric B, Mekic H, Biocanin R.Monitoring and prevention of anemia relying on nutrition and environmental conditions in sports. Mater Sociomed. 2013;25(2):136-9.

181. Sagoe D1, Molde H2, Andreassen CS3, Torsheim T4, Pallesen The global epidemiology of anabolic-androgenic steroid use: a meta-analysis and meta-regression analysis. Ann Epidemiol. 2014 Jan 30. pii: S1047-2797(14)00039-8.

182. Sánchez Oliver A1, Miranda León MT, Guerra-Hernández E. Prevalence of protein supplement use at gyms. Nutr Hosp. 2011 Sep-Oct;26(5):1168-74.

183. Santos DA, Matias CN, Monteiro CP, Silva AM, Rocha PM, Minderico CS, Bettencourt Sardinha L, Laires MJ.Magnesium intake is associated with strength performance in elite basketball, handball and volleyball players. Magnes Res. 2011 Dec;24(4):215-9.

184. Saunders MJ. Carbohydrate-protein intake and recovery from endurance exercise: is chocolate milk the answer? Curr Sports Med Rep. 2011 Jul;10(4):203-10.

185. Sawka MN, Burke L, Eichner R, Maughan RJ, Montain SJ, Stachenfeld N. American College of Sports Medicine exercise and fluid replacement position stand. Med Sci Sports Exerc. 2007;39:377-390.

186. Schubert MM, Astorino TA, Azevedo JL Jr. The effects of caffeinated "energy shots" on time trial performance. Nutrients. 2013 Jun 6;5(6):2062-75.

187. Senchina DS, Shah NB, Doty DM, Sanderson CR, Hallam JE. Herbal supplements and athlete immune function--what's proven, disproven, and unproven? Exerc Immunol Rev. 2009;15:66-106.

188. Setaro L, Santos-Silva PR, Nakano EY, Sales CH, Nunes N, Greve JM, Colli C.Magnesium status and the physical performance of volleyball players: effects of magnesium supplementation. J Sports Sci. 2013 Sep 9.

189. Shuler FD, Wingate MK, Moore GH, Giangarra C.Sports Health Benefits of Vitamin D. Sports Health.

2012 Nov;4(6):496-501.

190. Siegel R, Maté J, Watson G, Nosaka K, Laursen PB. Pre-cooling with ice slurry ingestion leads to similar run times to exhaustion in the heat as cold water immersion. J Sports Sci. 2012;30(2):155-65.

191. Silva LA1, Pinho CA, Silveira PC, Tuon T, De Souza CT, Dal-Pizzol F, Pinho RA. Vitamin E supplementation decreases muscular and oxidative damage but not inflammatory response induced by eccentric contraction. J Physiol Sci. 2010 Jan;60(1):51-7.

192. Silva LA1, Silveira PC, Pinho CA, Tuon T, Dal Pizzol F, Pinho RA.N-acetylcysteine supplementation and oxidative damage and inflammatory response after eccentric exercise. Int J Sport Nutr Exerc Metab. 2008 Aug;18(4):379-88.

193. Smith AE, et al: Effects of beta-alanine supplementation and high-intensity interval training on endurance performance and body composition in men: a double-blind trial, J Int Soc Sports Nutr 6:5, 2009.

194. Smurawa TM, Congeni JA: Testosterone precursors: use and abuse in pediatric athletes, Pediatr Clin North Am 54:787, 2007.

195. Stear SJ, Castell LM, Burke LM, Jeacocke N, Ekblom B, Shing C, Calder PC, Lewis N.A-Z of nutritional supplements: dietary supplements, sports nutrition foods and ergogenic aids for health and performance--part 10. Br J Sports Med. 2010 Jul;44(9):688-90.

196. Stephens FB, Marimuthu K, Cheng Y, Patel N, Constantin D, Simpson EJ, Greenhaff PL. Vegetarians have a reduced skeletal muscle carnitine transport capacity. Am J Clin Nutr. 2011 Sep;94(3):938-44.

197. Sureda A, Ferrer MD, Mestre A, Tur JA, Pons A.Prevention of neutrophil protein oxidation with vitamins C and E diet supplementation without affecting the adaptive response to exercise. Int J Sport Nutr Exerc Metab. 2013 Feb;23(1):31-9.

198. Suzuki A, Okazaki K, Imai D, Takeda R, Naghavi N, Yokoyama H, Miyagawa T Thermoregulatory Responses Are Attenuated after Fructose but Not Glucose Intake. Med Sci Sports Exerc. 2013 Dec 2.

199. Tarazona-Díaz MP1, Alacid F, Carrasco M, Martínez I, Aguayo E. Watermelon juice: potential functional drink for sore muscle relief in athletes. J Agric Food Chem. 2013 Aug 7;61(31):7522-8.

200. Taylor NA, Machado-Moreira CA. Regional variations in transepidermal water loss, eccrine sweat gland density, sweat secretion rates and electrolyte composition in resting and exercising humans. Extrem Physiol Med. 2013 Feb 1;2(1):4.

201. ter Steege RW, Geelkerken RH, Huisman AB, Kolkman JJ. Abdominal symptoms during physical exercise and the role of gastrointestinal ischaemia: a study in 12 symptomatic athletes. Br J Sports Med. 2012 Oct;46(13):931-5. Epub 2011 Oct 20.

202. Tomlin DL, Clarke SK, Day M, McKay HA, Naylor PJ. Sports drink consumption and diet of children involved in organized sport. J Int Soc Sports Nutr. 2013 Aug 19;10(1):38.

203. Torres-McGehee, T, Pritchett, K., Zippel, D, Minton, D, Cellamare, A Sibilia, M. Sports Nutrition Knowledge Among Collegiate Athletes, Coaches, Athletic Trainers, and Strength and Conditioning Specialists. Athl Train. 2012 Mar-Apr; 47(2): 205–211.

204. Trenton AJ, Currier GW: Behavioral manifestations of anabolic steroid use, CNS Drugs 19:571, 2005.

205. Tscholl P, Alonso JM, Dollé G, Junge A, Dvorak J. The use of drugs and nutritional supplements in top-level track and field athletes. Am J Sports Med. 2010 Jan;38(1):133-40.

206. Turocy, P et al. National Athletic Trainers' Association Position Statement: Safe Weight Loss and Maintenance Practices in Sport and Exercise. Journal of Athletic Training 2011:46(3):322-336

207. USOC http://www.teamusa.org/About-the-USOC/Athlete-Development/Sport-Performance/Nutrition/Resources-and-Fact-Sheets

208. VandenBerg P, Neumark-Sztainer D, Cafri G, Wall M.Steroid use among adolescents: longitudinal findings from Project EAT. Pediatrics. 2007 Mar;119(3):476-86.

209. Vanheest JL, Rodgers CD, Mahoney CE, De Souza MJ.Ovarian suppression impairs sport performance in junior elite female swimmers. Med Sci Sports Exerc. 2014 Jan;46(1):156-66

210. Van Loon L J C et al. J Physiol 2001;536:295-304

211. Vertalino M, Eisenberg ME, Story M, Neumark-Sztainer D.Participation in weight-related sports is associated with higher use of unhealthful weight-control behaviors and steroid use. J Am Diet Assoc. 2007 Mar;107(3):434-40.

212. Volpe SL, Poule KA, Bland EG. Estimation of prepractice hydration status of National Collegiate Athletic Association Division I athletes. J Athl Train. 2009 Nov-Dec;44(6):624-9. Br

213. Wall BT1, Morton JP, van Loon LJ. Strategies to maintain skeletal muscle mass in the injured athlete: Nutritional considerations and exercise mimetics. Eur J Sport Sci. 2014 Jul 16:1-10.

214. Wall BA, Watson G, Peiffer JJ, Abbiss CR, Siegel R, Laursen PB. Current hydration guidelines are erroneous: dehydration does not impair exercise performance in the heat. J Sports Med. 2013 Sep 20.

215. Warber JP, Patton JF, Tharion WJ, Zeisel SH, Mello RP, Kemnitz CP, Lieberman HR. The effects of choline supplementation on physical performance. Int J Sport Nutr Exerc Metab. 2000 Jun;10(2):170-81.

216. Watson TA, et al: Antioxidant restriction and oxidative stress in short-duration exhaustive exercise, Med Sci Sports Exerc 37:63, 2005.

217. West NP1, Pyne DB, Peake JM, Cripps AW. Probiotics, immunity and exercise: a review. Exerc Immunol Rev. 2009;15:107-26.

218. Wierniuk A, Włodarek D. Estimation of energy and nutritional intake of young men practicing aerobic sports. Rocz Panstw Zakl Hig. 2013;64(2):143-8.

219. Williams M: Dietary supplements and sports performance: metabolites, constituents, and extracts, J Int Soc Sports Nutr 3:1, 2006.

220. Williams J, Abt G, Kilding AE. Effects of Creatine Monohydrate Supplementation on Simulated Soccer Performance. Int J Sports Physiol Perform. 2014 Jan 15.

221. Williams M: Dietary supplements and sport performance: minerals, J Int Soc Sports Nutr 2(1):43, 2005.

222. Wilson JM, et al: Acute and timing effects of beta-hydroxy-beta-methylbutyrate (HMB) on indirect markers of skeletal muscle damage, Nutr Metab 6:6, 2009.

223. Wilson M, et al: Effect of glycemic index meals on recovery and subsequent endurance capacity, Int J Sports Med 30:898, 2009.

224. Wolk BJ, Ganetsky M, Babu KM. Toxicity of energy drinks. Curr Opin Pediatr. 2012 Apr;24(2):243-51.

225. Wong SH, et al: Effect of pre exercise glycemic-index meal on running when CHO-electrolyte solution is consumed during exercise. Int J Sport Nutr Exerc Metab 19:222, 2009

226. Woolf K, St Thomas MM, Hahn N, Vaughan LA, Carlson AG, Hinton P. Iron status in highly active and sedentary young women. Int J Sport Nutr Exerc Metab. 2009 Oct;19(5):519-35.

227. Wu T1, Qi X, Liu Y, Guo J, Zhu R, Chen W, Zheng X, Yu T. Dietary supplementation with purified mulberry (Morus australis Poir) anthocyanins suppresses body weight gain in high-fat diet fed C57BL/6 mice. Food Chem. 2013 Nov 1;141(1):482-7..

228. Wylie LJ, Mohr M, Krustrup P, Jackman SR, Ermıdis G, Kelly J, Black MI, Bailey SJ, Vanhatalo A, Jones AM. Dietary nitrate supplementation improves team sport-specific intense intermittent exercise performance. Eur J Appl Physiol. 2013 Jul;113(7):1673-84.

229. Xia N1, Pautz A1, Wollscheid U1, Reifenberg G1, Förstermann U1, Li H2.

230. Artichoke, cynarin and cyanidin downregulate the expression of inducible nitric oxide synthase in human coronary smooth muscle cells. Molecules. 2014 Mar 24;19(3):3654-68.

231. Yeo WK, Carey AL, Burke L, Spriet LL, Hawley JA. Fat adaptation in well-trained athletes: effects on cell metabolism. Appl Physiol Nutr Metab. 2011 Feb;36(1):12-22.

232. Yfanti C, Fischer CP, Nielsen S, Akerström T, Nielsen AR, Veskoukis AS, Kouretas D, Lykkesfeldt J, Pilegaard H, Pedersen BK. Role of vitamin C and E supplementation on IL-6 in response to training. J Appl Physiol (1985). 2012 Mar;112(6):990-1000.

233. Zanchi NE, Gerlinger-Romero F, Guimarães-Ferreira L, de Siqueira Filho MA, Felitti V, Lira FS, Seelaender M, Lancha AH Jr. HMB supplementation: clinical and athletic performance-related effects and mechanisms of action. Amino Acids. 2011 Apr;40(4):1015-25.

EPILOGUE

Congratulations. You are one step closer to living Legally Lean.

Thank you for investing your time into learning more about the latest, scientifically based strategies for reaching optimal health and performance. You are now armed with performance nutrition formulas, a guide to super foods, grocery lists, and menus to attain a Legally Lean physique and to maintain and sustain your personal best in health, sport, and life.

Along with a library of resources, online links, newsletters, and websites, you also have a quick guide to safe supplements as needed when your diet falls short of your daily needs, whether that is due to health issues, high-volume training, travel, or the everyday stresses of life.

There is no quick fix.

As you learned, the consequences of taking the fast lane for reaching your goals—leanest body, fastest speed, and greatest strength—with steroids, performance enhancing drugs, or tainted supplements can include illness and even death. In addition, adhering to extreme dieting over time can sabotage your looks and your nutritional status.
Taking the fast track can deplete your energy levels and cause hair, skin, and bone loss. It can also ultimately lead to vitamin and mineral deficiencies and compromise your immune system and your ability to attain and maintain your body composition for competition, your high school reunion, your wedding day, or at any other important time in life.

Being a great athlete and a healthy individual is a continuous, lifetime journey which requires dedication, time, and consistency in your training and your diet to fuel the course.

Keep in touch; send your stories, recipes, strategies, and tips at twitter@ LegallyLean, Instagram@LegallyLean, Facebook@LgeallyLean, or at the website www.legallylean.com.

Cheers to a Legally Lean life!
Lisa